HEALING
&
HOPE

HEALING & HOPE

Six Women from the Betty Ford Center

Share Their Powerful Journeys of

Addiction and Recovery

BETTY FORD

G. P. Putnam's Sons

New York

Although the stories of the six women featured in this book are true, names, residences, the names of their family members, and certain events in their lives have been changed to protect their privacy.

While the author has made every effort to provide accurate telephone numbers and Internet addresses at the time of publication, neither the publisher nor the author assumes any responsibility for errors, or for changes that occur after publication.

G. P. Putnam's Sons
Publishers Since 1838
a member of
Penguin Group (USA) Inc.
375 Hudson Street
New York, NY 10014

Library of Congress Cataloging-in-Publication Data

Ford, Betty, date.
Healing and hope : six women from the Betty Ford Center share their
powerful journeys of addiction and recovery / Betty Ford.
p.   cm.
ISBN 0-399-15138-9
1. Betty Ford Center.
2. Substance Abuse—Patients—Rehabilitation—Case Studies.
I. Betty Ford Center.   II. Title.
RC564.74.C2F67   2003   2003047041
362.29'18'082—dc21

Printed in the United States of America
1   3   5   7   9   10   8   6   4   2

This book is printed on acid-free paper. ∞

Book design by Chris Welch and Stephanie Huntwork

To Beatrice, Claire, Harriet, Jacqueline, Paula, and Laurette for having the courage to retell the past so that others may have a brighter future. To all women—particularly those struggling with addiction—that they may see a reflection of themselves in these stories of survival and from them, find the strength to live a life free from the chains of addiction. May these intimate testimonies demonstrate that you, too, have the strength inside to begin anew.

Acknowledgments

I wish to express my personal thanks to the women in this book, who allowed themselves to be interviewed, patiently answered all our questions and trusted us with the intimate and profound experiences recorded in these chapters.

I wish also to express my deep gratitude to Damian McElrath, whose wisdom and experience helped guide us through the complex tasks of translating and portraying the sometimes bewildering and always powerful journeys from addiction to recovery. I'd also like to thank Russ Patrick at Patrick Communications and Martha Bushko at G. P. Putnam's Sons for bringing it all together.

Contents

I

INFERNO
What It Was Like Before

II

PURGATORIO
What Happened?

III

PARADISO
What It's Like Now

HEALING

&

HOPE

Introduction

by Nancy Waite-O'Brien, Ph.D.

A woman's experience with addiction is different from a man's. The voices of the women in this book testify to those differences. They describe how our culture reinforces the shame and guilt associated with being a female alcoholic or addict, the devastating physical complications of this illness on women, the impact women's economic circumstances have on their access to treatment, and the psychological problems that add layers of complexity to the treatment of this illness in women. The six women profiled in this book also describe the incredible life change that occurs when a woman begins the road to recovery.

The women in this book are not celebrities. One is a schoolteacher, another a housewife, one is a former gang member. They are black, white, Hispanic, lesbian and straight. Their "drug of choice" ranged from alcohol to prescription pills to heroin. For some of the women, treatment was successful the first time around. For others, the path to long-term sobriety was much more arduous.

In short, these women are the faces of addiction. Taken together, they represent the complex journey female alcoholics/addicts must take if and when they decide to challenge their disease.

There is an old adage that addiction is an "equal-opportunity disease." After working in addiction treatment for more than twenty years, I certainly know this to be true. That said, I do believe that addiction affects men and women differently Men have historically been the "identified patient" vis-à-vis addiction; women have tended to be the "invisible victims."

Alcohol and drug consumption and abuse by men tends to occur in groups, often in public (for example, in bars). For men, the consequences of excess use are likely to be played out in either a courtroom or place of employment, or both. Women tend to use and abuse alcohol and/or other drugs in isolation. Instead of recognizing that the use/abuse is a symptom of the disease of addiction—and needs to be treated as such—lots of euphemistic "causes" are cited when it comes to drug abuse by women, for example, the need to cope with "physical pain" or "emotional problems."

A review of the scientific literature of the last forty years relative to women's alcoholism provides information about how female alcoholics/addicts are viewed within the scientific community. The assumption is that women's drinking is more frowned upon than men's drinking and therefore is more likely to be hidden. It's hidden by the woman drinker and denied by her loved ones. When it can no longer be hidden, the physical consequences are more severe.

At some time in our lives, we've probably all heard the old maxim, "Nice ladies don't drink (too much)." Our culture (until recently, at least) has very much frowned on the female alcoholic/addict. Even though it's much more acceptable now for women to drink alcohol and/or use other drugs than it was in the past, the remnants of bias exist, as you'll see in the chapter "Conduct Unbecoming a Lady."

Women who lose control while consuming alcohol and/or other

drugs are thought of in particularly harsh terms. They are assumed to be sexually available or to be indiscriminate in their sexual choices, to have failed in their roles as mothers or partners, and they are generally viewed as having violated the "laws" (or at least conventions) of gender behavior.

This is substantially different from how male alcoholics/addicts are viewed. They are more likely to be viewed as having failed at a *task* (work, being a law-abiding citizen), not as having failed *as a human being.* Many women hide their drinking or drug use in an attempt to avoid having "Life Failure" stamped on their foreheads.

When examining the issue of culture, it's important to remember that the harshest critic of the female alcoholic/addict isn't society in the abstract, it is the woman herself. She sees herself as a failure in the important roles she's chosen for herself: mother, professional, wife, partner. These harsh internal and external judgments result in higher levels of shame and guilt in women alcoholics and addicts than in men.

There are other ways women's addiction differs from men's. Female alcoholics and addicts are likely either to be living with another user or to have been abandoned by a non-using partner. Again, our cultural zeitgeist affects the dynamic. Seldom does a man stay with an alcoholic spouse. The sense of helplessness and loss of control associated with living with an active alcoholic or addict often drives the non-alcoholic man out of the relationship. He may leave by moving out or by plunging deeper into his work. Either way, he effectively abandons the relationship.

A non-addicted woman living with an addicted man is not as likely to leave that relationship, mostly for economic reasons. Salary levels for women are lower than for men; the role of homemaker and mother is seen as having little economic value. As a result, women have less money and less choice about leaving or staying in a relationship.

A woman's access to drugs or alcohol is often through her male partner. She may have been introduced to illicit drugs by him; she may maintain her supply by having a sexual relationship with him; she may stay in an abusive or emotionally empty relationship because it expedites her using.

Throughout history, the most reliable access to mood-altering drugs has been through a woman's doctor or pharmacist. In the early 1800s, the typical opium user was a middle- or upper-class Southern woman. Physicians and pharmacists freely dispensed elixirs containing opium and alcohol to anyone who complained of any number of physical or emotional maladies. Their most reliable customers were women. A woman could then experience intoxication and euphoria without the cultural opprobrium associated with drinking in public.

Today, the number of prescriptions written to women for pain medications, antidepressants, and tranquilizers is much greater than those written for men. The prescription from the doctor continues to provide an accepted way to relieve emotional or physical pain without the cultural judgment associated with drinking or illicit drug use.

I'm haunted by something I read just this weekend in *New York* magazine (June 9, 2003), a profile of a young woman who lives on and for pills. Prozac in the morning, Klonopin in the evening, Neurontin at suppertime. "Look," she told the reporter, "I take a minimum of fourteen pills a day. It's not attractive. It's not something pleasing. It's something you have to explain to people when you start dating. I'd prefer they make one little pill that I could swallow casually, because really I do think it's the volume of these pills—the way they're all different sizes and shapes—that makes people think it's like I'm in Candyland and I'm playing. But I'm not. I'm trying to keep myself sane."

I want so badly to say to that young woman, "You should consider reaching out for professional help—and not from Candyland!

Popping fourteen pills—or one superpill!—is like treating cancer with a Band-Aid. As a matter of fact, Candyland could very well kill you. You need to address your problems, not medicate them."

Physiology is a significant factor in how alcohol affects women. Women become more intoxicated than men after consuming equal quantities of alcohol (adjusted for body weight). This is due, in part, to the fact that women have lower body water content. This creates a greater concentration of alcohol and a higher blood alcohol level.

Women also have lower levels of alcohol dehydrogenase in their bodies. This chemical breaks down alcohol in the digestive system before it moves into the bloodstream. Because the alcohol isn't broken down, it moves into the bloodstream undiluted and is broken down and excreted by the liver and kidneys. These two organs have to work harder to remove the alcohol from the body. The overall result of this is earlier development of cirrhosis, the scarring that reduces and finally shuts down liver function.

There is some evidence that alcoholic women have virtually no alcohol dehydrogenase. In these women, the liver is solely responsible for breaking down and removing the alcohol from the body. In this scenario, the likelihood of significant impact on the liver from drinking is remarkably high.

Women alcoholics and addicts are likely to present complex psychological issues. In the population as a whole, women report more depression and anxiety than men. In the population of alcoholics and addicts this is also true.

Most alcoholic and drug-addicted women were abused physically, sexually or emotionally earlier in their lives. They may well be living in abusive relationships, or they may have experienced assault in another part of their adult lives. These experiences leave emotional scars in the form of psychological distress. Depression, anxiety, posttraumatic stress, chronic relationship difficulties, distrust of others are all marks of the struggle. They are evidence of psychic wounds inflicted at a time the woman could not defend herself. Drug or alcohol use provides moments of respite from the pain of dealing with these problems. In the longer term, though, the attempt at problem-solving with drugs or alcohol just creates more problems.

For women in treatment, it's the most wonderful and frightening time imaginable. Frightening, because problems are addressed, head-on. Wonderful, because most women who come into treatment have never taken any time *for themselves;* they've spent years balancing the demands of others with the demands of their disease. Caught in a trap, they've lost sight of who they really are. They've become lonely, isolated, and separated from their real self.

In treatment, the focus is on discovery and reconnection: with the self, the soul, with hope, and with others. Recovery allows a woman to learn to act with courage, to learn to connect with those around her. Feminist psychologists describe connection to others as being central to psychological well-being. Addiction disrupts these connections because the demands of the disease make having genuine relationships with others impossible. To those around the addicted woman, it's as if they are trying to connect with someone who's just about to leave the room.

The image of the circle, mentioned so often in this book, describes perfectly the sense of healing and wholeness that emerges as women discover the world of *possibility* that opens up during treatment and recovery.

It is in connection with others, with women who have walked the path of recovery, that the alcoholic, drug-addicted woman learns to trust, learns to value herself and learns to create a life closer to the one she once dreamed of.

Prologue

How might your life have been different if there had been a place for you,
a place for you to go to be with your mother, with your sisters and
the aunts, with your grandmothers, and the great- and great-great-
grandmothers, a place for women to go, to be, to return to,
as a woman? How might your life be different?

JUDITH DUERK, *CIRCLE OF STONES: WOMAN'S JOURNEY TO HERSELF*

When Leonard Firestone and I started thinking about the possibility of establishing a hospital in the Southern California desert for persons addicted to alcohol and other drugs, far from the noise and distractions of urban and suburban life, the concept of gender-specific treatment was just an academic one. Although we saw a need for it, after all, Leonard and I had only experienced treatment with mixed groups and weren't quite sure how well gender-specific treatment would work. Also, most persons seeking treatment had traditionally been men. How could we possibly fill 50 percent of our beds with female patients, living in separate residential halls?

Two of the first four patients admitted to the Betty Ford Center on the day we opened, October 4, 1982, were women. Soon thereafter we were overwhelmed by the number of women applying for admission. The realization began to dawn that perhaps we could, in time, offer gender-specific treatment.

But in the short term, when I presented a plan for separate halls for men and women to the staff for their input and consideration, the reaction was mixed. Fourteen staff members voted for gender-specific units, fourteen voted against. I cast the tie-breaking vote in favor. But the board of directors, still concerned that there wouldn't be enough female patients to fill 50 percent of our beds, tabled the request at two meetings in 1983.

I persisted, and finally, in the spring of 1984, West Hall (now called Pocklington Hall) was set aside exclusively for women. Eventually, Fisher Hall also was designated exclusively for female patients.

I thought—and think—that the argument for gender-specific treatment is pretty simple. So often, female patients are reluctant to discuss their failures, fears and anger, their flights of fancy, their shame and guilt, their abuse experiences openly in front of men. Living in separate halls and undergoing gender-specific treatment provides women with the physical and psychological space they need to share their life stories.

We found in those early years that men patients often exploited the women's eagerness to please. Believe it or not, one woman had to be told to stop ironing shirts for a male patient! We also found—no surprise!—that when the sexes mixed it was a recipe for distraction. Getting sober is tough, tough work. What you *don't* need is to be sidetracked by preening for—or being chased by—members of the opposite sex.

Providing an environment for our female patients where it was safe to speak openly and honestly was just the first step. I am very proud that during our first twenty years the staff has developed a host of gender-specific services that are directed toward healing the whole person. Besides the disease of addiction, women who come to us often have a broad range of issues that need special attention if the healing process is to take hold and the possibility of relapse be significantly reduced.

A woman's search for wholeness is made more difficult by the culture in which she finds herself. So often, women—when they're growing up, when they're wives and mothers, when they're at work—find themselves playing subservient, secondary and dependent roles.

Our culture is slowly changing, but that hasn't been much help when it comes to rebuilding our fragile self-esteem and strengthening our self-image as we women attempt to recover from the disease of addiction. I'm afraid it's safe to assume that a chemically dependent woman is on the bottom rung of the ladder of self-esteem.

I'm so proud of the fact that one of the real "signatures" of the Betty Ford Center is that we've evolved a treatment process for female patients that's been crafted by female professionals in order to address the specific needs of our sisters.

The Betty Ford Center has been described as a "Healing Circle" where men and women can come and rediscover their journey to wholeness. I like to think of the women's halls as sanctuaries where women can gather in circles and feel safe. It is also sacred space where a woman's own personal self-revelation becomes a burning torch that warms the hearts and illuminates the minds of the other women present. It is a safe place where each woman can tell the truth about herself, allowing her to face up to the powerlessness of her addiction and to be embraced and strengthened by the power and legitimate pride of everyone else present.

Jean Shinoda Bolen, author of *Crossing to Avalon*, expressed it so well: "For a women's circle to work as a spiritual and psychological cauldron for change and growth, we need to see every woman in the circle as a sister who mirrors back to us reflections of ourselves. This means that whatever happened to her could have happened to us, that whatever she has felt or done is a possibility for us, that she is someone toward whom we feel neither superior nor inferior nor indifferent."

Many of you know the story of my own experience with the use of alcohol and prescription drugs. In my book, *A Glad Awakening*, I spoke about some of the issues that women face in dealing with this deadly disease: "We feel guilty because we haven't been able to fulfill the role society has established for us, we feel depressed by our failures and our inability to cope without chemicals, we feel angry because we lost control of our lives.

"The disease impacts women faster and more intensely, so when we finally seek help—and we hide in our denial longer than men do—we're sicker physically and emotionally. Once we leave treatment we may need intensive aftercare. But what we will have learned is that, wherever we go, there will be other women who will understand."

One of the patients who went through treatment at the Center in 1986 gave me her diary and told me I could use it. We published a few of the pages in *A Glad Awakening* as well. They paint a decent but incomplete picture of what a patient's days are like in the first days of treatment. But the stories of the women in this book are much more detailed.

What it comes down to is that essentially the women love one another and talk almost nonstop! As that woman wrote in her diary, "My head still hurts, but I am happy. I like the safety and the structure, of which there hasn't been much in my life, and the process. I really have begun to love these people. I have worked hard for a long time at the cost of having no personal relationships. Or maybe because I wanted to avoid personal relationships. Except with scotch, or Demerol. I feel myself becoming humanized."

The powerful stories told by the women in this book reflect what the Betty Ford Center does best—it provides a sanctuary for women. A place to feel safe, to heal and recommence life's journey toward that unique and special wholeness to which each of us has been called. I and every other recovering woman owe these six brave

women—Paula, Jacqueline, Claire, Harriet, Laurette and Beatrice—
a special debt of gratitude for sharing their stories with us.

To demonstrate my gratitude and love for them, I agreed, reluctantly at first, to serve as a guide for the reader as the women travel
their journeys. The editor suggested a structure that has overtones of
Dante's immortal *Divine Comedy.* I liked that idea. The lives of our
women are divided into sections that mirror Dante's journey: what
their lives used to be like, what happened to transform their lives,
and what their lives are like now.

Our women will tell you that their lives were "hell," that their pas-
sages out of "inferno" through "purgatorio" were painful, that they
are now blessed with a happiness they never thought possible—think
Dante's "paradiso," or Bill W.'s "fourth dimension."

So we divided the book into three sections: Inferno, Purgatorio
and Paradiso. I've tried to present the stories without getting in the
way. My comments serve simply to assist the reader in some further
understanding of the disease of addiction with reflections on my
own recovery and the treatment process for women at the Betty Ford
Center. My voice and comments are *italicized.*

I

INFERNO

What It Was Like Before

*There sighs, lamentations and loud wailings resounded through
the starless air, so that at first it made me weep; strange tongues,
horrible language, words of pain, tones of anger, voices loud
and hoarse . . . made a tumult which is whirling through
that air forever dark, as sand eddies in a whirlwind.*

THE DIVINE COMEDY

1

Homecoming

L ike the swallows of Capistrano, more than one thousand Betty Ford Center alumni return to the Rancho Mirage, California, campus every autumn
to celebrate their sobriety and to express their gratitude to the place where
they found the strength and tools they needed to get and stay sober. While a patient at
the Betty Ford Center, each person found a community of fellow sufferers whose experiences matched her own. As they gather again on campus, they look for the people
with whom they shared so much during their stay here.

I take great pride in the Alumni Reunion, which started in 1983, on the first-
year anniversary of the opening of the Betty Ford Center. It's a celebration, really, a
celebration of recovery. The weekend begins officially on Friday afternoon with the
sign-in at the hospitality center on campus; unofficially, it begins Friday morning
with golf, tennis and organized hikes in the nearby San Jacinto Mountains. Saturday
morning there's a large outdoor Celebration of Recovery, the highlight of which is a
chip and medallion ceremony at which alumni receive medals appropriate to the length
of time they've been sober. Saturday afternoon there are all kinds of workshops where
alumni can "upgrade" their recovery and life-coping skills.

The huge Saturday-night banquet is the highlight of the weekend. It's an amazing
event, a huge "sober celebration." My husband and I haven't missed a single one. The

spirit and energy of a thousand-plus "sober celebrants" from all over North Amer-ica—and the world—gathered together in one hotel ballroom is awesome.

We're all survivors in that room. We've faced head-on, with eyes wide open, an illness that can maim—and, if not treated, kill—the mind, body and spirit.

The women we meet in this book have had their minds clouded, their bodies bro-ken, their spirits bent by the disease of addiction. Their return to the Betty Ford Cen-ter every fall is a demonstration of their healing and their gratitude for having their lives—and families—put back together.

The men and women returning to the campus reflect a colorful spectrum of two decades of patients now in recovery. Many feelings and memories accompany them as they return "home" and wend their way through the oleanders to visit Firestone Hall where they were admitted, the Serenity Room where they meditated or prayed, the swimming pool and gym where they began to get their physical health back.

This annual homecoming serves as a metaphor for another kind of home-coming, a coming home to self. All of us feel the need to be at home with ourselves. Addiction and the addicted self cause us to lose our moorings, cut the tethers to our real selves and induce us to drift aimlessly in space with no sense of purpose or direction. The "vision quest" that women embark upon at the Betty Ford Center is a transforma-tive process that allows them to see more clearly how their addictive selves have robbed them of health and happiness, and a future. But I will talk more about this "vision quest" later on.

Each of the women narrating her story here has carved out a different journey and each journey has a hundred different paths, byways, one ways, U-turns and, yes, dead ends. And yet they all marched in the same direction—toward home. One of the earliest female members of AA wrote in the Big Book (the formal title of which is actually Al-Anon: The Story of How Many Thousands of Men and Women Have Recovered from Alcoholism) *describing a meeting she attended in Bill W.'s home on Clinton Street: "I went trembling into a house in Brooklyn filled with strangers . . . and I found I had come home at last, to my own kind . . . I had found my salvation. I wasn't alone anymore."*

The woman had come home to herself by discovering a common shelter with others.

The women whose stories I am privileged to introduce are a representative cross section of all the women who have gone through the Betty Ford Center during its first twenty years: black, white, Hispanic and Asian; single, married, divorced and widowed; young, middle-aged and older adults; heterosexual and lesbian. Some were addicted to alcohol, some to prescription medications, some to illegal drugs and some suffered from cross addiction. Some are "old-timers." Others completed treatment relatively recently.

None of the six women in this book are celebrities—but they're all stars as far as I'm concerned! And they all received star treatment.

In the lives of many of the women, the mother-daughter relationship is most poignant and in a few cases the neglect, abuse and hurtful attitude of their own mothers prevented access to their own true natures. Most were ready indeed for treatment and subsequent sobriety when they arrived at, and departed from, the Betty Ford Center. A few were not. Those unfortunate souls had to return to their previous lives of being slaves to their disease—until they truly surrendered and admitted they were powerless before alcohol and/or other drugs.

◆　◆　◆

Paula entered the Betty Ford Center for the first time in 1986. She came back for treatment again in 1994, and has been sober since.

As I learned when I talked to Paula at our Twentieth Anniversary Alumni Reunion in October 2002, she sometimes doesn't feel worthy of the "together" life she now leads. As you read the story of her life you'll be astonished to learn, for example, that she now loves to golf. As a matter of fact, during the Alumni Reunion she and her husband played golf Friday morning in a foursome with Dr. James West, our former "tough-love" medical director (at age eighty-six, he's still our outpatient medical director and vice chairman of our board of directors!) and his wife, Maureen.

Paula's previous life still has the power to haunt her with sudden, ugly nightmares and some of the scar tissue from her long, tortuous journey to sobriety remains. One incident in particular is printed indelibly in her memory.

Now it's time for Paula to tell her story.

Paula

I was born in a small town in Idaho. My father was an alcoholic and
pill addict. My mother fits the description perfectly of a "rageaholic."

Nothing could interfere with my father's daily dosage of alcohol.
When he was drinking it was not unusual for him to be physically
abusive to my mother and me.

One of my earliest memories is of the severe beating he gave me
when I was five years old. I was playing with my sister Judy, who is
seventeen months older than I, when Father warned us to stop gig-
gling. As hard as I tried, I couldn't. His eyes clouded over. That always happened when he drank. His face got red. That was the sign I
really dreaded. As he leaned over to smack me I raised my arm to ward
off the blow—and managed to spill a glass of milk.

I was frightened to death. He pulled out his belt to whip me.

To this day I can hear the click of the buckle and the snap of his
alligator belt as he pulled it out of his trousers and whipped it again
and again across my back. Judy was terrified and fled to the living
room. My mother did nothing to stop him. Finally, I scrambled
around the table and escaped upstairs to my room.

My back was throbbing and bleeding from the welts. I was sobbing as I packed my doll suitcase and sneaked out of the house, in-
tending to run away. My little patent-leather purse contained my
entire fortune: two pennies.

It was snowing, and like the soft flakes tossed by the wind, I
drifted aimlessly, not knowing where I was going. To this day I get a
sinking feeling whenever I remember how lost I was and how abandoned I felt. Still sniffling from the beating and the open, bloody
wounds on my back, I was invited into a neighbor's house. They'd
seen me wandering down the street. They called my parents.

When my parents came to take me home, they scolded me. Mother took me upstairs and told me to take off my blouse, which stuck to my back. It hurt terribly when I pulled it off. Not a word of sympathy came from her, only disgust and anger about the stains, which she would have to wash out.

No one held me or comforted me. There were no apologies. The next day my hungover father looked at me sheepishly with bloodshot eyes, but didn't say anything. That's what happened after every beating.

Abuse from my mother was different, but in its own way, much, much worse. Daddy's was physical and eventually healed; Mom's was mental and emotional—and, I suppose, spiritual. Those wounds have lasted a lifetime. Her verbal abuse and barbs were like poisonous arrows shot into my soft flesh that could only be removed by painfully pulling them back out.

I was finally able to heal myself from within, but the scars remain to this day. Sixty years later my mother's denunciations of me echo in my memory, if no longer in my soul. I can hear her now: "You little bitch; you're so ugly and stupid. You will never amount to anything." I was forever in the shadow of my older sister, who was the smart one, the cute one. It was no contest, in terms of beauty or otherwise. We would fight over toys and dolls and Judy would always win, as Mom would tell me to give them to her.

As hard as I tried I could never win my mother's love. Many times when Dad was drunk he would beat her up, and she would call to me for help. I tried going to her aid, but Dad was too big for me. He would pull my hair and bang me up against the wall. One time he broke my nose, which never healed properly.

Mom never thanked me for trying to help her nor did she sympathize with my injuries. When she really got angry at me she would pull my hair, slap me, call me a bitch and scream: "If it weren't for you, I wouldn't have to put up with this." Of course, that didn't make any sense, but I was too young—and intimidated—to realize it.

Things continued like this for many years, and I developed new ways to cope. I was fairly popular when I was in high school, but I had to be sneaky when my dates brought me home because I never knew what to expect. Dad might stagger out on the porch in his underwear to wave me inside, or Mom would start yelling at me. If neither of them appeared, my sister Denise, who was eight years younger than I, might run out frantically calling to me to come inside, because Dad was hitting Mom.

To distract my date I would keep talking a mile a minute and make sure that he kept looking at me. One time my future husband, Robert, put his head on the steering wheel and moaned because I wouldn't stop talking. Of course, I was too embarrassed to invite him into the house, fearing Mom's tirades or Dad's drunkenness.

Mom never ceased to tell me how stupid and ugly I was. One of her favorite refrains was "I can't for the world understand how any boy could be interested in you." Whenever she had guests over she would send me to my room because, in her own inimitable words, "I'm ashamed to have them even look at you."

Mom often berated me for being either too thin or too fat. I felt like a loser, worthless, a nothing. One of my earliest goals in life was to make myself look pretty despite my mom's insistence that I was "forever ugly."

When Dad didn't come home, my job was to drive Mom around in the car with my younger sister, Denise, in the backseat, looking for him and the woman my mother said he was seeing.

One time she hired a detective to follow my father. Despite my protestations that I had to do my homework, she forced me to drive her to the motel where the detective was waiting. When he forced open the door, my mother shoved me into the room ahead of her so that I would be the first to view the sordid scene. Then she screamed at me, "Look, there's the filthy bastard, there's your father."

And there, indeed, he was, sitting on the edge of the bed in his shorts, drunk and dazed, trying to shield a frightened woman who had a sheet pulled up to her chin.

At the end of my senior year we moved to Nevada. I felt suffocated; my spirit was slowly dying. All the physical and verbal abuse convinced me that I had to get out of that house.

Fortunately, Robert was determined to marry me, even though we had dated only once or twice. He complained that I never had time for him because I was always cleaning the house or taking care of my younger sister, a task that had been delegated to me by my mother. He was persistent, though. He drove back and forth from Idaho to Nevada on weekends.

When he proposed to me it was as if Prince Charming had come to rescue me. His love and devotion counterbalanced (but unfortunately did not erase) all the negative stuff that my mother had filled my head and heart with. Robert loved me for who I was. He thought I was the most beautiful person in the world, perfect in every way, his dream girl, his Cinderella. His love stood in sharp contrast to the steady stream of criticism I received from my mother, who never turned off the spigot of verbal abuse.

When we were married, I had just barely turned twenty. I didn't mind a bit that the wedding was a comedy of errors, like a hillbilly sitcom. Of course Mom said no to a wedding dress. She claimed the family couldn't afford one. So I bought one myself. A justice of the peace married us at my parents' home. It was 110 degrees outside, and I remember that the dog was howling away in the heat.

Mom had been in charge of sending out invitations, but she didn't send any to Dad's side of the family since she hated his mother. Of course, she came anyway, which added to the already tense situation.

For the nuptial entrance my father played a Hawaiian wedding song. The record was badly scratched and made a god-awful sound.

When the moment came to escort me into the living room, he tried to walk beside me instead of letting me go first. We got stuck side by side in the door. It was a scene right out of a Laurel and Hardy movie.

Despite the fiercely hot temperature outside, my father decided a roaring fire in the fireplace would add a little atmosphere to the celebration. But as he squirted starter fuel into the fireplace a huge burst of flame sent him reeling backwards onto his rump.

His escape from serious injury was the excuse for several toasts. There was plenty of alcohol since my dad worked for a leading liquor distributor. At that time I drank very little.

Mom was great at playing what I call "the secret game." She would tell me a secret and forbid me to repeat it to my sister Judy. She'd tell Denise something and forbid her to tell it to Judy or me. Then she'd try to catch us by making believe that Denise had told me something, which I was to keep secret from her. She would say that she knew that Denise had shared a secret with me and I was not to pretend that she hadn't. All these permutations made us dizzy, trying to remember exactly what secrets could be shared and with whom.

Much later in life I learned that alcoholism and drug addiction are all about secrets and they, too, often compound the effects of our disease.

•   •   •

Many of the women who come to the Betty Ford Center for help with their chemical dependency are victims of abuse: emotional, physical and/or sexual. One of the secrets that so many women carry with them is a history of childhood sexual abuse. There appears to be a direct correlation between abuse and chemical dependency. Our counselors make it a point to explore abuse issues with our patients and to deal with them both in the treatment setting itself and in the patient's continuing-care plan.

•   •   •

While Paula was playing golf Friday morning, Jacqueline was setting up the hospitality suite (no—"drinks" were not served there!) outside the Firestone building. Firestone's the "hub" of the Center, in many ways. It's where new patients check in, where the medical staff is based and, until recently, was where everybody came to eat meals.

Jacqueline, who's been sober since 1994, had volunteered to steer returning alumni to the sign-in books. There are books for each of the four residence halls, another one for persons who've been through the Family Program, as well as one for those who've been through the Intensive Outpatient Program.

After signing in, alumni inevitably search through the signatures to see if there are names they recognize; joyful shouts are heard over and over again as alumni spot familiar names.

Conversations often turn to those who are absent. "Have you heard from so-and-so?" There are sighs of relief when someone says yes, she's okay; expressions of sadness when there's news of a relapse—or worse.

After the hugs and handshakes, alumni often walk along the circular path behind Firestone Hall. They reminisce about the happy and painful times they experienced at the center and, of course, about their lives since leaving the center.

The paths are not laid out in a circular pattern by accident. "The circle" plays an important part in treatment. The residential halls are laid out in a circle connected by circular paths. Another circular path goes around the perimeter of the center's grounds, which patients walk every morning. When alumni recite the Serenity Prayer Saturday morning during the annual reunion, they form a giant circle on the lawn.

The circle has a long and honorable history. People gather into circles to celebrate, to hold council, to create community, to govern by consensus. Sitting or standing in a circle fosters the idea within the entire group that anyone and everyone is part of the whole. The circle draws from the peer group's collective wisdom, conscience and experience.

I'm proud that the circle finds such a prominent place at the center because it is the most refined representation of unity, so important in the AA tradition.

I remember when we opened the Center, the first four patients and twenty-one staff had to walk carefully on campus, lest they stumble while traversing the uneven paths among the three completed buildings—Firestone, McCallum and West Hall (later named *Pocklington*). Today the 100-plus inpatients and their family members, young people from the Children's Program, Professionals in Residence, as well as our 240-person staff, walk unimpeded through a magnificent twenty-acre campus of nine buildings landscaped with a variety of trees, shrubs and flowers of every color. Some of the walkways are now lined with "building bricks," which feature the names of those who are living lives of sobriety. Alumni proudly point to these bricks as they tour the campus during the reunion.

For the past six years Jacqueline has volunteered her time every Friday to help in the alumni office. Everyone who meets her notices the sparkle in her hazel eyes, her winsome smile and the striking, prematurely gray hair. She is one of the miracles of recovery. She felt especially good on this day and thought how wonderful it was to be alive, well and sober. Her memories of her first reunion and the two following ones were not at all pleasant. She was pretending that she was sober, sporting a mask of sobriety. But we are getting ahead of ourselves. I shall first let her introduce herself.

Jacqueline

While admiring the wonderful sunny days here in the desert during Alumni Weekend, I thought that no one in the Coachella Valley really knows what a winter is like unless they've been to South Dakota, where it could get to fifty degrees below zero even before the windchill was factored in.

I can still remember sitting in the cab of my dad's pickup truck, with my brothers, waiting for him to take us to school, and not being able to see over the snowdrifts. It was Dad's job to take us to and from school—and more often then not, those trips home involved Dad stopping in for a "quick one." It got frigidly cold inside that truck while we waited for our father to finish warming himself with liquor and the conviviality of friends. His words as he parked the truck and headed into the bar were always the same: "You children wait here, I'll only be a few minutes."

When it got too cold and my two younger brothers and I were chilled to the bone, I would go inside to fetch my father. If he wouldn't come I'd at least grab the keys so I could start the engine and get the heater working. Then we'd do our homework under the dome light or just horse around the way brothers and sisters do. Occasionally I would screw up my courage and bring my brothers into the bar. It was like most other country bars in South Dakota with about twenty stools around the bar itself. There was a pool table in the middle of the room and a couple of tables against a wall. There we would sit, sipping Cokes.

Invariably, Mom would call and the bartender would fib and say Dad had left fifteen minutes ago. That was our cue to pack up and get on the road. At home, Mom would be worried sick during those "missing" fifteen minutes. She knew full well that her husband had been drinking and that he was driving home sloshed, with the kids in the truck.

This routine was acted out repeatedly for about a year until Mom returned to teaching. Then she took over driving us to and from school.

I didn't know then—but certainly know now—that my father was an active alcoholic, and it was from him that I inherited my own genetic predisposition to what would be for me a very serious illness.

When he wasn't drinking, my father was a farmer. I was the eldest of five children (two brothers and two sisters) whom he fathered and my mother raised while also teaching and at times working in the fields. Even after Dad had "gone on the wagon" (as it was called in those days), he was never able to achieve a state of inner peace. As an adult, reflecting back on Dad's behavior while drinking and after he stopped, I began to understand the important difference between "getting sober" and actually living a life of serenity.

There are great benefits to being raised in a small town in South Dakota. I enjoyed school, I got good grades. But every year my report

card would point out that I talked too much. And I did. I was a
people person and later a people pleaser. I participated in everything:
track, basketball, volleyball and eight-person football.

I was hurt when my father failed to attend my sporting events, but
I soon prayed for his no-shows because when he did appear, he was
always drunk. The hurt was particularly poignant when he failed to
attend my graduation, but even then I had mixed feelings—relief because, had he been drinking, I would have been embarrassed, and a
combination of anger and hurt because Dad wouldn't or couldn't
stop drinking long enough to show how proud he was of me. The
legacy of this wounded father-daughter relationship continues to
this day.

Because of Dad's drinking the rest of us did everything without
him, visiting relatives, going in to town on Saturday afternoons after
we'd done the morning chores. We were and still remain a close-knit
and supportive family, as the later intervention on me will clearly
demonstrate. But Dad was difficult to be around. His sarcasm had a
razor-sharp edge when he was drinking and he could cut us to the
quick with his verbal barbs—something I became quite adept at as
well when I started drinking.

There were only forty-five kids at our high school. We were all
friends. But I was jealous of Jane, my closest and dearest friend. I
would stay with her a lot. She seemed to have the perfect family and
I thought her parents were wonderful, particularly her father, who did
not drink and who showed up at all the high-school activities. I was
flattered by the attention that he paid to me. Jealous feelings kept
popping up and I couldn't seem to push them away no matter how
hard I tried.

I had to hold my breath when Jane told me that she hated her parents. It really baffled me, but who really understands the shifting
tides of the adolescent mind and soul? It was my first encounter with
life's darker side. I was ashamed of my father's behavior and could

not fathom Jane's attitude toward her dad. I even wondered at times what exchanging parents would be like!

Then when we were sophomores, Jane was in a terrible car accident from which she never fully recovered. She suffered severe head injuries and had to have brain surgery. She wasn't the same after the accident. I felt so bad for both Jane and her parents. I've often thought that Jane's postaccident situation was similar to my own. We were both locked into worlds separated from others—she was trapped physically, while I was trapped emotionally and mentally.

•   •   •

A great deal has been written about "predispositions" to alcoholism—biological, psychological and social. It's easy to see how this genetic predisposition may have played a role in the lives of Paula and Jacqueline, given their fathers' alcoholism. I suppose there could have been a genetic predisposition in my case as my brother was an alcoholic. But it is clear that my addiction to prescription drugs was the result of my medical disabilities and my alcoholism was a case of crossing the thin line from social drinking to dependency.

•   •   •

As Jacqueline was still signing in visiting alumni, Claire was on her way to Fisher Hall, the residential unit built especially for women in 1986. I paid close attention to the design of this building and made sure that bathtubs were installed, something omitted in the first three halls. Fisher Hall women, who like to refer to themselves as "Fisherettes," call it "Betty's Hall" because of the attention I gave to it while it was being designed and built.

Claire is one of the great ladies of the Betty Ford Center. One of the main reasons I agreed to be her sponsor when she completed treatment is that her history is much like mine. Every year at the reunion she volunteers to tell her story to current patients. Claire looks at least ten years younger than her seventy-six years and she greets everyone with that husky voice that made her such a great solo singer. She has a great sense of humor.

It was just about four o'clock on Friday afternoon when Claire headed for Fisher Hall to share her story with the female patients. She also lets them know how lucky they are to be in an all-women unit instead of sharing McCallum Hall with men, which was how it was when she entered treatment in 1984.

Claire

I grew up in a loving family, the youngest of three children. The whole clan was musically oriented and while the sounds of music at our grandparents' summer home hardly resembled the Von Trapp family, the harmony was exceptional and the music always raised our spirits. Dad and his two brothers never lacked for an audience when they performed as a trio.

We lived in a small suburb outside Chicago, Illinois, where we had the biggest backyard in the neighborhood, ideally suited for kicking the can and all sorts of fun games. Then when I was eleven, we moved to a larger home on a nearby street. My mother allowed me to pick out the colors and the materials for my own room—Wedgwood blue and white stripes and a white chenille bedspread. I had a bay window that looked out onto the street and my own dressing table and bathroom.

Scott, the oldest boy, shared a room and bathroom with Ben, my other brother, at the other end of the hall. There was a wonderful landing at the top of the stairs where Mom had her own desk. Looking over the railing from above we could see the family room and the library with its tiled floor. Our house had a spacious screened porch at the back where we spent a lot of time in the summer. Mom let me pick out some of the features for the beautiful rock garden that she made in back of our home. My mother and I were very close.

I associate World War II with a lot of tragedy in our home. That's when Mom was diagnosed with cancer. She died at the young age of forty-three. Then both my brothers went off to war. Dad and I were left alone at home with our loving housekeeper, Donna. I was entrusted with the task of juggling the ration coupons. Dad had bought Mom a new car shortly before she died. Since she hadn't used it much, we had an extra supply of gasoline coupons. I remember going to the butcher and exchanging some of them for food. I would say, "My dad needs a pork chop and you need gas. Let's cut a deal." The butcher smiled but treated me as a grown-up, even though I was still in high school.

One day we received a telegram from the War Department. Donna was there, and we didn't know what to do. I had a sinking feeling in the pit of my stomach. We opened the telegram and it said that Ben had been wounded in battle. I started to cry and asked Donna if we should call Dad at work or wait until he came home. She told me to go next door to the neighbor, who was one of our dearest friends, and ask her what to do. When I ran into the kitchen to tell her what had happened, I was out of breath and white as a sheet. She told me to call my dad right away. When he came home, he took charge and said that we should wait until we found out more about the wound and not to anticipate the worst.

Well, the wound was pretty bad. Ben was with the 101st Airborne and he had lost his left leg just below the knee. We met him at the train station when he came home. He was struggling to become accustomed to crutches. I remember the cabdriver saying to my brother, "Well, at least you still have your knee." It was not the smartest thing in the world to say, but at least he said *something*. I didn't know what to say.

I felt sad and ill equipped to deal with the situation. I remember how desperately I wanted my mother to help me through this, to help me understand, to tell me what to say. Ben missed Mom also.

He was her favorite. He had to be fitted with an artificial leg and then undergo intensive rehabilitation. He took to drinking more and more and eventually died from alcoholism.

When I graduated from high school, I was lucky to get into a highly regarded college in New York. I chose the school because some of my friends were going there. I missed my dad, but was excited about leaving the dull Midwest for the glamour of New York.

Encouraged by one of my teachers, I became interested in theater and drama. On weekends we went into Manhattan. While my friends shopped, I would make the rounds of the theaters, where I would make friends with the ushers. At intermission they would sneak me in and allow me to stand at the back of the theater and watch the second half of the show.

I loved to listen to Billie Holiday, my idol, who was at the end of her career, and Sarah Vaughan, another of my favorites.

We used to do a lot of drinking when we were permitted out. I discovered that I could drink more and hold it better than most of the other girls. They looked to me to escort them back and sign them in when we returned to the college after a night of carousing.

I returned to Chicago in 1947, having completed two years of college with majors in art, speech and radio. I had a new stepmother whom I did not find all that friendly. There was some jealousy between us. She was always finding fault with our home, which I took as criticism of Mom. For my part, I was envious of her relationship with Dad. Ben didn't like her at all and we both felt that she had invaded our turf. I tried to be a buffer for Dad, a role that provided early training for my later careers of caretaker and codependent. I got busy being busy.

I was hired by a major department store in downtown Chicago, and because of my training in art, I was assigned to the Display Department, decorating windows, doing interior design and in general learning the business. I did so well that nine months later I was put in charge of decorating the Toy Department for Christmas. In my leisure time, I was singing with a small combo on weekends and then given a fabulous fifteen-minute radio spot on WTMJ after the Cubs' game on Sundays.

And then the gods were especially kind. Some advance men for Matt Matthews and the Sophisticates heard me auditioning for the amateur hour on the Philip Morris show. They considered me a perfect fit for a "single" in the band and offered me the job. Recovering from my astonishment, I told them that I would have to ask my father.

Dad wanted to speak with Mr. Matthews personally. He was playing at a local club so I took Dad there and introduced him. Dad told Mr. Matthews that I had been raised in a good Christian family and that he didn't want me involved in any monkey business. Mr. Matthews told him that he and his wife were also good Christians and that I could stay with them in California. I was to be paid $125 a week—a fabulous sum.

Dad gave me his blessing. I took my own car, a red Plymouth convertible with black leather seats, a black top and whitewall tires. The down payment for the car came from the checks from my grandmother that I'd been saving; the monthly installments were $56. The tenor in the band and his wife drove with me to California.

I moved into one of the darling little cottages surrounding the Matthews home. The Matthewses were kind to me, particularly after I pitched in and helped paint a few of the cottages. After a couple of months Mr. Matthews invited me to accompany him to Palm Springs. He was aware of my background in art and design and wanted to ask my advice about some work that he was planning to do on a motel that he'd bought there. I told him I didn't think the decorating and color schemes that he had in mind were going to work.

He didn't take too kindly to that. I didn't realize how sensitive he was to criticism.

A few weeks after returning from Palm Springs I said my goodbyes and left my quaint little cottage. Truth to tell, I felt left out of the fun and good times that the rest of the band was having. They were staying at a hotel in Hollywood. I was young and wanted to enjoy the companionship of other members of the band.

In September 1948, we started working our way back east. I'd fallen in love with Joe, the lead bass player, who was the most attractive guy in the orchestra. He was very talented and had a feature spot in the band. We got married in Arizona. Mr. Matthews didn't like that one bit, and I could sense that my father was not happy when he came to meet the groom in Texas. It saddened me that the two favorite men in my life didn't like each other.

We continued the tour for a little while but soon Joe, whom I discovered was a heavy drinker, got fed up with everything, the travel in particular, and said, "Let's go home, we'll stay with my mom." "Home" was Kansas City and I was very excited to move there.

Joe got a job playing with a dance band at a hotel in downtown Kansas City. I soon became restless and marched down to the local TV station and told them that they had no programs for teenagers. "Bee-bop" and "hip talk" were much the fashion, and I was very good at that language. The station management decided to add something for the younger audience between four-thirty and five in the afternoon, and I was given the job.

I was thrilled when Beth was born although soon my husband was beginning to work less and drink more. He was often loaded when I came home, watching television while the baby was dirty and wet, screaming to beat the band. It wasn't long before he was getting abusive, spanking Beth when she cried too much.

Finally, I decided to leave. One day when Joe wasn't home, my friend came over and we packed up all my clothes and my sewing machine. That's all I took. That machine had been an anniversary present from Joe; I thought when he gave it to me it was a wonderful gesture. Boy, was I dumb. I soon learned that he'd only made a small down payment on it, leaving me to make all the monthly payments!

Beth and I stayed with my friend for a few months, and then boarded with a wonderful woman who knew me from TV. She soon fell in love with Beth and became her granny. I ran into a talented piano player and the two of us put a cabaret act together. We had a good run at the Black Hat, one of the classy nightspots in Kansas City. To pay the bills I was working at three jobs: commercials and voice-overs on radio and TV during the day, the Black Hat in the evenings and an upscale hotel in downtown Kansas City on weekends.

◆　◆　◆

Since it was getting close to dinnertime, Claire told the patients that she would break here and return after supper to finish her story. She left to a round of applause from the grateful patients. The sun was beginning to set, and the patients from the various residential halls began gathering in circles as they prepared to walk over to Firestone for dinner.

Patients never forget being introduced to the outdoor premeal circle. Together, they chant the antidrug, prolife mantra that's specific to their hall. The words of the chant might vary from one generation of patients to the next, but the ritual of the circle and the tradition of the chant itself do not change. Nor does the chant's message ever lose its punch, which speaks to transformation, change itself. "Change in a circle is circular, it embraces everyone."

As the sun went down on Friday, many alumni were still on campus, conversing with staff, sharing memories—some serious, some hilarious. I still laugh at some of the stories, no matter how often I hear them. One in particular is in my autobiography. A new female patient was shocked when the staff confiscated her mouthwash and perfume at check-in (because they contain alcohol). Then a counselor said that he would take her to her room. "You're in the swamp," he said.

Her reaction? "They think I'm going to drink my perfume and mouthwash and then sleep in a swamp. These people are crazier than I am!"

Of course, she was soon to learn that "the swamp" was hardly what she at first imagined. It's the name given to the one room in each hall which has four beds rather than the customary two.

2

Good Mommies, Bad Mommies

Saturday, the second day of the anniversary celebration, promised to be just as beautiful as the day before—perfect for the outdoor events that were scheduled that morning on the spacious lawn at the entrance to the Betty Ford Center. The "Celebration of Recovery" consists of the chip and medallion ceremony; alumni who've been clean for thirty, sixty and ninety days get a plastic chip; those with more than ten years of sobriety are awarded a bronze medallion. Then a parade of alumni make brief remarks to the rest of the crowd. It's always very moving.

Early Saturday morning before the chip ceremony I was in president John Schwarzlose's office in Firestone Hall. He was reviewing for me some of the contents of his "State of the Center" address, which is presented to the Betty Ford Center recovery community every year, usually just before lunch on Saturday. The audience is always curious about what's happened at the Center during the previous year, any changes or additions that were made as we continue our mission. I used to give the address, but for the past few years I have turned it over to John, a good friend, who has been with me since the opening of the Center. I and the rest of the board attribute much of the Center's success to his leadership.

As John and I were leaving his office, we saw Harriet exiting the nearby Serenity Room. We'll meet Harriet in a moment, but first let me say a word about the Serenity Room. It's one of the places that I'm most proud of on this campus. When it was built in 1986 (a gift from a grateful alumni) it became a visible sign of what recovery is all about and of the truly spiritual dimension to the program. It is there for the benefit of both patients and visitors.

When a person enters the Serenity Room, she or he is touched immediately by the silence that envelops him or her. It's as though they've entered a sanctuary, a place of solitude, where the inner and outer worlds meet. Like so many other things at the Betty Ford Center, it is shaped in a circle. One whole wall is glass, from floor to ceiling, allowing the visitor to gaze upon a small but beautiful rock garden almost oriental in its shape and dimension.

The eye is attracted to life-giving water falling over the rocks into a small pond surrounded by a variety of colorful flowers and desert plants. The waterfall is almost inaudible. The room is perfectly still and quiet, layered in three tiers with pillows allowing one to sit or lie comfortably facing the rock garden. Above the small concrete wall outside the window, guarding the privacy both of the space and the visitors, one can see the azure sky and the rugged mountain range that serve as nature's backdrop.

I remember on one occasion speaking with my sponsor and telling her that there was nothing much spiritual going on in my life. She said to me, "As a recovering person, when you tell your story to another human being, that is sacred ground." That comment has remained with me ever since. There is much that is spiritual about storytelling and nothing that is sensational. I always tell nonrecovering people that there is a vast world of difference between television talk shows and storytelling. Talk shows commercialize, sensationalize and degrade the AA genre of storytelling, which by its nature is sacred ground, spiritual and deeply personal. They glory in the quick fix, the drive for instant attention, fortune, fame and glamour. They are intended to satisfy the public's insatiable appetite for the sensational.

Storytelling, as conceived by Bill W. and Dr. Bob, the cofounders of Alcoholics Anonymous, provides the opportunity for a circle of healing, for the storyteller to take first position and for the listener to take second. It is a private affair, noncommercial, bereft of fame and fortune. It is a sacred moment between sharer and listener. It is *not an end in itself, but rather the beginning of a circle; nor is it carried out in a carnival-like atmosphere but in a circular setting that promotes healing through self-forgiveness. No one derides, boos or hisses; everyone simply listens, identifies and respectfully applauds the courage and humility of the storyteller.*

Not by the farthest stretch of the imagination is the talk show a sacred moment. The attempt at instant intimacy is, in my opinion, a complete failure and a bunch of nonsense, often ludicrous. Having experienced a spiritual awakening myself, I've learned that a recovering person's story suggests and invites a profound intimacy and mutual nurturing bond between narrator and listener.

During the first year of my recovery, I said very little at AA groups. But gradually, as I began to experience the joy that can be found in recovery, I wanted to help others discover that same joy. Both Leonard Firestone and I embraced the tradition that the best way to express thanks for one's personal recovery is to pass the message on to "the millions who still don't know." I came to understand that people relate to someone who has the same problems and has overcome them.

◆　◆　◆

Now it's time for you to meet Harriet. When she finished her stay in Fisher Hall, she decided to remain in the desert instead of returning to Georgia, where she worked.

Harriet

To remind me of how much she loved me, my mother would paint in vivid verbal detail a graphic picture of my birth, and say, "See how much I love you? I went through all of that."

The saga she recounted sounded both melodramatic and nightmarish. She described a cesarean delivery supported by saddle-block spinal anesthesia and complained that they did not block her high enough. Even though she screamed to everyone in the operating room that she felt the knife, the surgeon wouldn't stop. Moreover, she claimed that they used an airway on her and knocked out all the beautiful porcelain caps on her teeth. So there she was in pain with a mouthful of sharp shards of teeth when the nurse handed me to her, "a wrinkled red mess," to use my mother's own words.

She described me as "disgusted looking" when I left her womb to face a new world. Dad, however, recalled her muttering "disgusting looking" when she described me at birth. That made him cry because he concluded that his wife didn't like their newborn daughter. While I never pictured myself as "Rosemary's baby," I always felt that I caused the pain she endured forever after. I was ashamed for any misdeed I committed or inadequacy I exhibited, anything that caused Mommy additional pain. Early on I became accustomed to retreating to my hiding places so as to avoid causing trouble.

To outward appearances my family was the prototype of the American dream: businessman father, beautiful mother, two well-dressed daughters in matching outfits, a uniformed maid and two sets of grandparents. Dad's folks were sophisticated and wealthy, Mom's earthy and old-country.

But nothing was as it appeared. Every player had his or her own secrets, which sabotaged the normality I longed for.

We lived in a beautiful house in Putnam County, New York. It was a large lot with plenty of old and beautiful oaks, maples and elms. My room, smaller than my sister's, was under an alcove on the top floor of the house. I could always isolate myself by hiding there when there was tension in the house. There I would settle down with my authors as companions: Jane Austen, Shirley Ames, Nancy Drew. I loved to read and was attracted to stories about independent living. My grandfather would get all the books on *The New York Times* bestseller list so he could make them available to the family, even though he himself could not read.

My mother was very beautiful, a former model in the 1930s. She was also a typical Jewish mother. The "good mommy" was glamorous, always impeccably dressed, perfectly manicured, coiffured and made up. She would be gushing with "I love yous" and smothering us with kisses.

The "bad mommy" stumbled about in a housecoat with rollers in her hair, her face splotchy and puffy, venting her wrath on the weakest of targets, which was usually me. My sister and I could never be completely sure when we were about to see the "good mommy" and when we'd see the "bad mommy," just as later in my own life I couldn't be certain whether my addicted or real self would appear on the stage.

One time my mother was cutting my hair while I was sitting in front of the mirror which sat above her dressing table. All of a sudden she started laughing crazily and began chopping off huge chunks of my hair, first on one side and then on the other. I looked as though I'd been scalped.

Another time, she overheard me tell my sister I hated "bad mommy." She grabbed me by the hair and pulled me over to the sink where she washed my mouth out with soap. Then she stood me in front of her and pinched my cheeks so hard the welts lasted all day long. Then she triumphantly demanded, "Now do you love me?" With tears streaming down my cheeks, I whimpered, "Yes, Mommy, I love you a lot." She let me go and said with visible disgust, "You're a little liar."

Other times "bad mommy" would come home when I was in bed, enter my room, turn on the lights and empty out all my drawers on the floor. Then without a word she would leave. My fear and resentment of "bad mommy" carried over to "good mommy" because I couldn't predict the Jekyll-Hyde transformations.

My mother's parents, Nanny and Papa, lived in a small, dark apartment that always contained the lingering smell of fried herring and a cloud of ancient dust. Nanny was a large woman with a bad knee and one eye. She wore a perpetual expression of disapproval and always smelled unwashed. She whined all the time. I remember Papa for his dirty, long, gray overcoat, soiled old clothes and a bright, frayed, hand-knit bow tie.

For a long time I tried not to remember the times when Papa was baby-sitting, and would take me upstairs to my parents' big bed. It had a green velvet-quilted bedspread and a huge white carved headboard upholstered in the same fabric. He would place me on the bed or on his lap and would rub his hand over me everywhere. When I was seven, I became aware that he did this to my sister, too.

Papa would warn me not to tell Mommy, because "she wouldn't understand." My little heart told me there was something wrong about what he did. The one time I got the courage to tell my mother what Papa did, she screamed at me that this was impossible because Papa had always been the favorite of all the children in the neighborhood. He entertained them with his tricks and his magic, she said. She didn't know that after his tricks he would have us reach into his pants' pocket to feel his "roll of nickels." My sister and I seldom agree on anything but we are united in our disgust, shame and anger over Papa's treatment of us and our mother's denial of it.

When we were young, Lisa and I were always paraded like talking parrots before company and made to recite the words that Mommy made us memorize: "You're the best mommy and daddy in the world."

But I was different from Lisa. When she told them she loved them, I believe she meant it. As far as I can remember, I did not. My parents never trusted me, and let me know that. I was not allowed to play outside our yard, or walk the one block to and from school without the maid. I had few friends; sometimes I wonder if I had any real ones. I invited no one to my home because I was ashamed of Nanny and Papa and afraid "bad mommy" might be in residence. Ironically, "good mommy"—and she was always "good mommy" while chaperoning school trips—was popular with my classmates.

My dad was an enigma. I remember once being in a highchair eating and making a mess as young children do. He couldn't handle it and turned away looking sick. Mom said, "Just don't look at her." From that day on he ate in the dining room, while Lisa and I ate in the kitchen with the maid. Daddy wasn't really aloof, just oblivious—especially while watching sports on TV. He could be very sweet with our mother, who stood between him and everyone else so much that she even answered for him in social situations and conversations. I couldn't help but feel ignored (some would interpret it as being rejected) by him.

Otto, my grandpa, used to call my dad a "pansy" and would berate him constantly. Otto liked to drink Chivas Regal and used to give me a nice tall tumbler of it weakened with a lot of club soda, saying with a wink, "Here's your ginger ale, young lady." That started at the age of fourteen. He and Grandma Sally had an elegant apartment on Fourteenth Street in Manhattan. I loved to visit with them and to sip my scotch. At our own home we had cocktails every night at 5 P.M. It was a ritual—scotch on the rocks. The ritual would include a discussion as to whether one more was in order; if so, then my mother would sing to a "captive" audience.

Just before my senior year in high school I met my stepbrother, Tom, for the first time and became attached to him immediately. (He was my dad's son by a previous marriage, which neither my sister nor I knew about. Tom was five years older than me.) He came to my assistance several times later in life when I was in serious trouble.

Mom didn't like Tom and demanded that I avoid all communication with him. She went so far as to intercept all the letters that he wrote to me. In one of them he mentioned a pot bust at his home, but I never saw the letter. Mom did, however, and broadcast this juicy piece of scandal throughout the family. For a long time Tom was ostracized. He blamed me for divulging the information and breaking his trust. I had never seen the letter and I felt betrayed by my mother—not to mention hurt that Tom thought I had done this to him. This invasion and abuse of my privacy was but one of many examples of our wounded daughter/mother relationship. I couldn't wait to leave home and get away from her.

When I was twelve, my mother took me for the Mensa exam. A few weeks later she took me out shopping and bought me three fancy dresses, something that she had never done before. Then she took me to lunch at a fancy restaurant. While we were eating she gave me a letter that she had already opened (even though it had been addressed to me). It informed me that I had scored in the top 1 percent of those who had taken the Mensa exam. I will never forget my anger and resentment at what she had done. It was another shameless violation of my privacy, and I hated her for it. For her part, she was pleased with me only when I existed as an extension of herself and she could take credit for all the applause that came my way. Such was my mother's control over me.

For me, the culminating example of her control occurred at my high school graduation. I wanted to go to college and be a writer. The University of Miami was on the top of my list. My mother wanted me to go to Hofstra, on Long Island, so that I wouldn't be too far away. When the headmaster handed me my diploma and announced the college at which I had been accepted, it was—sure enough—Hofstra. I don't know how she managed it, but she did.

In the end, though, she won the battle but lost the war. Hofstra, yes, but I wouldn't be living at home; I'd live on campus. It was the first step toward emancipation.

My freshman year was a fabulous time to be in college. Student rage was being directed against the Vietnam War. Communes, hippies, long hair, flower children, Woodstock—it was all magic to me.

I didn't study much in college. I majored, really, in politics and drugs. I was literate and cool and became politically savvy. I hung out with older students and professors, smoked pot, skipped classes,

helped organize antiwar rallies and wrote for an underground newspaper. I felt gloriously free, vital and happy—and nearly flunked out.
When my English professor asked me if I was coming back for my
sophomore year, I said yes. He said he wondered why. I was taken
aback and began to wonder why myself.

Somehow I came to realize that the only reason I was in school
was to get away from home and that there were other ways to do that.
Browsing through the newspapers one morning, an ad for a school
for paralegals caught my eye. I asked my grandfather, who was fond
of me, if he would underwrite my endeavor. He liked the idea of his
granddaughter starting out on her own, working for a living, and
said that he would.

My parents were aghast at the career that I had chosen but I stood
firm. I lived at home and commuted to Manhattan for class. Thor-
oughly enchanted with my new vocation, I devoted myself to it.
However, along with my paralegal career, I began also to develop a
few other interests, including drinking after school with my teacher
and before dinner with my parents.

Having scored very high on my New York license exam, I was offered a job in Atlanta, Georgia, as a paralegal for a prestigious law
firm at a very attractive salary. I was proud of myself, and moved to
Georgia at the age of twenty. I had my own job, my own life, my own
apartment and was no longer dependent upon my family for money.
My life included hard work and its rewards—and hard play and its
penalties. My reputation as a reliable and accurate professional paralegal continued to grow. In truth, though, I was materially secure but
emotionally at risk. I looked to men for my self-esteem.

◆   ◆   ◆

When Harriet arrived at the chip and medallion ceremony Saturday morning, I
watched her take a seat in the back next to Laurette, a close friend of hers. The stage
contained a podium and microphone for the master of ceremonies and the speakers.

There were about five hundred people present, including the patients from all the halls. It made a huge impact on those patients to see the alumni proudly stand up in groups according to the number of days or years that they'd been continuously sober.

The chips and medallions are a big hit with former patients now in recovery. I remember one of them telling me the great feeling he has when he goes through airport metal detectors and the guard smiles knowingly at him when he (the guard) notices the medallion in the little plastic bowl. He said he's especially proud to be a recovering person when little things like that happen.

After the chip and medallion ceremony, selected graduates representing all the programs—inpatient and outpatient, the family and children's programs—give their testimonials, reflecting on what it was like before, what happened at the Betty Ford Center, and what it's like now. After each story the audience gives the speaker a standing ovation, not just because it's the customary thing to do, but because the speakers clearly touch the souls of everyone listening. It's as though the speakers are exhorting the listeners, "Dare to take the risk. What I have done is something that you also can do."

♦ ♦ ♦

Harriet and Laurette are among my favorite Betty Ford Center alumni. Laurette's stay in Fisher Hall preceded Harriet's, but her reputation lived on. Laurette had been angry with everybody, pushed everyone's buttons, including the staff's, and all without exception had expected her to be unceremoniously thrown out sooner rather than later. Few expected her to survive. But there are many roads to recovery, and Laurette found one of them. Some magic occurred during Laurette's journey from the confinement of prison to the sanctuary of the Betty Ford Center. Her story is miraculous.

Laurette

Whenever I recall the time I spent at the Betty Ford Center, I cannot help but contrast it with the time that I wasted in jail. The image of the judge shaking his head as he looked down at me will never leave me. As he sentenced me, he said, "I'm tired of seeing you here in court. One year in county jail!" And with that he banged his gavel. Hard. I tried to stare him down, but inside I was really frightened.

I was only nineteen but I already had four previous arrests for driving while intoxicated or for being drunk in public. On those occasions, my friends would bail me out the next day. When I went to court, I would get a slap on the wrist and be released. I was young and looked pretty innocent, although I certainly wasn't.

This time was different. I had assaulted a police officer while resisting arrest, and it took three of them to put me in the squad car and take me into custody. By the time they put me on the prison bus and took me to the county jail, I was pretty darn meek. There they took everything away from me; I was strip-searched and put in orange jailbird clothes three sizes too big for my small frame. I was given a blanket and a few other things and taken down the catwalk. The door to my cell opened automatically. The three women inside just looked me up and down when I walked into the cell. Their faces were hard, and they all wore the same sickly orange uniforms. It was surreal.

There were two double-decker bunk beds, an open privy and no windows. Even though I was zonked, I remember feeling scared shitless. I went immediately to the bed that was unoccupied, pulled the blanket over my head and slept for twenty-four hours. On and off I heard the women talking about me. They wondered if I'd managed to smuggle any drugs into jail. As they gathered around my bunk, I tried to figure out how to handle this situation. Suddenly, the pregnant one stopped the others and said, "I know her." Turns out she was a gang member whom I knew in high school. We often bumped into each other in the streets, doing drugs.

Nobody bothered me after that. That girl saved my butt. Otherwise it would have been three against one. I later discovered they were really tough broads.

I knew that I'd have to play a hard-ass if I was going to survive. That wasn't such a tough task, really. I'd grown up so full of anger that I already had that "hard" look. I may have only been nineteen, but I was determined to strike the first blow if anybody came at me. Even though I put up a good front, the first few days I was so frightened that I didn't even feel the effects of my withdrawal from the large amounts of drugs that I had consumed right up until I was jailed.

I further won the women over by giving them my food, unwrapped baloney and cheese sandwiches on white bread. I thought it was gross the way the sandwiches were passed from dirty hand to dirty hand.

That probably sounds strange. Here I was a junkie, often not bathing for days, a person who slept in dirty clothes in dirty alleys, queasy about eating a sandwich that others had touched. Strange, I know.

Occasionally I'd find some drugs in the sandwiches, probably intended for someone else on our cellblock and distributed to me by mistake. I gave them to my cellmates. They liked that.

The commissary cart came around every Thursday. I would buy boxed cereal, packaged peanuts and chocolate bars with money that my friends had sent me. I'd store a week's supply of goodies under my pillow. We were given a package of tobacco and zigzag paper to roll cigarettes. Funny—they wouldn't give us toothbrushes but they did give us tobacco. I didn't smoke so I gave it to my cellmates, which made them even friendlier and more protective of me. We were confined to our cells except for one hour a day, and were allowed to watch television until the guards shut it off. The inmates talked, yelled and screamed all night and slept during the day.

I kept pretty much to myself and had plenty of time to think. Full of self-pity, I kept staring at the whitewashed ceiling and asking myself, "Why me? My mother is the maniac who should be behind bars in a mental ward. What am I doing here?" All the gang members and "friends" I'd lived with were nowhere to be found. I was all alone again.

One of the female guards once said to me, "Kid, you don't belong here. Get rid of your loser friends and get some help." I had no idea what she meant. Often during my drugging days her words would come back to me.

Most people would say that my road to lockup was pretty much predetermined. I was born in Stockton, California. My mother was but a teenager when she brought my brother and me into this world. She was both physically and verbally abusive to us. She used to make us feel that we weren't wanted; that we were both accidents and that if it wasn't for us she would have been able to have a happy life. I actually doubt that very much, though, because she was suicidal; after her husband (our father) left, she tried to hang herself a number of times. Her favorite spot was the garage. She tossed strips torn from sheets over the rafters.

I'll always remember how the police would take us away after each suicide attempt and then return us home after a time when Mom was better. I was filled with dread that she would never come back, and when she did, another type of fear would consume my brother and me—the fear of verbal abuse and the deeper anxiety that came with rejection because we were a burden to her.

As a kid I was withdrawn, nervous and shy. One time I was so hurt by Mom's behavior that I wished she would be successful with one of her many suicide attempts so that we could get on with our lives. But later, I would be ashamed that I ever thought that.

Our grandparents loved us very much. Being Hispanic, we considered family very important. They tried to make up for what Mom did not or could not give us. My grandfather had a good job and was well off. But there was a lot of drinking and codependency in my extended family. Sitting in my jail cell, I thought about how many funerals I had attended over the years of family members whose lives had ended in violence or suicides. I never once heard of any of them getting help. There was never mention of AA. The only way out of the terrible lives they lived was just to die.

It wasn't long into high school before I realized that I would have to look after myself. I always felt alone. My mother made fun of me whenever I tried to share my feelings. She would say that I was too dramatic, or hysterical, or that I was prone to blow everything out of proportion. If I got hurt she told me to be tougher, if someone picked on me at school she'd say I must have provoked it. She never stood up for me or took my side. I felt I always had to stand alone.

It was only natural that I turned to my peer group for my survival. When I joined an all-female gang, I was no longer alone. We were low riders with creased clothes and practiced movements and stares. We kept ourselves segregated from the Aggies and Blacks. We were proud of our Hispanic culture although we knew nothing about it and were probably poor examples of its rich tradition and wonderful customs.

At the beginning I was picked on and pushed around because of my small frame. This only further angered and toughened me. We were a bunch of messed-up kids with a lot of rage but no direction or goals in life. We were products of our parents' dysfunctional lifestyles, passed on from one generation to the next. It was one hell of a legacy.

I started drinking and sniffing as soon as I got to high school. It was the normal thing. I hardly ever went to class and would write my own notes to excuse myself. Nobody at home cared.

One time, soon after my mother had tried to commit suicide yet again, I overheard my grandparents talking and wondering what they were going to do with "those kids"—referring to my brother and myself. It seemed like we were extraterrestrial. The casual remark wounded, and I still carry the hurt and the rejection that I read into the phrase. A small thing, but I seized on it to cement my ties with the gang, with those kids my grandparents called "losers." I believed that the gang cared for me, and I felt that I could trust them with my life.

Because I had to support myself and pay for the alcohol and drugs that I was getting into, I became a thief and deep-sixed my conscience. Over time, I found it easier and easier to walk into a store, steal what I wanted and saunter out again—without getting caught. I earned the respect of the gang and I felt like a "big shot." It was a sick way of fostering self-esteem.

When I ended up in jail, I'd ask myself, "If you're so clever, how did you end up in this cell with this community of losers?" I knew that I wasn't playing the game right. I had no intention of going straight when I got out—but I was determined to avoid getting caught. I had to stay out of jail. Of course, the smartest way to do that was to change my behavior, to stay clean and sober. But those words were foreign to me; the old way was still the most appealing. I would just have to be more careful. I would continue drinking and drugging but make sure to avoid the cops.

After six months in the Big House, I got another break. The jail was overcrowded, so my sentence was reduced for good behavior. As a parting gift I was released from jail at three o'clock in the morning. I had to hold up my pants with my hands, I'd lost so much weight. I was left standing outside in the rain. It was a fitting background for the mood that I was in. I was pissed off and I was determined to punish everyone, which I did by almost killing myself over the next two decades.

There was a pattern and a cycle to my self-defeating behavior that tended to repeat itself. I dropped out of high school and left Stockton for Chico, California. There Shoshanna found me on the streets, befriended me and brought me to her home. I've saved a photograph of myself from that time, sitting on a couch in the living room with this ugly baseball cap on my head, sporting a gruesome black eye with bruises all over my face. I'm wearing a T-shirt under a plaid wool shirt. A pair of army boots from the Salvation Army adorns my feet.

There were five of us in the house—me, Shoshanna, another young girl and a couple of guys who would sleep on the couches in the living room. One or two others would occasionally drift in and out. The traffic through the commune was so constant that I never could be sure who was living there. We would sleep all day and go to the bars at night. Shoshanna became my lover and supplied my drugs. Sometimes I worked, but for the most part I stole to feed my habit. My drugs of choice were coke and heroin, but I would use anything to get wasted. Eventually I was consuming about a thousand dollars of drugs a week. I became so addicted that it's a miracle I'm alive today.

Someone was always overdosing. I myself had to be taken to the emergency room seven times. Drinking a fifth of Black Velvet a day, snorting cocaine, as well as speedballing, I suffered all sorts of hallucinations.

For my twenty-first birthday, Shoshanna and the gang threw a big drug party. I used so much coke and booze that night that I had to be taken yet again to the emergency room.

Emotionally and mentally I was like a zombie wandering through the hallways and rooms of the drug house. The drugs took their toll on me physically, as I didn't take care of myself and was a habitual mess. I didn't shower, I was full of lice and I contracted herpes. I was wasting away and slowly dying. I stayed in my room for a month, never leaving, just doing heroin and coke. I was repulsive to everyone but myself. I started stealing from Shoshanna to feed my habit, and she too became disgusted with me. She owed everyone money be-

cause of me. I knew that my welcome was at an end, and I even became paranoid that someone was going to kill me.

What saved me this time on my disastrous merry-go-round of life
in a commune was the love and concern of my grandparents, who
had been searching for me since I left home five years earlier. My
grandmother, whom I loved dearly and who had tried to help me on
and off for years, was dying of cancer. Somehow I managed to get
my shit together for a little bit so that I could return home. For the
most part I was able to stay off the hard drugs and confine my using
mostly to alcohol, which I needed for maintenance.

I knew that my family—in particular, my mother—felt that I was
a loser. I caught everyone by surprise when I came home and began
to help care for and nurse my grandmother. In reality it was the other
way around; my grandmother actually helped me by telling me before she died how much she loved me and worried about me. Whatever strength I had was coming from her. She carried enough faith
and strength for both of us.

I was drinking and occasionally I would go into the bathroom to
shoot up with the drugs that my friends, who would sometimes visit
on a weekend, had brought me. I had to do it for the maintenance of
my system and to be able to get through the daily routine of helping
my grandmother while watching her die.

I was struck by how grateful she was for the little things, like being bathed and looking at the flowers in her garden where I settled
her wheelchair and sat with her in the sunshine. She was a very special lady, and it was all very painful for me. She had even made all her
own funeral arrangements, selecting the casket and paying for the
cemetery lot so we wouldn't have to worry about all those details.

Everything and everyone was so rational as my grandmother died
that it drove me crazy, even crazier than I already was with all the
chemicals in my system. I couldn't understand how she could have

faith in anything. I couldn't believe that she wasn't angry with God for causing her such pain and me such grief. During her last week she needed to have everything done for her, and I had to back off and turn her completely over to the nurses. It had become too much for me, both physically and emotionally.

My grandmother died while the priest was on his way to our home. She was a devout Catholic. I hated the priest and his church and everything that they stood for. I wouldn't talk to or look at him as he came through the door. I hated the God who I believed had punished her with this terrible illness. No one was excluded from my hatred and my blame. I hated everyone for being so calm about her death.

During the wake I got totally wasted and suffered a tremendous hangover. The church service and the burial at the cemetery are just a blur. After the funeral, my friends and I drained a keg of beer and I began to help myself to the contents of the big bag of drugs that my grandmother had accumulated during her sickness. For the next six months, while I stayed with Grandpa in Stockton, I would drive to Chico to visit Shoshanna to see if she would take pity and provide me with some heavy stuff.

When I'd return, the house felt so empty without my grandmother. Grandpa, too, was lost without her: wouldn't eat, couldn't sleep and didn't pay attention to the household bills or the routine chores of the home. Then all of a sudden he started seeing a woman who had been a friend of Grandma's and he came alive once again. One night I was very drunk and Grandpa and I started screaming at each another. Things got so bad that we actually had a fistfight. I stormed out of the house vowing never to come back.

To this very day I feel the loss of my grandmother deeply. I still get angry about the fact that she is not here for me, to care for me, to protect me. My search is filled with anguish. "Who is there for me?" I ask myself. My best friend who helped care for Grandma told me recently that she had a dream about her and that in the dream my grandmother pointed out a way to help her resolve something that she had been struggling with. I had some feelings of jealousy and wondered why my dreamcatcher couldn't conjure up a comparable vision where my grandmother would hold me and tell me what to do. I still haven't had closure about the grief of her loss. Sometimes I wonder if I have dealt with it at all.

3

Downhill

Watching the chip and medallion ceremony and hearing the stories, I thought about how the journey from addiction to recovery is both different and the same for all of us. It is the same, in that all of us go through similar stages. We are introduced to the drug or drugs of our choice, are captivated by the way they can change our moods, by the highs they provide.

For me, alcohol came first, as I progressed (or regressed!) from nondrinker to social drinker to dependency, as prescription drugs and painkillers entered the equation. It's insidious how they imprison the body, mind and spirit, and soon we no longer have the freedom to live without the chemicals.

In Dante's hell, no one escapes ("All hope abandon, ye who enter here"). But anyone and everyone can escape the hell that addiction has created for them, if they dare to take that first big step. The incentive to take that step is usually some major crisis in one's life. Standing on the edge of a precipice, the women in these pages became willing to do anything to change.

After the Celebration of Recovery I went to listen to the Center's president, John Schwarzlose, give his address to the alumni. John was there at the beginning of the Center when the lake did not exist, when there were no ducks to feed, when the circular paths were not yet completed. The old-timers among our alumni remember the cramped quarters of the original Admissions Office, staffed by only three people.

Since the extension and renovation of Firestone Hall, the admitting area is expansive, inviting and comfortable, with a large staff and many volunteers. In the beginning, everything was done by hand; now computers are everywhere.

But everyone—whether they entered treatment back in 1982 or twenty years later—recalls how kind the Admissions' staff was to them. People remember the gentleness of the admitting team, the feeling of having entered a safe place.

Claire, who began telling her story Friday afternoon to the patients in Fisher Hall, never fails to tell her listeners, "When I arrived here, I didn't know what to expect. But the relief I felt at finally taking that big first step to getting my life back was overwhelming."

About a month before any patients entered treatment, John Schwarzlose organized what he referred to as a "shakedown cruise." Eisenhower Medical Center staff, local AA members and a few others—including Leonard Firestone and me—volunteered to act as patients so the newly hired staff could practice how they would handle the real patients.

At first, no one knew what to do with the Secret Service agents assigned as my guardian angels to be with me all the time. Unfortunately, unlike angels, they were not invisible. Finally the decision was made to put them in the "swamp" close to my room. As for Leonard Firestone, he was seen by one of the staff leaving the grounds after dark, something that the real patients would not be allowed to do. The next morning the staff held a mock confrontation. Leonard sheepishly told them that he forgot to bring his pajamas. He phoned his wife who brought them to the entrance of the grounds late that evening.

Whenever I tell that story to the patients, the image of the Honorable Mr. Ambassador Leonard Firestone being confronted and reprimanded by staff always brings the house down.

◆　◆　◆

Walking over to hear John Schwarzlose's talk, Paula—whom we left playing golf yesterday—caught up with me. I have a special fondness for Paula; in many ways *her story resembles my own. Pain medications did both of us in, and we both refused initially to admit that we were alcoholic. Here, Paula tells what it was like before she got help.*

Paula

A month after my marriage to Robert I was pregnant with Nancy. That's when my secret romance with pills began. My doctor gave me amphetamines to help me through my pregnancy. Nancy turned out to be a very colicky baby, and I was unable to nurse her. I walked her all day and all night. An extra dose of the "uppers" gave me the energy to keep going, and I liked the idea that I was losing so much weight.

Between Nancy and my second daughter, Victoria (Vicky), I had six miscarriages and it wasn't until later that I was able to make the connection between those misfortunes and the amphetamines. With all that poison in my body it's a wonder that as a baby Vicky turned out to be the opposite of Nancy. She slept all the time and hardly ever cried—to my and Robert's great relief. Nancy's need for attention had been the cause of many sleepless nights and endless exhaustion.

Now, with two children, the pills were more necessary than ever to keep me going. There was always so darn much to do: caring for the infants, washing dishes, preparing meals, doing yard work, shopping, entertaining and socializing as my husband began to climb the corporate ladder.

In 1969 we drove to Sun Valley, Idaho, on business. While Robert attended a seminar, he insisted I go skiing with some of the other wives. I begged him not to make me go, saying I'd just wait for him at the hotel. He got angry and insisted it was important that I associate with the other wives. I didn't know how to say "no," people pleaser that I was. The plan was to meet later at the lodge for cocktails, supper and dancing at the Boiler Room.

Even though there was plenty of snow, it was an awful day for skiing. It was freezing cold and the wind was blowing up to eighty miles an hour, at least that's what it felt like to me. As we made our last run, the visibility was down to almost zero. I wasn't too far down the slope when I hit a hidden mogul, lost control and came crunching down on my back. I later discovered that I'd blown out my spine, shattered my tailbone and ruptured some of the discs.

People quickly gathered around. I was embarrassed to see them staring down at me, especially when I got sick to my stomach and started throwing up. Some of them had seen me flip and hit the snow hard and were concerned that I'd seriously injured myself. I protested that I was fine. Nonetheless, the ski patrol took me down the rest of the way on one of their sleds.

When we got to the bottom, I somehow put a smile on my face and told the helpers I was okay, just a little bruised, and the only help I'd need would be getting in the van that would take me to the lodge. But I was delivering an Oscar-level performance; the pain was excruciating. I felt like I was moving through a minefield and bombs were exploding every time I took a step.

From that point on, the ski slope became the metaphor for my life. Everything went downhill. I lost control and was unable to manage even the smallest mogul.

I don't know how I carried on the next few days. I filled myself with whatever pills I had. It was as though someone had taken a baseball bat and smashed my back with all their might. The painkillers got me through the dinner that evening and somehow I kept from my husband the full extent of my injuries. On the drive back home, I tried every outlandish position imaginable to get comfortable. I was like a contortionist. Robert kept asking if I was all right and said he would take me to the emergency room as soon as we got home. I talked him out of it. I was too frightened and too stupid to seek medical help.

Finally, I could no longer stand the pain. I drove myself to the doctor's office. He took one look at the deep black-and-blue contusion that covered my back and said, "This is very serious; you should have come to me right away."

I wouldn't let anyone touch it. The doctor injected some painkiller and then sent me for X rays. After viewing the pictures, he told me the most serious damage was a shattered tailbone, and that an operation would be necessary. I refused to consider it. The doctor said I was just delaying the inevitable. He prescribed large amounts of Percodan to make the pain bearable.

Eventually, I did have the surgery, as the doctor predicted. During the long recovery process the pain was constant, and only gradually subsided thanks to large numbers of mood-altering painkiller pills.

I established a daily routine. I had my amphetamines to help me wake up, my Percodan to help me manage pain, my muscle relaxant and Valium to help me calm down; my Seconal and Nembutal served as the magical potions to guide me to slumberland. I also had my alcohol. That provided me with pleasant feelings of serenity and security whenever I needed to be in a social environment.

Lo and behold, Cinderella had turned into Sleeping Beauty, inured to pain, affable to all, empty of all but pleasant feelings. I had mastered the twenty-four-hour cycle, had control over day and night with the use of drugs, all of which had been prescribed by doctors. For a long time they helped me change and control my moods.

When I entertained, everything was in perfect order—the house was spotless, the table was a work of art, the lights were dimmed, and the proper music was selected for the proper ambiance. I made a good impression on people, my husband seemed to be pleased, and I enjoyed the daily roller-coaster ride the pills provided, allowing me to function.

By 1974 the number of pills I was taking was a matter of serious concern to both my doctor and my husband. Even I noticed that my consumption of downers and uppers had increased at an alarming rate. The doctor recommended a psychologist to review my case.

Looking back, I realize the psychologist knew nothing about the disease of addiction. His recommendation, believe it or not, was that I stop taking pills and in their place consume only alcohol! I thought it a rather bizarre prescription for recovery and I was quick to reply that I needed my amphetamines to get going in the morning as well as my pills for the pain. He said that whenever I'd been accustomed to taking a pill, to just substitute a drink!

He gave me forms to fill out; I was supposed to record my booze consumption: when I had a drink, how many ounces I consumed, at what level the pain was and whatever other circumstances accompanied the drinking. Had I had an ounce of the common sense that came later with treatment, I would have realized this was all complete nonsense.

For a short time I tried to followed the shrink's wacky "plan for recovery." I went out and stocked the house with Jack Daniel's, vodka, wine and liqueurs—the higher the alcohol content, the better.

Before too long—no surprise!—I was back on the pills, now combining them with the alcohol. My husband tried monitoring my alcohol consumption, moving the bottles and drawing lines on them to show how much I'd consumed the day before. I'd fill them with water to bring them up to the mark. We never spoke about it face-to-face.

After giving birth to Vicky I had dropped from 110 to 86 pounds. I liked the compliments. People said I looked like Audrey Hepburn. Because of Robert's work we moved after Vicky's birth to a small town in Idaho, very close to where I had been born. It felt like I was going back to prison. But we had to go.

I had to accompany Robert to many company conventions where the husbands would attend training sessions and the wives were left pretty much to themselves. In the beginning it was scary trying to determine what I should wear, what I should say, how I would do my hair. I took my amphetamines to get to the party, had my cocktails to get through the party and then when we got back to our room took my sleeping pills to get through the night.

Robert's concern increased. He scheduled a meeting for me with a psychiatrist, whose recommendations were that (1) I stop drinking alcohol, and (2) he carefully monitor my consumption of pain pills. He scheduled two sessions a week, but I never opened up to him. When he asked me why I drank, I told him it was because it made me feel good.

We had to get all the alcohol out of the house. I decided to drink tea. I went out and bought all sorts of teas: ginseng, lemon, mint, orange pekoe, Earl Grey. To encourage me, my daughters gave me a huge iced-tea glass.

But my abstinence lasted only a few weeks. Soon I was sneaking vodka into the giant tea glass. Then I phoned Robert and asked him to bring some wine home because I'd had a strenuous session with the doctor, discussing Mom. God bless him, he agreed to do it—if I promised I'd only drink one glass. Soon I was having three or four, and he'd blame himself.

In no time at all, of course, I was pounding back a full bottle—and blaming it on those painful memories of my not-so-dear mom! Excuses, excuses, excuses . . .

One day I was on pins and needles, waiting for Robert to come home from a visit with the psychiatrist that he'd had on his own. He sat me down and took my hands in his and said gently that the doctor was recommending that I go into the hospital for observation and possibly for a series of shock treatments.

Well, I didn't need any shock treatments! Robert's announcement was shock enough! "Please," I begged, "I can't go." I pleaded and promised, "No more alcohol. No more extra pills!"

I fled to our bedroom and stayed there for I don't know how many days, sweating, shaking, thrashing about in the bed, trying to detoxify myself. I was in and out of consciousness. At one point during my agony, Robert came to the room and said my father was on the phone and wanted to talk with me.

Well, Dad may have been a drunk, but that didn't stop him from yelling into the phone, "My God, are you a damned junkie?" I was shaking from withdrawal, my heart was racing, I wanted desperately to get off the phone. I heard my mother yelling like a banshee in the background, "I don't want to talk to her, she's no good, nothing but a fall-down drunk!" I hung up the phone and felt horrible, devastated. I wanted to die. Life was hell.

What saved me that time—for the short term—was a geographic change. In 1981 Robert was transferred to Irvine, in Orange County, California. The move helped, but my greatest fear from that point forward was that my supply of pills would run out. I was up to around fifty to seventy pills a day and I was drinking.

Changing towns and physicians should have made getting drugs easier. After all, I had a whole new population of doctors and pharmacists I could lie to. But it didn't work out that way. I simply needed too many pills. One savvy doctor refused point-blank to write a prescription for me. Another wanted to reduce the dosage drastically. I tried to manipulate others by offering pathetic, phony excuses like my pills had been stolen at the beach or had blown away when I had my convertible top down. I felt dishonest, and the look in their eyes confirmed my assessment of myself.

When I finally couldn't face the local doctors and pharmacists any longer, I called my guy back in Idaho, who agreed to send me a supply of 500 Tylenol #4 codeine pills every two weeks. My lifesavers came in a plastic bag in a little white box. I had to scrounge, scrape and steal $20 here and there to accumulate the $185 in cash that I had to send him every two weeks. I didn't dare use our telephone because Robert would want to know why I was calling our old pharmacist on a weekly or biweekly basis. By this time Robert was becoming suspicious of everything I did.

I'd panic if the pills didn't arrive on the day I expected them. I remember crying when two pills were missing from one shipment of 500. Pathetic but true.

Every time Robert told me we were going to a business convention the following week, I'd panic. I was never certain I'd have enough pills to get me through the trip. "Robert," I'd say, "I don't have enough time to get ready." He'd look at me with disbelief. "Honey, that's foolish. We'll be gone for only a few days and you have a whole week to prepare and pack."

I'd immediately call my pharmacist and request a backup supply. Then I'd look out my window every day, waiting for the postman to appear. I'd heave a sigh of relief when he turned the corner three blocks away. My heart would begin to pound if he were late or if I'd forgotten it was a holiday.

So powerful was the hold the drugs had over me that I could not stop or control my usage despite the deterioration of my relationships with those I loved the most—my husband and my daughters.

Frequently when Vicky came home from school I'd be in the kitchen cooking, but she could see that I was in a zombie-like state. She'd say, "Mom, I can't talk with you when you're like this." She'd walk out of the kitchen, leaving me feeling ashamed and hurt. The harder I tried to act natural, the more frustrated I'd become. Vicky withdrew further and further. She knew what was in that little white package that came in the mail every two weeks.

My relationship with Nancy, who was away at college, seemed to deteriorate even faster and further.

When I went to visit Nancy at her school, I thought I looked

quite smart. I was wearing a cream-colored suit with a burgundy silk
shirt, and I thought Nancy would be proud of me. But when I walked
into her sorority house, she gave me a disgusted look. "Mom," she
said, "you've been drinking again, and I refuse to go to lunch with
you." Those words hurt so much the tears just cascaded out of my
eyes. Eventually we went, but the conversation was restrained and
cool during the luncheon.

Later, when Nancy announced she was going to get married, I
didn't know how I'd get through all the pre-wedding socializing and
the ceremony itself. Miraculously, there were no mishaps, but I felt
Nancy was constantly on edge lest my speech or behavior betray me
in front of the wedding guests.

Early one morning, at 3 A.M., I woke up with a start sitting alone
in front of the TV set. Both girls had been home watching TV with
me earlier that evening, but had gone to bed and were sound asleep. I
had no memory at all of their leaving the room. Either I'd suffered a
blackout or I'd slipped into one of my deep, drug-induced sleeps. It
scared the daylights out of me when I looked down and saw that a lit
cigarette had fallen onto the carpet next to an overturned ashtray. I
thanked God that the carpet hadn't gone up in flames.

Shame and terror filled my heart! I had jeopardized the lives of my
loved ones with my carelessness. Still, I was in full-blown denial. I
didn't connect the accident with my drug and alcohol use.

Robert was distancing himself from me. He felt helpless. Visits to
psychiatrists hadn't helped. Their diagnoses and "remedies" had been
largely useless—in fact, they seemed to make things worse. One of
them, as I've recounted, prescribed alcohol, as if I could drink my way
out of my dilemma! He hadn't a clue about the nature of my illness.
The other prescribed a plethora of pills, shock treatment and divorce. That's right—he recommended that Robert divorce me. He
also managed to coyly let me know that he liked me better when I

was drinking! That shrink's own penchant for alcohol reminded me of the age-old maxim: "Physician, heal thyself."

Meanwhile, Robert couldn't figure out why his accounting of our household expenses was off by $370 each and every month. Once when I heard him saying he thought he was going crazy because he couldn't square the accounts, I thought to myself, "My God, if he goes crazy, then both of us are lost." I was terrified.

Because of my condition, Robert often had to cancel social obligations. Of course then I'd be embarrassed when I ran into a friend who innocently inquired why I had not attended this or that social event. I'd mumble another excuse, another lie—I'd built up a storehouse of hundreds of them. My life had become one big lie, a total sham, to conceal my addiction, and no one, least of all me, knew what to do about it.

One day Robert came home from work and made a casual remark about the fact that his company had medical coverage for people to get treatment if they had a problem with pills or alcohol. That's all he said, nothing more. My heart dropped as I waited for the executioner's blow, for him to say, "Honey, you need help."

He never directly linked "treatment" and "Paula," but the seed had been planted. I now knew there might be a way to get help.

Physically, my body was finally reacting to the terrible blows the alcohol and the pills were inflicting on it. It was way worse than the strappings my father had administered. In the spring of 1985 I began to bleed rectally, slightly at first and then more heavily. One time when we were at a social gathering I could feel the blood coming through the packing I had used; I was horrified at the thought that people would see a stain. I rushed to the bathroom just in time to prevent a major catastrophe.

My confusion and state of denial were so powerful that I didn't tell my husband and I didn't go to the doctor, hoping against hope that whatever the problem, it would miraculously disappear. Talk about delusion!

On a flight home with Robert from a convention in West Virginia, I remember I couldn't wait for the attendant to come around so I could order a Bloody Mary. By that time in my drinking life I'd started to gag when I drank alcohol, but it didn't matter if it took five painful swallows to get my Bloody Mary down, I had to have that drink. I'd heard how alcohol could affect the esophagus, but not even that could deter me.

Not only was I physically a mess, my spirit was dying too. The master bedroom became my sanctuary, my shelter, my cave, my bunker, my refuge in this "vale of tears." Night became day and day became night as I drifted in and out of sleep. I didn't know what day of the month it was; days and months all ran together. Much as Lady Macbeth wandered the halls of her castle seeking relief from the nightmares that haunted her, I wandered around my bedroom in my lavender robe trimmed with burgundy—a lost soul.

I felt isolated, trapped. I cried continuously. The shutters were always closed. My bedroom cave was dark, except for the small amount of light given off by the lamp at our writing table.

My life was like a bad movie. One night Robert came home, walked into the bedroom, saw me wasted, a bottle of liqueur at my side, aimlessly spreading all my jewelry on top of the bed. He took a look at the disaster before his eyes and finally said, "Honey, we have to get you some help." But he really didn't know what help I needed.

The next day I woke up with a start. I was frightened, trying desperately to come out of a dense fog, struggling to get my bearings. It was pitch-black. All the shutters were closed. I thought it was early morning. As I looked at the clock on my bed stand, though, I realized it was three-thirty in the afternoon. My tongue was thick, and even though I felt chilled, my nightgown was clinging to my sweaty body.

Instead of waking refreshed, I felt like I was drugged. My heart was pounding. I was desperate for a drink, even though I knew I'd gag repeatedly before I could get it down.

I needed ice for my vodka. No problem, I figured. Since no one was home, I'd just walk from the bedroom to the fridge in the kitchen, get the ice and go back into my cave.

But when I entered the kitchen, my knees almost buckled when I saw Vicky at the stove with her back to me. She'd come home early from school and was heating up some noodle soup.

I wanted to scurry back to the safety of my room before she saw me. But it was too late. She'd heard me come into the kitchen and had already turned around.

I expected the usual head shaking, registering displeasure and disapproval at my awful condition and disheveled appearance. Instead, Vicky totally disarmed me with a look of love and concern. She asked if I wanted some soup. To put it mildly, it was not the reception I expected, given that she'd caught me sneaking into the kitchen for my ice and a lime.

It was an amazing moment. Like water breaking inside me, there was a huge release. Her love and angelic smile broke through all my defenses, all my lies.

I walked to her a bit unsteadily and wrapped my arms around her. I hugged her hungrily, with my head nestled into her shoulder so she couldn't see my face.

Finally, I managed to utter these words: "Honey, I feel so ashamed. I've tried to stop but I can't. I need help."

After that, I couldn't speak any more. Deep, sorrowful sobs emerged from a cavern way down inside me.

I'll never forget what Vicky said in response. "Mom, I'm so proud of you, telling me this. That's great!"

We sat down at the kitchen table. I felt such love radiating from her.

When Robert walked through the front door, Vicky said to him, "Dad, Mom has something to tell you."

I walked over to him, put my arms around him, buried my head in his chest and whispered, "I need help."

After all the years of denial and lies, the poor guy was in a bit of a daze. Vicky helped him comprehend what I'd just said. "Mom wants help with her pills and alcohol."

He looked at me and said, "Thank God." And then, knowing what it had cost me to say what I'd just said, he repeated the exact same words Vicky had spoken when the floodgates had opened up several minutes earlier: "Honey, I'm so proud of you!"

Vicky came over. The three of us stood in a tight little circle and held on to one another. I remember the three of us walking into the living room, trying to figure out the how, when and where of the form "help" would take.

• • •

I'm amazed at how much Paula's story resembles my own. I'd already taken to drinking every day when I developed a pinched nerve in my neck. I had to have constant medication and when I developed a tolerance for one drug, the doctors gave me a prescription for another. I used the prescription drugs to wipe out my physical pain and the alcohol to bury the emotional pain as I began to feel sorry for myself and found that I could not live up to my own expectations. The drinking was the quick fix. It temporarily relieved me of my feelings of inadequacy, and I felt a sudden surge in my self-esteem and a boost in self-confidence. But the negative feelings returned when the mood-altering chemicals gradually lost their grip.

About a year after I began mixing my pain medications and my alcohol, I visited a psychiatrist who diagnosed my problem as low self-esteem. He paid little attention to the troublesome twosome that were my constant companions—alcohol and pills. Many psychiatrists still believe that if you relieve emotional problems you'll take care of drinking problems.

I can really identify with Paula waiting for that little white package from the pharmacist and having to be certain that she had enough pills on hand. The pills stored in my little black case were my salvation. As my neck problem got worse, I made sure that it was filled at all times and panicked when it was only half full.

I didn't feel guilty about taking pills for the pain. It's easy to convince yourself that you're an innocent victim, that you're not to blame because you need the pills. Besides, they were being prescribed by the doctors, so they must be all right.

With my own addiction, it got to the point that everybody was relieved when I started to decline invitations to social events. My husband adopted the enabler's role and made excuses to the effect that I was suffering from a cold or that I had the flu. I was so tranquilized that I had become totally passive and lost my enthusiasm for doing anything.

. . .

But enough about me! Let's continue with Claire's story. We left her Friday at Fisher Hall, recounting the story of her recovery to the patients.

Claire never had a problem with pain mediations or drugs. As a matter of fact, she never thought she had a problem with alcohol. I never really thought that I had a drinking problem, but then most alcoholics don't think they do.

We rejoin Claire as she returns after supper to continue telling her story to the "Fisherettes."

Claire

I met David, my second husband, at the Black Hat in Kansas City. He would come to hear me sing and after my performance would invite me to his table. Over drinks we would tell each other our embellished war stories. On Sundays, my only full day off, he would take me to brunch. He was a fund manager and took care of the large family portfolio. Despite his wealth he drove a funny old Ford. He dressed well but wasn't showy. He was always the gentleman and had a great sense of humor.

Over lunch on St. Patrick's Day, two years after we started dating, he gave me a five-karat emerald-cut diamond ring. I kept staring at its sparkle, which resembled the glow on my face. The engagement ended my singing career as David didn't want me working at the club any longer. But I was glad to get out. I was tired of the routine and the long hours involved.

We were married later that year. My dad and my brothers thought David was wonderful and that I'd made a great catch, especially when they compared him with the previous barracuda. My stepmother gave a wonderful reception but I was surprised she didn't come herself. My brother, Ben, remarked sardonically that after the second drink she was in the habit of falling flat on her face.

The honeymoon that followed was fabulous. We went to St. Thomas where we entertained a lot, drank a lot, made love every night. I loved him to death. We had the world by the tail. I loved St. Thomas and convinced David that we should buy a house there. We went back to Kansas City, settled temporarily in a big suite at a downtown hotel before we eventually moved to a new house. Then it was back to St. Thomas to enjoy its beauty and to search for a home. We brought Beth, my daughter, with us.

Although I had sensed it before, it was during this trip that I first understood that David and Beth would not be compatible. She was four years old when we were married and he never really took to her. He wanted her to be a perfect little girl, which she wasn't and couldn't be. I remember how we used to fight, especially after drinking, about his aloofness from her. In a funny way, they were jealous of each other. David came from a family where perfection was expected of everyone—and I think as much as he wanted to live up to that ideal he also highly resented it. A sure cure for perfectionism was alcohol. He got heavily into drinking, and I followed right behind him.

The birth of Cindy did not help Beth. David doted on Cindy and gave her all the hugs that Beth had so desperately wanted. When Beth was old enough she was sent to camps and boarding schools to get her out of harm's way, namely David's silent treatment of her.

As Cindy grew older she didn't understand the merry-go-round that we were on, but she remembered that her daddy had promised on one occasion to stop drinking when we returned from one of our frequent trips to St. Thomas. But he didn't, and one day, in tears, she confronted him. He was repentant for about a week, but then started up again.

David was turning into a verbal bully with me, which got worse with the drinking. In turn, I was drinking more and more "to cope," as I rationalized it. David broke his hip in St. Thomas and then reinjured it, so it took a long time to heal. We drank a lot and fought even more. I was getting fed up. I began seriously to entertain the idea of walking out on him. He knew what I was thinking, and taunted me about being too old to go back to singing for a living. He let me know in plain terms that I would not get a nickel of his money.

Then David was diagnosed with colon cancer. They had to keep him in the hospital for a bit before they could operate. I didn't understand why then, but I know now—they had to detox him before they could proceed. It was frightening when I look back on it. The colostomy was very painful and humiliating for him, and I couldn't run away from a sinking ship. I again donned my Florence Nightingale cap, tended to his every need and cleaned up after him.

After three months the colon was repaired, the sack was removed and the doctor told us that the cancer was in remission. My husband celebrated by having a drink and the vicious cycle started all over. He was soon drinking heavily, with his wife following closely behind. His verbal abusiveness heightened my feelings of worthlessness. When Cindy went away to boarding school our isolation was complete.

With the cancer in remission I figured that David was out of the woods and I had done my job. I went to the family lawyer and told him that I wanted out. I couldn't take David's drinking anymore, and I was turning into a lush myself. We had both been passing out at night and drinking early in the morning. The lawyer asked me if I would give AA a chance, rather than pursue a divorce. Knowing next to nothing about the fellowship, I said that I would try anything.

Shortly thereafter, a recovering alcoholic rang our front doorbell. I didn't know what I'd expected, probably someone dressed in a uniform like the Salvation Army. On the contrary, he looked very normal. I let him in and told him that my husband was all his. Then I left the house and walked around the neighborhood until I thought he was finished.

I'm still not sure what happened that day, but I was the recipient of a great gift. I remember thinking this wouldn't last, but David stuck with it. He told me that I didn't have to stop drinking because of him. But I did cut back, and I really felt good when I heard him praise me in front of some his AA friends. It was nice to get a pat on the back. We went to some open meetings together, and I sensed that the people there were glad to see us. They included us in their plans and we began to have a social life again, something we hadn't had for years.

Then the cancer returned. David decided, with my blessing and support, that there would be no more surgery and that he would undergo chemotherapy treatments. I put my nursing cap back on and every five weeks he took a fistful of pills and received another vaccination or whatever they were called at that time. We went back and forth from Kansas City to St. Thomas. I was so glad to have the AA people around, both in St. Thomas and in Kansas City. We had a wonderful time sitting in the sun and wading in the water. AA members would come to visit.

I was once again with the guy with whom I had first fallen in love. I had no more thoughts of divorce. What really frightened me now was the thought of losing him.

Nineteen eighty was a lousy year. My Dad died that summer, and at the same time David was very sick and I was caring for him. There were times when it was overwhelming and I didn't think I could carry on. Toward the end, I was medicating David every four hours. Finally, I had to get a nurse to help out. Cindy was able to return home before David died, so they had a chance to talk. But Beth was too late. I knew David wanted to make amends to her, but by the time she saw him he was unconscious.

As the end approached, David was pretty stoic. Our AA friends were there for us. His last words before he lost consciousness were, "Well, you've been a good wife." I replied, "Well, I tried." We loved each other very much, even though for a long time we had to suffer the pain inflicted by the barbed wire that surrounded our drinking.

After David's death I busied myself with a lot of different activities. I did the civic thing by accepting an invitation to join the board of a highly regarded local playhouse. Another man, Harold, entered my life and became my constant social companion. We commuted back and forth to Las Vegas in his private plane where he gambled and I went to all the shows and listened to all the singers, including Frank Sinatra. We had a great time. My drinking made it even more glamorous, or so I thought.

My drinking had gotten progressively worse, although I didn't pay too much attention to it. I thought it was just a habit that I could break any time I wished. I never thought of it as an illness. I'd forgotten most of what I'd learned from the recovering people who were so good to us when AA came into David's (and my) life.

It's interesting how small things stick in my mind. I do remember one incident very clearly that gave me pause even if it was only for a moment. Every night at ten o'clock, my housekeeper who'd been with us since 1955 would join me as we watched *The $10,000 Pyramid* on TV. We loved the show. I would have orange juice and spike it with vodka. Then one night I didn't want her to see that glass. I felt that I was sneaking drinks and it didn't seem like the grown-up thing to do.

Beth and Cindy always tried to be with me at Christmas, since my birthday is the day before. Harold had taken it upon himself to tell Beth that he thought that I was drinking a little too much. On New Year's Day, the girls sat me down to do a "petite intervention," with no consequences attached. In the most loving and caring way, they plied me with examples of my excessive drinking. Since it was non-threatening, I was not terribly upset, although I was hurt. At the end, I told them I would stop for a while although I did not believe that I was drinking all that much. But my resolution was halfhearted.

Soon I returned to my customary watering holes, where I did not discourage the bartender, when he saw me, from saying, "Hi, Mrs. B., here's your scotch."

Months later, when Beth was again visiting, she secretly tape-recorded one of our evening conversations. The next morning she said she had something she wanted me to hear. I was both surprised and upset at what she'd done and then terribly embarrassed as I listened to myself on the tape. My speech was heavily slurred. I was holding forth like a philosopher and issuing what I thought the previous night to be great and profound statements. Of course it was gibberish when I heard it the next morning.

The image of W. C. Fields kept running through my mind. I wondered, "My God, how often have I acted like this?" I laughed, trying to make a joke about my behavior. But I was the only one laughing.

Beth said, "Mom, this isn't funny." I felt a deep flush spreading across my face, not from alcohol but from shame.

Again I tried to cut back and again I thought that I was doing pretty well. Then one morning I discovered that Cindy had left her apron at my place. She lived nearby, so I decided to deliver it personally to her apartment. When I arrived she opened the door, thanked me for bringing it, but didn't invite me in.

She paused and then said, "Mike's here." Well, when Cindy and Mike had separated a year earlier, I'd helped Cindy move her things out from their apartment, so I was shocked that they appeared to be back together. I turned around, went home and immediately poured myself a large drink. I asked myself, "What in the world is happening?" When Cindy called a little later she said she'd planned to tell me about the reconciliation several times, but that every time she was at my place, I was too drunk to hold a conversation. This was September 1984.

After that phone call I sat down for a while, thinking that everything around me was crumbling, including myself. I felt as though I'd lost my grip on the edge of a cliff. I went to the phone and called a friend in AA. Her name was Lou Ann, and she'd been calling me up from time to time since David's death. Occasionally we'd have lunch together, and she'd make sure that we went to a place where I could have a drink. That's what I liked about her: She never preached at me. Only on rare occasions would she say that she was worried about me, but she seemed always to have the knack of doing it gently, so I wouldn't take umbrage at her remarks.

This time I told Lou Ann that I was worried about myself, that I was drinking too much. My daughters, the two people whom I loved most in the world, were telling me that I needed to do something about my drinking. I said to Lou Ann that I thought maybe I had to "check into the bin." We agreed to have lunch the next day.

When we met, I had a simple request: "Tell me what to do." Lou Ann suggested a number of treatment centers. One was in the South. I told her that wouldn't work; I couldn't understand southern people. Another one was in Minnesota; "God, no," I told her, "I'll freeze to death." Finally she mentioned a new place in California, the Betty Ford Center. "That's where I'll go," I told her. "It'll be warm there."

To this day I never tire of telling people that I came to Betty Ford for the weather—and they gave me back my life!

• • •

I like to repeat what I've heard so often: Alcoholism is the most democratic of all diseases. I suspect that I had a biological predisposition to it, but for a long time I would have considered myself a social drinker. At some point, however, I crossed the line and alcohol became important to me, a necessary part of my day, and no longer a social activity that I could take or leave. I don't know when I began to be preoccupied with alcohol, but preoccupation is one of the clear signals that a person has crossed over into dangerous territory. It's very easy to ignore the danger signals, and the point arrived where having cocktails every evening, whether I was out with friends or home alone, became the norm. Alcohol had become my constant companion. The same thing happened to Claire.

Later in her recovery Claire realized how ignorant she had been about the power of alcohol and how, slowly, it took control of her and her second husband, and eventually the lives of her children. It took a long time for her to realize that she and David were destroying themselves and their marriage with alcohol.

Claire and Paula both experienced with their families what is described in the Big Book: "An illness of this sort involves those about us in a way no other human sickness can. The alcoholic is like a tornado roaring his way through the lives of others. Hearts are broken. Sweet relationships are dead. Affections have been uprooted. Selfish and inconsiderate habits have kept the home in turmoil."

4

The Funeral Cortege

My heart goes out to Jacqueline, whose story we continue from chapter 1. I hadn't a clue what an intervention was when I became the focus of one a quarter century ago. Like Jacqueline's—but for different reasons—the first one didn't take. While Jacqueline was docile and submissive, I was angry with both my daughter, Susan, and Dr. Joe Cruse, who dared to trespass into my home and suggest that I had a problem. I rose up on my high horse and threw them out. I try not to think about it too often, as I feel ashamed and embarrassed when I do.

But the second intervention had a different ending, although many of my feelings remained the same. Surrounded by the family who loved me and knowledgeable professionals who cared about me, this intervention saved my life. When they all marched into the house together, I was startled and for the life of me could not figure out what the occasion was for this gathering. Then my husband led me to the couch, sat down close beside me and said they wanted to talk about something important because they loved me very much. And that's how the intervention started. I listened, and my self-esteem—which was already at rock bottom—descended to even lower depths. All I heard was that I had failed. I managed to block out those very important words that everybody uttered, over and over again: They loved me.

A lot of people at the center of an intervention are very angry, and show it; others appear to be docile, but underneath the peaceful façade they're angry, too. Once the person gets into treatment, though, these anger issues are dealt with and usually resolved.

It took Jacqueline a long time to come to an awareness of how badly she was hurting herself and her family with her drinking.

Jacqueline wasn't "The Housewife Who Drank at Home." She was the working mother who risked everything for that first drink. And when she took that first drink her husband and her children saw the other side of her, the addicted side. It made her want to crawl in a closet when she thought of all those people who had come to her intervention as a demonstration of their love and how disappointed they must be at her failure.

Jacqueline

Drinking became a part of my life after I graduated from high school and went away to nursing school. It felt good to get away from the small town I'd grown up in, and from the ranch and my dad's drinking. Still, I went home most weekends to visit with my mom, whom I missed a great deal. On one of those weekends my dad and I had both been drinking and we got into a horrible fight. We started off being sarcastic and ended up screaming at each other. I left the house vowing never to return. It was an idle threat, as Mom was too important to me. When I did visit, and it was quite often, I did my best to avoid contact with Dad. Our relationship has remained strained to this day.

I could never understand why my mother put up with him. "Why do you let him treat you that way?" I would shout at her. "The S on your forehead is either for 'saint' or 'stupid,'" I'd say. My mother is a very giving and forgiving person and she was always there for me, even during my most unforgivable alcoholic performances.

At school, I would go out a lot at night with a group of people who liked to visit bars, to dance and drink. It was not unusual to get back to the dorm at three or four in the morning. Just before graduation I was hospitalized for ten days for pancreatitis. The doctors couldn't pinpoint the cause, since I hadn't admitted to them how much I'd been drinking.

I returned to the family homestead to recover. The doctors had told me it would take a month to recuperate, but even during that time I was out most nights with friends drinking and partying. It wasn't the smartest thing I've done my life, but I was young and, I believed, indestructible. The pancreatitis should have been an early wake-up call but most medical people are not very bright when it comes to diagnosing alcoholism—and although I knew my drinking was the cause, I never once considered asking for help.

◆ ◆ ◆

I feel the need to add a commentary on Jacqueline's story at this point. When I was hospitalized the first time, the doctors were unable to find anything wrong. But along came a specialist who diagnosed pancreatitis and recommended that I stop drinking for a time. I remember when my husband asked those original doctors if drinking could have been the cause of my pancreatitis, they said it was a possibility. As a matter of fact it was a prime cause, but they avoided talking about it with me. Such enabling still continues in the medical profession.

◆ ◆ ◆

I worked and drank in South Dakota for the next couple of years, until the summer of 1979, when I accepted a job in southern California at a Coachella Valley hospital. When I drove into the desert that first night, I thought I had died and gone to hell, it was so hot. I was convinced that I had made the biggest mistake of my young life. But my first day at the hospital, there was a party for the new staff members. I began to feel that life in the desert wouldn't be so bad since there seemed to be plenty of watering holes and a lot of drinking companions.

I proceeded to get drunk at the first-day party, and I knew I'd never make it home on my own, so I called someone to come and get me, not because I was reluctant to drive while inebriated, but because I couldn't remember where I lived.

I didn't drive that night, but there were plenty of other times when I drove under the influence. The last time it happened I was jailed. That disgrace and the humiliation that accompanied it ended not a life of crime but a life of addiction. The disgrace became a grace. But I'm getting ahead of myself.

In June of 1979 I got really sick once again. I began throwing up bright-red blood, and passing fairly large clots of blood. The diagnosis was a bleeding stomach ulcer. When the doctor asked about my drinking habits, I told him I was only an occasional drinker. Later my treatment counselor told me I had the wonderful knack of looking people right in the eye and denying the truth. And that's what I did with that doctor.

But as with the pancreatitis, I knew that the ulcer was caused by excessive drinking. I believed that I could *stop* drinking whenever I wanted to. Problem was, I didn't want to! There didn't seem to be a good reason to quit. After all, I'd never been beaten up or gotten pregnant and I never used hard drugs. As a matter fact, hard drugs scared me, and I stopped going to a lot of parties frequented by medical people where heavy-duty drugs were being used.

My life had settled into a comfortable pattern of work, socializing and drinking with friends who liked to visit bars, dance and usually stay out late. That left little time for sleep since I had to rise early for work. But I was still young, and my body recovered quickly.

In April 1980, Michael, the man who eventually would become my husband, decided he preferred the weather in the Coachella Valley to that of upstate New York. We met on the job. He was an X-ray technician, and he swears the first time he saw me he knew he was going to marry me. We were, in fact, married on Valentine's Day, 1981.

I continued to drink, but not as heavily as before. I didn't want my new husband to think he'd married a lush! But once I had a drink or two I needed more, so I started sneaking extra hits from the always handy box wine. I thought I was being pretty clever with that cardboard box because there was no way you could see precisely how much had been consumed from one day to the next.

Rationalizing knows no bounds. When Michael went to karate practice at night, I'd be home all alone, and I'd say to myself, "Poor thing, God knows you deserve a few extra glasses of wine." For years, I'd concealed my drinking problem from doctors; now I was concealing it from my husband. As for myself, I was suffering from full-blown denial. What, me? A problem? No way!

I did temporarily stop drinking during my two pregnancies. But immediately after the two cesareans, I celebrated with champagne. I continued to drink while I was nursing both my little girls. Emily was born in 1988 and twenty-two months later I had Anna. Both Michael and I were surprised Anna was conceived without the use of fertility drugs, as had been the case with Emily.

So here I was with two lovely little girls, only twenty-two months apart. I should have been thrilled. Instead, I felt overwhelmed. Now I *really* needed the alcohol to keep me going.

One day Michael came home early. The babies were crying, the house was a mess. I'd been drinking all day, and he was clearly annoyed. While he made a business phone call, I poured myself a whole tumbler of vodka, which I guzzled down. Almost immediately, I passed out.

Michael was at his wit's end. He had no idea what was going on with me. He put me to bed and tended to the babies. Sometime after midnight, when I felt like I was going to be sick, I got up to go to the bathroom. Michael got out of bed to help me. In the process of pushing his arm away, I slipped and fell, cutting myself just below the eye.

We couldn't stop the bleeding. Blood was everywhere! Every time he tried to put pressure on the wound I screamed at him to let me be. The children were awakened by the commotion, and they started to cry. Finally, Michael called our friend and neighbor, Karen, who dressed and came over. She was afraid I'd dropped one of the babies.

Karen quickly surveyed the bloody scene, inspected the cut and knew immediately that stitches were going to be necessary. At first I refused to go to the hospital, arguing that I couldn't leave the children. Finally they persuaded me to leave the house and go with them to the hospital. On the way, at a stoplight, I tried to jump out of the car.

It was two in the morning. Why was I acting so erratically? Because I was terrified that the emergency room people would do a blood test, and they'd know that I was a fall-down drunk. And here I was, on maternity leave from my job at the hospital, supposed to be home caring for my two little babies.

When they didn't insist on drawing blood, I calmed down. The head wound required 16 stitches. My black eye lasted for months.

The next morning, of course, I was filled with remorse and shame.

Michael didn't have a clue as to why I drank to such an extreme, but he did insist I make an appointment with my obstetrician, who diagnosed the problem as postpartum depression. He, in turn, sent me to a psychologist. She "diagnosed" me as being the adult child of an alcoholic.

Throughout all this, no one said out loud that I was just plain drinking too much alcohol! Thanks to my black eye, I later discovered that some of my friends whispered that the problem was spousal abuse. Poor Michael!

There was no fooling my mom, though. She'd had firsthand heavy-drinking experience with my father.

In my denial, I concluded yet again that I couldn't have been drinking too much. After all, I'd never called in sick and never missed a day of work. In the fall of 1989, I went back to work.

It was at this point that I decided to change my drinking habits. I no longer drank in public or at cocktail parties—but was usually six sheets to the wind when I arrived. Here was my pattern: stop at a liquor store on the way home from work, buy a half pint or two of vodka, park in the lot at the country club, put my Volvo in neutral, stretch out under the dashboard, twist the top off the bottle and gulp the vodka down while it was still in the brown paper bag. (Years later when I described that ridiculous ritual to someone, she had a very commonsense question to which I didn't have a ready answer. "Why didn't you just use a paper cup?")

Then I'd go home, dress the babies, put them in the car and take them to one of the school sports events that Karen, our good friend and neighbor, was coaching. I'm sure that oftentimes I made a complete fool of myself at the games. I'd scream and yell, God knows at or about what. Afterward, I wouldn't remember a thing.

Looking back, I was drunk virtually all the time.

In May 1990, Karen invited me to the McCallum Theater to hear Reba McEntire, whose singing I loved. By the time that we were ready to go, I'd put back two half pints. In the lobby, I knocked back a glass of wine. And all this booze on an empty stomach. After Reba came on the stage, I remember nothing—until I got sick and threw up, not on Karen, but all over the woman sitting on the other side of me.

At that moment I don't know what I was feeling or thinking. But whenever I recall the incident I cringe, mortified at how awful the scene must have been.

I would have gladly accepted a life sentence of changing diapers rather than having thrown up on that stranger. Karen tells me now that she got me out of there as quickly as possible and took me to her home to clean me up and wash my clothes.

I announced that I was going to walk home. And that's what I did—wearing only my underwear! Imagine, walking down the street in my underwear! Fortunately, Karen managed to turn me around and get me back into her house.

I don't remember a thing about that nightmare episode firsthand. All I know is what people told me afterward. And to this day I am mortified when I relive it in my mind.

The next day at the hospital, my boss took me aside and told me that I had to do something about my drinking. "While I care about you, what I'm *really* concerned about is the girls," she said. I was angry and indignant but said that I would stop drinking.

And I did—for a month. Then we went to South Dakota on vacation, and it was party time all over again! I got so drunk the first night that I was babbling and crying. My mother and sister said that I needed to talk to someone. They made an appointment for me with a priest who just happened to be a recovering alcoholic. We talked and again I lied about my drinking, throwing in the old chestnut— "I just don't know who I am."

In hindsight, this was the reality. The addictive self who was emerging more and more was pushing my real self into the shadows. Later in my recovery, I discovered that recovering people could see right through the verbal smoke screens that drinking people hurl at them. The priest gave me a list of AA meetings. I pretended I was happy to be receiving this invaluable knowledge. Of course, I knew that in a million years I'd never go.

For heaven's sake, why would I go to a gathering of alcoholics, when I certainly wasn't one! When we got back to the desert, I started worshiping again at my under-the-dashboard altar.

Thanksgiving, 1990. My sister, Donna, and I went to the airport to pick up our other sister, Dawn, who was coming from Kentucky. I was driving; the girls were in the backseat. I was drunk and almost had an accident. Donna was a nervous wreck. The trip and the anxiety were for naught because the airline had rescheduled Dawn's flight for the following morning.

Donna went to the airport to meet Dawn in the morning. I went to work. On the way back from the airport Donna told Dawn about the harrowing experience the night before. She added, "Something's very wrong with Jacqueline." Donna then called the Betty Ford Center, asking for help. They gave her the name of Ed Casey, an interventionist based in Los Angeles, who works with the families of people who need help because of their drinking or other drug use. Donna quickly phoned Ed and then spent the remainder of the day begging friends and family to come and participate in the intervention that was scheduled for right after Thanksgiving.

Meanwhile, I continued drinking, quite oblivious to all the frantic phoning and arrangement-making that was taking place. With the help of my sisters I prepared the Thanksgiving meal feeling comfortably spaced out. Had I not been drinking, I might well have intuited that something was going on; my sisters and husband were especially solicitous and ingratiating.

On Sunday I drove Dawn to the airport and dropped her off at the departure ramp, where we said our good-byes and promised to see each other before too many months went by. Little did I know that Donna drove up shortly after I left to chauffeur Dawn back to her home.

I later learned that on Monday everybody got together for a dress rehearsal of the intervention!

When Donna came over Monday night to give me a perm—a loving, unsolicited and seemingly spontaneous gesture—I was drunk and belligerent. What she was really doing, of course, was getting me ready for my stay at Betty Ford.

Years later, Donna confessed that I was so nasty that night she felt like drowning me!

The next morning I got up at my usual time, five-thirty, and took my shower. I noticed that Michael—who was not an early riser—was already up. So were the girls. "What are you girls doing up this early?" I asked. "Get back to bed."

Before they could move, the doorbell rang. It was 5:55 A.M. Michael said he'd get it. He walked across the living room and opened the door. The first person who stepped in from the dark was my mom. She was crying and my first thought was, "Oh my God, Dad has died and Mom has come to get me."

Then Dawn came in. I thought she was back in Kentucky; after all, I'd dropped her off at the airport just two days earlier. My sister Donna was next. Then came two special friends from South Dakota, Amanda and Joe, whom I hadn't seen in eight years. I'd served as a bridesmaid for Amanda; Joe is a doctor.

On and on they came. Karen, our neighbor. Colleagues from the hospital. An aunt and uncle from Los Angeles.

Finally, a stranger walked in and said, "I'm Ed Casey. You don't know me, but all these people here love you."

It struck me like a thunderbolt. *They're here because of my drinking.*

By this time I was truly terrified. I'd retreated back into the kitchen and was pressed against the stove, crying and whimpering, "No, no, no." The girls were crying, but when I went to comfort them Michael picked them up to take them across to Karen's place where he had arranged for a baby-sitter.

I was crushed and thought I would die. My babies were being taken from me! But Michael was adamant that he didn't want them there. The next thing I remember was sitting on the couch between my old friends Joe and Amanda; the rest of the people formed a circle around me. Some sat on chairs, some parked themselves on the floor.

Ed Casey started the whole process by telling me that this was an intervention by people who loved me. It was the first time I'd ever heard the word. He said that everyone was there to help me, and that each person was going to read a letter they'd written to me about my drinking. They did, and I sat there and listened as each told horror stories. As I listened, I felt both helpless and ashamed. Helpless, because I was cornered. Ashamed, because these were people I loved, people whom I'd obviously hurt.

As the folks from the hospital read their letters, I could hardly look at them. I had thought I was such a great actor! I'd thought I'd fooled them! Truth is, I hadn't fooled anyone. I wanted to feel betrayed, but incident after incident revealed how *I* had betrayed *them*.

The *pièce de résistance* was a tape Ed Casey played. On it were messages from twenty-five other relatives, including Dad and my two brothers.

The person whose presence affected me the most was Amanda's. I hadn't seen her in eight years, yet she'd known about the hell that my life had become. She cried so hard that someone else had to read her letter. She'd come to the intervention at great sacrifice to herself. She was terrified of flying, but took her first plane trip ever to be with me. I sobbed while her letter was being read and as she held my hand.

After what seemed like an eternity but was only an hour and a half, there was a long pause. I was numb and trembling. Ed Casey started talking again. Oh, how I hated his presence and despised his voice. How dare he intrude upon my life and enter my home.

Ed said I had two options. The first was to go into treatment. A bed had been arranged for me at the Betty Ford Center, where the family could visit on Sundays. Or I could go to Hazelden in Minnesota. In either case, my mother had volunteered to take care of the babies while I was gone. The other option was to do nothing and continue with my self-destructive behavior. If I chose that route, I couldn't remain in my home. My husband and children were not about to watch me destroy myself.

I felt such hurt at my husband's betrayal. I thought he'd been the ringleader in pulling this intervention together. Yes, my drinking had been a definite strain in our relationship. Yes, my drinking prevented me from being a full partner in our marriage and prevented the real communication necessary for a solid relationship. But did I deserve *this?*

For his part, Michael couldn't do anything to control my behavior. He hated that feeling of helplessness. He felt that he loved me more than I loved him and that he was getting the short end of the stick in this marriage. In retrospect, he was right.

Michael was very quiet at the intervention. Turns out he was not the ringleader. As a matter of fact, he wanted to back out the night before the intervention. He told the family and friends that had come from all over that he thought that we, husband and wife, could work things out. He began to think that the intervention and the truth that would be revealed—namely his inability to control his wife and her drinking—would reflect poorly on him. However, my friends and family were determined to see this through and convinced Michael the help I needed was not something he could give.

How does one measure success? In one sense the intervention was successful because I resigned myself to going to the Betty Ford Center. What else could I do? I couldn't disappoint all these wonderful people who'd disrupted their lives and paid a lot of money to travel to help me.

The funeral cortege that followed me to the Betty Ford Center included my husband, my sister Dawn, Amanda, and Joe and the avenging angel Ed Casey.

I have never in my life felt as alone as I did when they drove off after depositing me at the Center. When I was young and dropped off at summer camp I felt homesick, but this time I felt completely abandoned, left to myself to face the unknown. Not even the friendly face and voice of the Admissions counselor, Malcolm, could erase that feeling. The only friend who could have made me feel better at that moment was dear old alcohol. And even that had abandoned me!

Deep down inside I was nurturing a bitter, boiling, resentment: *I had not been allowed to have my last drink.*

. . .

It's impossible to single out one factor that compels people to seek help. The story in the Big Book, "It Might Have Been Worse," probably sums it up best: "There comes a time when you don't want to live and are afraid to die. Some crisis brings you to a point of making a decision to do something about your drinking problem. Try anything. Help which you once rejected, suggestions once turned aside are finally accepted in desperation."

This is a good description of what happened to Harriet and Laurette, whom we last encountered at the chip and medallion ceremony. Their accounts of what it was like before treatment describe experiences as "hellish" as anything Dante could create with his inspired pen.

Harriet

Life in Atlanta was a ball. As a paralegal, I met and dated lots of young attorneys but found them self-absorbed and fickle. I enjoyed the company of older men who admired my youth and conversational skills and—ten scotches later—my drinking capacity as well. It was cool to be able to drink with men, and to keep up with them as we downed drinks.

A friend who was a judge once asked me, "How many men have died trying to get you drunk?" He passed away from liver cancer. A doctor I had been dating lost his brilliant career to drink. The end of each relationship hit me hard. I now drank both to enjoy and forget.

When I swore off dating, I turned to trips and cruises for recreation and vacations. I traveled to London and then Cairo for a cruise up the

Nile. Scotch was my medicine to "kill those microbes," even when brushing my teeth. The next year, I traveled to Scandinavia with a girl-friend. We partied everywhere with everyone. My friend got so drunk one night in Copenhagen she was mistaken for a hooker. Fun, eh?

On my thirtieth birthday, I flew alone to Singapore where I joined the Orient leg of a world cruise. On the trip I met Winston, whom I called "Mr. Churchill." He was a very polished Brit. We began a ro-mantic adventure that grew more serious as the cruise continued. Af-ter thirteen days, I flew home to Atlanta. He followed me, first with flowers and telephone calls, then in person. He proposed; I agreed to marry him. Back in London, sober, he had a change of heart and ended the engagement. He was sixty-five; I was thirty and devastated.

Then began the depressed or morose stage of my life. I threw my-self into my work, which carried me through this period. I prospered financially. When my grandfather died, I inherited enough money to buy a condominium. I underwent therapy and analysis, wrote poetry and drank alone. To overcome my social isolation I took three more cruises on the same cruise line, where I became a "regular." I looked forward to the steady relationship that I had with the ship's bartender. Nick was a kindred soul, a musician and a drinker, and not bad in bed. But at the end of each voyage, the great emptiness returned.

My parents encroached upon my independence when they retired to Atlanta three years after I had moved there. Following my mom's operation for cancer, I played nurse for a whole year to both of my parents and my grandmother. Dad's bypass, Nanny's sickness and death, Mom's mastectomy, hemorrhoidectomy and cosmetic surg-eries, such as a face-lift and skin peel—it was a bad year. Dealing with Mom was especially hard as her "bad mommy" side came out a lot more often when she was sick.

One afternoon I entered my office eating an ice-cream cone. Jerry, who worked at the same firm, followed me and closed the door behind him. He put his arms around me, pinning me to the desk and kissing me for a long time. All the while I was holding the ice-cream cone as it melted in my hand.

It was a steamy moment, and I felt swept away. That evening he came to my apartment, and we began our affair. At the core of our relationship was a fabulous intuitive sexuality. We seemed to meld into each other emotionally. Outside of the office we were inseparable, but I insisted that no one at the office know about it. I was sensitive to the fact that both my business partners had been very protective of me over the years and didn't like Jerry.

Then for Jerry's fortieth birthday, we went public. I threw a surprise party at the office and the cat was out of the bag. I was proud and happy. Mom and Dad seemed to enjoy his company until I announced our engagement. It was like a scene out of *Who's Afraid of Virginia Woolf?*, with my mother playing Elizabeth Taylor. Having spent so much time caring for my parents during the previous two years, I was really hurt.

I suspected their hostility grew out of the possibility of "losing" me, although Mom accused Jerry of being a fortune hunter interested only in my money. Dad was disappointed that Jerry hadn't gone to him first to ask for my hand.

They forbade me to marry Jerry. I told them to go to hell. They declared me dead. After Jerry and I eloped, my parents and I didn't talk for ten years.

Since my business partners didn't trust Jerry, I left that firm. I wasn't willing to listen to anything negative about my loving spouse, and I felt they were jealous.

I soon discovered Jerry had a speed habit. I started indulging, too, which increased our marital bliss. I felt wild and free, like a renegade.

Jerry had been married previously and had a child. I made the two of them the focus of my life. By entering their lives, I believed that I

was "fixing" things for them and making them happy. Classic codependent behavior. Same thing I'd done with my mother.

Jerry and I moved with Atlanta's fast crowd. While we spent too
much, partied too much and drank and used too much, we paused
hardly at all to reflect on what was happening—we were destroying
our lives, together. We found ourselves bankrupt, not only financially, but also spiritually and physically. Since I couldn't blame myself, Jerry became the indicted person and unwilling scapegoat. He
had a long history of addiction to speed. He promised to stop using,
and for a year he convinced me that he had.

One day I sat down at his computer and accidentally stumbled
across some speed while I was searching for some paper for the
printer. When he came home, I told him I'd found his stash. He was
angry and accused me of sneaking around his things. I later discovered that instead of playing poker Friday nights, he was taking speed
and doing who knows what else with a girlfriend.

His sister and I intervened with Jerry and told him that he had to
stop using and start going to meetings or he had to get out. That finally did the trick. One year later, I went to a meeting where he got
a medallion for his one-year clean date. There were about one hundred people present, mostly hippies and bikers, and I sat in the back.
I don't think he knew that I was there.

I remember two things from that meeting. When he spoke, I expected to hear how "his wife had saved his life," but that didn't find
a place in his story. I resented that omission. I also remember being
struck with the thought that this program could work.

Unfortunately, things didn't get any better. As the months passed,
we both seemed to realize that we would never trust or forgive each
other. I couldn't forget his countless deceptions, and almost every
evening he'd tell me how miserable it was to come home to a wife
who was either drunk or on her way to getting drunk.

I hated him for saying that. Didn't I have the right to have a drink after a hard day at the office? He kept harping on my drinking, telling me that I was in denial and that I should be going to AA.

Things got worse and worse between us. We agreed to separate and eventually signed divorce papers. I continued working full-time, but it was a serious life situation for me—bankruptcy, divorce and depression. To relieve the stress, I drank every night, day *and* night on the weekends.

I moved to a nearby town with a marina and bar where I made friends with a woman in my building. She and her husband took me boating every weekend. The excursions always included their friend Chris. I was having fun again. Chris was very versatile. He was strong and smart, sensitive and handy. He helped me clean up my apartment, which had been a mess ever since I moved in. I began to relish life once again. We had a relaxed and mellow relationship. Eventually he became a frequent overnight guest.

In the summer of 1993 I met with my mom and dad, after our long estrangement. As usual, she did almost all of the talking. Turns out Dad had congestive heart trouble and Mom wanted me to help her care for him. She didn't like it when I suggested a professional nurse.

Nine months later my sister Lisa left a message for me at the office, telling me that Dad had died. I called my mother. "Would you have liked to have seen him?" she asked. "Of course," I replied. "Well, you can go to the hospital," she shouted. "His body's still there."

My dad died before I could say good-bye. Once again, "bad mommy" was running the show.

Soon after Dad died, Chris lost his job and I invited him to stay with me until he decided what to do. We soon became contentedly domestic. He built shelves, washed windows, did the shopping and instructed me on the mysteries of the computer. I was working full-time. We were financially secure and enjoying our life together.

In the summer months, business slowed down and I was able to spend more time at home. I loved baking a variety of cute homemade muffins for breakfast, creating light lunches and concocting fun dinners preceded by cocktails and accompanied by wine. As my drinking continued and now extended to the daytime hours, Chris expressed his concern for my health and I felt him distancing himself emotionally from me. This was probably in reaction to my brushing off his concerns and building a wall around myself. I would raise the drawbridge whenever he commented on my drinking.

Then the day before Thanksgiving, he told me gently but firmly that he was returning to Missouri, where his family was located. He didn't stay for the holiday, and now I had nothing at all to be thankful for. Even though he was affectionate and loving when he phoned, I couldn't stop crying. He knew that I was suffering, but the calls came less and less frequently. When I called him, I was drunk and incoherent. For a while after his departure I had this fantasy that he would call and ask me to come to Missouri to be with him. When he didn't, I felt crushed and completely isolated.

The downward spiral that had started with the death of my father got worse. I had been on Xanax, an anti-anxiety medication, popping about sixty milligrams a day. Then I went to a psychiatrist who knew that I was drinking—but not how much. He prescribed the antidepressant Prozac and said that I could continue drinking. He didn't know that I was drinking every day and getting hammered on the weekends.

Even though I had the shakes and suffered anxiety attacks, I managed to get through work. I couldn't wait to get home, have a few cocktails with my neighbor and then lock myself in my apartment and drink myself to sleep. Although I looked okay on the outside, my apartment was a stink hole that embodied how I was feeling on the inside. Chris's departure reinforced the sense of abandonment that I had felt when Dad died.

I began to get really sick. I missed work, telling everyone I was struggling with "the flu." In February my doctor diagnosed hepatitis and told me to rest for three months. I became a recluse, an unwashed one at that. My apartment became my refuge, a filthy refuge. I closed the blinds, unplugged the phone, put a towel under the door so the light wouldn't show through. I stopped taking pills, but stayed in bed drinking all day, and eventually all night. I no longer left the building except to sneak down and buy liters of wine. Occasionally I ordered food sent up.

I kept the wine at the side of the bed, next to the bucket I used to throw up in. Sometimes I would awaken and just want to die. It was hell. I took all my pills and put them in a beautiful crystal bowl on the dresser. I thought gulping them all down at once would be the easy way out. But I didn't have the courage.

By late May, I'd get violently ill if I went more than a couple of hours without a drink. One morning I rolled out of bed and fell among the bottles that covered the floor. I landed on my knees. I really wanted to live, but not like that. I sobbed and managed to pray, "God, please help me."

Somehow I manage to ratchet up my courage, get dressed and go to the doctor. I told him that I thought I was an alcoholic. He'd been concerned about me for a long time. We went over the symptoms and with tears rolling down his cheeks, he told me that I had to stop drinking and go to AA if I wanted to get better.

I'll always remember that scene. *I* should have been the one who was crying.

I went back to my room and looked through the Yellow Pages for the names of treatment centers. I didn't want a local place. I tried a few others; then the name "Betty Ford Center" popped into my mind. It was the only place I called where they didn't first ask me about insurance or how I would pay for treatment. Lucy was the person's name on the phone. She called back the next day to see how I was and to tell me that it would take a while before a bed opened up at the center.

I was broke and had no insurance. I called my stepbrother, who unhesitatingly and lovingly said that he would provide the funds. I called my mother and told her what was happening. Without missing a beat she said, "Why are you doing this to me?" and hung up.

To help firm my resolve to get help, I told my colleagues at the office that I was going to the Betty Ford Center. Now I couldn't back down. Still, during the weeks I had to wait for a bed to open up, I couldn't stop drinking. Finally, the call came. I was to report to the center in one week.

. . .

A phrase that is commonly used in recovery circles is "hitting bottom," which signifies the point at which the pain has become so great that a transformative process begins that allows the alcoholic or the chemically dependent person to shed his/her destructive behavior and begin the long journey home. As these stories illustrate, that point of recovery is different for all of us.

. . .

Laurette credited Ann, one of the counselors at the Betty Ford Center, with turning her life around and keeping her on the straight and narrow path. Ann was one of the counselors who—because of her own recovery—was able to accomplish wonderful things with the patients. Laurette's life had been spiraling downward toward disaster before her encounter with Ann in Fisher Hall.

Laurette

After my grandmother died and the shameful fight I had had with my grandfather, I went back to Chico, California, to live with a girl I'd met who enjoyed partying and doing coke, a lifestyle similar to mine. I thought it would be like that every day, but she and her friends partied only on weekends. Thanks to buying heroin, in no time at all I'd used up all the money I'd inherited from Grandma. It wasn't long before my lover told me that I had to get a job and pay my way. I remember looking at her and saying, "A job? *You want me to get a job?* I don't believe this!"

She returned my incredulous stare with one of her own and said that she wasn't going to support me—either I found work or she was kicking me out.

So I agreed to get a job. And because she made me do that, I owe her a real debt of gratitude. The job I got started me off on an interesting—and ultimately life-changing—path.

I went to a local restaurant and bar I knew called Lionel's. It was in an area where prostitutes hung out, a drug-happening spot. There was a HELP WANTED sign in the window. The owner, Frank, was a black homey from my hometown who knew my cousins. He took pity on me when I couldn't even fill out the job application, led me into the kitchen, pointed to the pots and pans and told me to start there.

I know it seems hard to believe but in some weird way this was, for me, the start of the long road back—even though I wouldn't stop drinking and using for a long time. Turns out I liked working. It was better than stealing and no matter how lowly the job, it provided me with some sense of self-worth.

A few months later Frank asked me if I wanted to learn how to cook. I said yes. When he saw me making muffins, he asked if I wanted to be a baker. I loved baking and pretty soon I was the assistant kitchen manager working the graveyard shift, still doing drugs and drinking beer, though.

I thought life was great, couldn't get any better. Never in my wildest dreams did I imagine that sobriety would be a thousand times more fulfilling.

One night I accidentally bumped a pot against my breast and I felt a sharp pain that took my breath away. While passing my hand over the spot, I felt a lump. Fortunately, for the first time in my life, I was covered by insurance, so I went to a doctor. He said I was too young to have cancer, it was probably benign, but he did a biopsy anyway on my left breast. I didn't have a clue what "benign" meant; I thought maybe he meant I had a chest cold!

When the test came back positive, the doctor's office spent a couple of weeks trying to find me. I didn't realize I was supposed to call in to get the results. They finally tracked me down through the insurance company to Lionel's and told me to come back in. I sat down in front of a group of doctors, and they looked back at me and I looked back at them with that glazed look that any savvy person would know was drug related. One of them told me that I had cancer in my left breast and they were recommending a mastectomy. I didn't show any emotion and really had no idea what they were talking about. Nor did I understand the implications of such an operation.

This same doctor who gave me the news knew about my drug habit. He grabbed my arm and pointed to the needle marks. "This is going to kill you," he said. "Unless you stop shooting up, you're going to kill yourself and we can't help you. Think about it and give me a call." He gave me his card and walked out. I felt totally confused. Everything seemed to be mixed up. I hadn't a clue what a mastectomy was and I still thought that I had nothing more than a serious cold.

When I returned home I was in a daze, my usual frame of mind. My partner held me in her arms for a long time and explained the gravity of my condition. After about a week I called the doctor. He told me I had to get clean before the operation. I sensed in his voice that he didn't think I could. But he gave me meds to detox myself.

The withdrawal wasn't easy. Several times I was tempted to forget the whole damn thing.

I was twenty-four years old when my left breast was removed. (It was only when I was in recovery and after I had my other breast removed many years later that I began to grieve over my loss.) I was in the hospital for eleven days. The pain was severe, so I had to have a lot of medications. How sweet it was, falling once again into the embrace of drugs.

When I was discharged from the hospital, I found that I could get all the prescription drugs I wanted for a dollar a pop. Vicodin, a synthetic heroin, was prescribed for me, which took care of that deepseated craving for heroin. And what could be better—a heroin high with no needle marks! I was in heaven! I thought life was wonderful. I was getting paid for not working and had an endless supply of cheap drugs. Since I was using only prescription drugs, I convinced myself I was clean and sober!

The next several years of my life were filled with cooking and baking. I loved being in a kitchen, and it gave some structure and direction to my life. But my head was far from healthy. Anger was still there, as well as feelings of inadequacy. I continued to drink and use.

It probably seems bizarre, but baking saved me. I even wrote an essay on my career in cooking that earned me a scholarship.

The owner of Lionel's wanted me to go to a culinary college, but I got turned down because I had a sixth-grade reading level. I persisted, though, and managed to get a grant to go to a baking school. I did poorly in the academic and classroom part of the program, but I excelled in cooking and baking and got straight A's. Whenever I was asked to demonstrate something, I seemed to know intuitively how to bake it. I took great pride in graduating fifth in a class of twenty-five. My friends at work who genuinely cared for me threw a party and for the first time in my life, I experienced a high without using drugs.

Still, I was searching for something, but didn't know what it was. When this sense of disquiet and boredom hit me hard, I'd sniff coke to deaden whatever was bothering me and to restore my spirit.

My life pretreatment was tied up in two things—cooking and getting wasted. I really don't know how I did it and how my body was able to survive the punishment that I meted out.

After cooking school, I was hired at a bigger and better restaurant. There again I learned fast, was accepted by the rest of the cooks and soon got into the swing of things: drinking on the job, closing down the restaurant, visiting bars and clubs, going home wasted and sleeping until it was time to go to work in the afternoon.

A hotel in New York tried to hire me, on the basis of a recommendation from the school. But I was too scared of the unknown—the thought of being three thousand miles away, having to meet new friends and, perhaps most important, needing to cultivate new suppliers.

But when another hotel, this one in Palm Springs, closer to home, called to offer me a job, I said yes. The salary was beyond my wildest dreams. I packed everything that I owned in my old MG and drove to the desert, totally unaware that my life would never be the same. I was heading in the right direction. Even though I was still frightened and felt out of place, I was determined to stick it out for a while. They called me the "muffin scooper" because at first that was all they let me do in the bakery—cook three hundred muffins a day. That made me even angrier than I already was. Every morning I went to work determined to master everything that could be learned. By the end of my seventh year I was the sous-chef at the hotel's classy Italian restaurant.

I had earned a reputation for excellence, but a sense of restlessness still pursued me. I was still drinking and doing some drugs now and then. I was making nice money, had my own new car and apartment.

I was successful, but I was feeling stressed. The head chef at the hotel had befriended me and offered me the opportunity to move from
a staff to a management position. It was a critical juncture for me.
They interviewed twenty people, some of whom were graduates of
prestigious culinary schools, very talented and with enviable résumés.

Soon after they promoted me, I had a meltdown and started to act
out. I got into fights with my employees; I choked one and hit another over the head with a sauté pan. Every night there was something. It seemed as though I was out of control and out to get
everybody. I called in sick because I'd been drinking or had had a car
accident. One time I blacked out, drove my new car into a tree, totaled it and walked away unharmed. My license, however, was taken
away. I didn't know why I couldn't stop drinking and drugging. I'm
not sure I wanted to.

Amazingly, I wasn't fired. My boss treated me with great kindness
and understanding. Finally he called me into his office one night and,
on the verge of tears, told me that the hotel had decided that I needed
help. Arrangements had been made for me to enter the Betty Ford
Center, but I had to wait a week until a bed was available. I needed
to sign a paper that said I would complete treatment, otherwise I
wouldn't have a job to come back to. I signed it without reading it.

I intended to continue work while waiting to be admitted to the
center, but that lasted only a day and a half. On New Year's Eve, I
asked one of my friends at work to drive me to the liquor store and
then home, promising to stay there until it was time to enter the center. There wasn't much else I could do—after all, my license had been
revoked after the last accident.

In my apartment I remember opening the liquor bottle, sitting on
the living room floor and crying for a long, long time. I couldn't recall the last time I'd cried. Something had opened up inside me. I felt
a little relief, maybe even a little hope.

At the same time I had no idea what I was getting into. I conceived of it as a thirty-day vacation, a much-needed rest. It would be nice to get cleaned up, take off some weight, get some exercise and sleep, give up the booze so that I could cut back on it when I returned to work. I brought bathing suits, suntan lotions, lots of reading material and a boom box to listen to while I was sunning myself.

Man, was I in for a surprise. A *shock*, actually.

• • •

Most people who come to the Betty Ford Center are in for a surprise, but the one thing that we do not do is "shock" therapy. All the women in this book, as we have seen, get to the Center through a variety of paths, having gone astray from the straight road and finding themselves "alone in a dark wood."

I have a special place in my heart for Laurette. We both suffered from the same illnesses, breast cancer and chemical dependency. In a later chapter, she will tell you of the special circumstances that brought us together for a number of years. That time we shared allowed me the opportunity to discover what a wonderful person she was and continues to be.

II

PURGATORIO

What Happened?

O human race, born to fly upward, wherefore
at a little wind dost thou so fall?

THE DIVINE COMEDY

5

It's All About Secrets

For a long time, women were considered second-class citizens by society at large, by the treatment industry and by Alcoholics Anonymous. If it's taken a lot of time to moderate the "moral reprobate" stigma that attached to the male alcoholic, it's taken even longer to accomplish that with women. As the disease concept slowly is understood and accepted as it pertains to men, women alcoholics and addicts are—for the most part—still seen as morally challenged, "weak" individuals. Only in recent years have we garnered some measure of respect and semblance of equality. High-profile people like AA's Marty Mann have led the way in bringing about this change in public perception. I'm told that my own book, The Glad Awakening, has contributed in some measure to the understanding of how the disease of addiction affects women.

I'm proud of the positive changes that have occurred over the years in the way women patients undergo treatment at the Betty Ford Center. One of the women counselors at the center once told me that some of these new treatment protocols mirror the new feminine perspectives that emerged in the latter half of the twentieth century.

If I were to single out the most important change that we made at the center, it would be the decision to create separate halls reserved exclusively for women, staffed *exclusively by women. Shortly after the opening of the center it became clear to me and the staff that there were important clinical differences between men and women that needed to be addressed separately in treatment. Today there are two halls set aside exclusively for women, Fisher and Pocklington. Living in these gender-specific environments allows the women to be more open, to feel freer to express themselves without wondering what the men are thinking or how they could win their approval. It was an eminently wise and practical move.*

From my experience at Long Beach I knew that in a coed group women tend to focus on the men instead of themselves. Moreover, there are personal subjects that women are not comfortable talking about in front of men—for example, sexual abuse and incest, to mention just two. Women typically have more grief issues to resolve than their male counterparts. Conflicts with their children are often more traumatic, and their guilt seems more debilitating.

The second innovative change was the creation of unique services that evolved over the years to meet the special needs of women, needs that the counselors began to identify as necessary to promote recovery.

Because of the social stigma placed upon women who drink too much, women tend to minimize their problems to the outside world. All kinds of secrets have to be unlocked before women can recapture their self-esteem and repair their self-image. In the beginning it wasn't always clear how to handle all these issues along with chemical dependency.

The addition of new services and groups designed especially for women divided the staff. On the one side stood some counselors who were schooled in the tradition that chemical dependency is chemical dependency is chemical dependency—that's what needs to be treated, not all the other stuff. That school of thought was in the ascendancy when Paula, Claire and Beatrice went through treatment.

But a new breed of counselors felt deeply that a more holistic approach was needed. They believed that unless some of the other issues like body image and sexual abuse were dealt with in treatment, the potential for relapse was strong. They were particularly concerned about the women's self-image.

Of course alumni discussed these issues too. Some took the side of the traditionalists; others sided with the holistic proponents. Some counselors complained that pa-

tients were being burdened with too many group sessions and the focus on chemical dependency was being lost. Laurette's and Harriet's stories allude to this. But through all this discussion, the disease of addiction, the sanctity of the Twelve Steps and the reality of a community of sister and fellow sufferers remained consistant.

The third thing that we did differently was develop and confirm the clear understanding that women are different from men. You're probably smiling as you read this since this is one thing that should be taken for granted. But that was not always the case when it came to the treatment of addiction. Take for example the First Step, the concept of powerlessness. Once female patients at the Betty Ford Center had their own halls, it made it easier for the counselors to stress the key notion of helplessness—which is a feeling so many women are weighed down by in our society.

Gradually the counselors sought to empower women in every way possible. A few years ago at the Alumni Reunion one of the Fisher Hall counselors was telling me about a book called Victims and Sinners, by Linda Mercadante, which she said had helped her immensely in dealing with female patients, many of whom hang their heads in shame, mired in self-defeat and victimhood. The counselor told me, "It's simple. When men come here, they need a good dose of humility; women need a strong shot of pride."

• • •

After the Friday-morning golf match was over, Paula had been asked to tell her story to the women in Pocklington Hall, at the same time that Claire was telling her story to the "Fisherettes." Paula's already told us how she finally surrendered in front of her daughter Vicky and husband, Robert, and asked for help. That's the first and the most important step on the road to recovery.

Paula had gone through treatment in West Hall (later called Eva Pocklington Hall) in the late fall of 1985. At that time West was reserved for women, which made her experience at the Betty Ford Center a little different from Claire's, who had gone through McCallum in 1984 when it was mixed gender. As I've already mentioned, trust takes root and grows more quickly when women are on their own.

The women who lived in West Hall referred to themselves as "the wild and wonderful women of West." After living, laughing, fighting, crying and playing together, they found themselves changed for life. The distrust that had atrophied their lives be-

fore treatment was cast aside, and they underwent a marvelous transformation. The medallion ceremonies were full of tributes like: "I would trust you with my life!" "I love you like a sister!" "You are truly a friend!"

Although she had told her story many times, Paula was still nervous when she entered Pocklington Hall and took her place in the "community room," where large group sessions are held. Paula started her story with her decision to seek help at the Betty Ford Center.

Paula

When my husband asked me where I wanted to go for help, I hadn't the foggiest idea ("foggy" was also the perfect adjective to describe the chemical haze that had engulfed me for the past several years). The company Robert worked for had an Employee Assistance Program so he called them the next morning. They recommended the Betty Ford Center as one of the best places for treatment. When he called me from work and suggested the Betty Ford Center, I hesitated for a few moments. I'd just had my morning pills, five of them, and my resolve to get help was wearing a little thin. The legacy of years of consuming massive amounts of alcohol and pills was encouraging my addictive self to second-guess the good intentions of the previous afternoon.

Again I wondered, despite all my past broken resolutions, if I couldn't really handle this mess myself. Robert's anxious voice sliced through my silence. "I hope you're not having second thoughts about this?" he wondered out loud.

Robert came home earlier that afternoon than I'd expected. I hadn't had a chance to down my midafternoon vodka. He told me that he'd called the center for information, but that part of the deal was that I myself would have to call the Admissions Office. He couldn't do it for me. I was terrified. My courage was dwindling fast.

I asked Robert if he was *certain* that he couldn't make the arrangements for me. No, he said, they had to talk to me personally. He urged me to do it right away and promised that he would sit down next to me for support while I made the call. When I picked up the phone, he held on to me tight.

Somebody named Malcolm answered the phone. I was surprised by his gentle manner. The tone of his voice conveyed a special care and understanding. He told me it would be two weeks before a bed opened up. After hearing that, I didn't know whether to be relieved or upset. Part of me wanted to be admitted immediately; the other part sought to prolong the agony so I could continue to find refuge in my pills and alcohol, even though they were no longer providing the comfort I sought.

Malcolm asked me what pills I was taking and in what quantity, as well as how much I was drinking. He suggested I continue to take the pills and consume the alcohol until I checked in. Any attempt to cut back without medical supervision would put me at risk for convulsions. I knew he was right; the few times I'd tried withdrawal myself the physical repercussions were awful.

I was scheduled to report to the center on Monday, November 4, 1985, at 8 A.M.

On that fateful day, Vicky got up at 5 A.M. to bake sugar cookies I could take with me. During the drive to Rancho Mirage, I kept saying to Robert, "Honey, we can't be late. They said eight A.M." I was worried sick that if we weren't on time they'd refuse to admit me. And then what would I do?! Vicky sat in the backseat whispering words of encouragement.

I could have saved a lot of nervous energy. We arrived in plenty of time.

After filling out several forms, I was given a white gown and told that the doctor would be along in a few minutes. Those minutes seemed like hours. Shame and relief battled for control of my emotions. The silences between Robert, Vicky and me were long but comfortable. I knew that eventually they had to leave, but I dreaded being left alone.

Eventually there was a knock on the door and in walked a tall, handsome man in his seventies. Dressed in a white hospital coat, he introduced himself as Dr. James West, the medical director of the Betty Ford Center. My initial impression was that he looked both kind and scary at the same time. I introduced my husband and my daughter. He then turned to me and after a few minutes of idle conversation began asking me about my drinking and using patterns—specifically, about how many pills and how many drinks I consumed during the course of a day.

I told him that I was uncomfortable talking about this sensitive subject in front of my family. "Perhaps it would be better if they left the room," I whispered.

My heart stopped when he said, "Oh no, Paula, you don't understand. That game is over."

I was mortified and felt that my family was embarrassed for me. My answers to Dr. West's questions were barely audible. But the cat was out of the bag, so to speak, and as I look back on it, answering those questions honestly (if quietly!) was the beginning of my recovery. *There would be no more secrets.* Once the questions were over, Dr. West told Robert and Vicky that it was time for them to say goodbye. After he stepped out of the room, there were hugs, kisses and tears—lots and lots of tears. We promised there'd be lots of phone calls and visits.

Then the door closed. And with it, a whole chapter of my life.

Here I was, terrified, left alone with sugar cookies and the formidable Dr. West. He explained that since I was going to have some blood work done and would have to go through a pretty extensive detox procedure, I'd begin my stay not at the center itself but next door at the Eisenhower Medical Center.

By the end of the week I was looking back at those days at Eisenhower as a fabulous break! I could sleep forever, my meals were brought to me on a silver tray (well, it wasn't silver—but that's what it seemed like) and I was waited on hand and foot. All this in stark contrast to the demanding schedule at the Betty Ford Center.

After my four days detoxing at Eisenhower, two volunteers, Gene and Byron, escorted me over to Betty Ford. They were sympathetic, courteous, caring and sensitive to my thoughts and feelings; I later learned they were in recovery themselves.

Gene and Byron loaded my suitcases on a little golf cart. It was raining, unusual for the desert, and the wind was blowing. I was carrying a fishing tackle box. Gene asked me if I thought I was going fishing and he laughed when I told him that my makeup was in it. His warm laughter made me feel better. But when they escorted me through the double doors of Firestone Hall, the point of entry for treatment, my anxiety increased. The temptation to turn around and go home was strong.

Standing by one of the chairs in the lounge area was a young woman, Donna, who escorted me to West Hall, where I would be living. She led me down a long corridor to my room. When she told me with a smile on her face that the room was called the "swamp," my heart took a nosedive and I knew that I wouldn't be able to catch a break the whole time I was here. The "swamp" was the only room that had four beds; all the others had two.

·   ·   ·

I can empathize with Paula. When I walked into the treatment center in Long Beach I was anything but happy to see that I'd be sharing a room with three others. I told the good doctor that I was accustomed to having my own private room. He called my bluff by saying that he would have the other three women pack their things and move to other rooms. Of course I couldn't allow that to happen, so I took the bed that was free.

Being in a room with three strangers is a very difficult thing. But what usually happens at the Betty Ford Center is that the people who need others the most end up there. I remember one time a self-important person arrived at the Betty Ford Center and was assigned a bed in the "swamp." She was raising hell with the Admissions people, outraged that she had to bunk with others. She announced that she was returning home. I told John Schwarzlose, CEO of the center, that if he thought it a good idea, I was willing to talk to her, to convince her to stay. Leonard Firestone and I had done that several times with self-important people. But it wasn't necessary with this woman. She showed up for breakfast the next morning, meek as a lamb.

◆ ◆ ◆

Another patient was in the "swamp" when we walked in. Donna asked her which of the beds was unoccupied. She didn't say anything, but pointed to the bed in the corner opposite the door. To its right was a sliding door leading outside to a patio with a breathtaking view of the mountains. Donna asked the woman where my towels were. She kept her silence, again simply pointing to the towel rack on which my towels hung.

Her behavior seemed rather bizarre. I later discovered that she had been "put on silence" for the day, not an unusual assignment for patients who don't listen and use their incessant chatter to block out what others are saying to try to help them. Donna then left me to unpack, a complicated task. How was I going to get the contents of my two large suitcases into the one small closet allotted to me?

My recollections of the first week at Betty Ford are rather hazy and disconnected. The pain in my back and one of my legs was intense. The first night was very hard, and the nurse monitored my vital signs every four hours. Even with regular doses of Librium, the withdrawal drained everything out of me. I was literally bouncing off the walls in the corridors. I remember sitting next to a heroin addict outside the nurse's office. He was shaking uncontrollably. He was also being treated for prostate cancer. He looked so uncomfortable that I gave him the cushion I used to support my tailbone. We were fellow sufferers and, despite my own pain, I recognized in him someone worse off than me.

Nights were the worst time of all. If I managed two hours of sleep, I was grateful. I spent a lot of the night in the kitchen area and the lounge (which I found out later was called the "pit"). I couldn't stop crying. I couldn't stand one of my roommates, who I felt was cold and distant. I saw myself as being an outcast and a prisoner at the same time. Every time that I thought about my family, I felt ashamed and guilty.

◆　◆　◆

Detoxification is a wrenching physical experience. As I listened to Paula's story about her withdrawal, I can actually squeeze right into her body. I still have some anger over the week before I entered treatment. My doctors decided that I could detox at home (versus a hospital). The first day, I kept throwing up. I was shaking the whole week. I couldn't keep my legs still. Despite all the best efforts of those helping me, I, like Paula, was unable to sleep. And, of course, I was having terrible pains because of the pinched nerve in my neck. In my first days at Long Beach, I couldn't go down the hall to get coffee I was still so shaky. My vitamins were ground into a powder that I could sprinkle on my cereal, as I wasn't allowed to take them in pill form.

◆　◆　◆

I wasn't ready for the orientation meeting that I had with one of the staff the first day in West Hall. Talk about tough love! She wanted to take a photograph of me to attach to my chart, but I was embarrassed about how I looked and asked if I could fix my makeup first. "No."

I was told my "therapeutic task" was to keep the kitchen clean and orderly. I was told to read to page 165 in the Big Book, paying particular attention to chapter 3, titled "More About Alcoholism." She then told me to read about the First Step in another book called

Twelve by Twelve. I asked if I could write down the assignments she'd just given me. "No."

It seemed like everything was in a foreign language. Ever since I was a child I'd had a problem reading and dreaded school assignments. My mother used to poke fun at me and make sarcastic remarks, like "She thinks she's so smart—yet she can't even read." I felt overwhelmed and started to cry once again.

I'll never forget that first Friday night in the auditorium. It was the day after I'd moved over to the center from Eisenhower. A woman about my age named Josie had befriended me and walked with me to the in-house AA meeting. At that time I knew nothing about AA meetings. The custom was for all the patients to introduce themselves at the beginning of the meeting. I was sitting in the first row, which was a mistake, as we were the first up. One by one the four patients to my right introduced themselves by their first names and then said that they were an alcoholic and/or a drug addict. When it was my turn I was paralyzed and tongue-tied.

People were staring at me. It seemed like an eternity. Finally, Josie prompted me with a gentle elbow nudge. Looking at the floor I whispered, "I'm Paula, and I'm an alcoholic." I felt like the dregs of the earth hearing those words come out of my mouth. I had become the real loser my mother had always told me I was.

◆   ◆   ◆

There are climactic moments in treatment that become the turning point for women. They are different for each one of us. I remember at Long Beach when I said in group, "I'm Betty and I know I am an alcoholic and I know that my drinking has hurt my family." It was the first time in treatment that I'd identified myself as an alcoholic. It came out quite spontaneously. I recall saying it with conviction because I had just listened to another patient say she didn't understand why her family was making such a big fuss about her drinking. It wasn't hurting them, she said. But I knew that her drinking was causing her family a lot of trouble; I'd heard them talk about it.

Each day in treatment is a learning experience, as we come to better understand the disease of addiction and how it affects us as well as our family and friends.

. . .

After my fifth day I was allowed to call home. I told my husband, "I can't do this. I think I'm going to die. Please come and get me and I promise I'll never drink or take pills again."

Robert was quiet. He didn't know how to respond, and was torn between coming to pick me up immediately and waiting until the end of the week. He was frightened. But Claudia, my counselor, called him later the same day and told him not to worry, that although I was still going through a very difficult withdrawal, everything would be all right.

Shortly after that I had just the tiniest sense that things might get better.

Dealing with the legacy of the dreadful relationship I had with my mother became a key part of my treatment plan. The years of dealing with her verbal and emotional abuse had left me deeply scarred. In one of the small group sessions I had to sit in the middle of a circle and express my feelings to another patient who was sitting opposite me. I addressed the woman as "Mom" and told her that I hated her when she called me "a beady-eyed, stupid milkmaid, a fat little bitch who would never amount to anything."

I told the stand-in for my mother: "All these years and you never said that you loved me. All I want is for you to love me."

Claudia told me I was like a child who keeps putting her hand on a hot plate and getting burned. Eventually, most children learn to stop doing it. "But you can't seem to unlearn that," she said. "You can only change yourself; you cannot change other people—and that most certainly includes your mother." She added, "You may be longing for the mother who never was, and more important, the mother who never will be." She then urged me to write a letter to my mother and read it to the group.

The letter contained all the pain, hurt and resentment that I had harbored over the years. We then had a ceremony outside at which I burned the letter. It was a ritual that signified the beginning of a healing journey for me which has extended over many years. While it is still not complete, as the wounds are still tender and the scars still linger, there is much less pain.

Isn't it amazing that even though the staff and other patients told me that I had to let go, I kept on sending postcards to my mother from the Betty Ford Center, with the simple message, "Hi, Mom. I love you."

She never answered.

A week after I arrived, Betty Ford gave a lecture that was outstanding. I concluded that she and I both have basically the same problem. She touched my heart. I talked with her after the lecture and asked if she called herself both an "alcoholic" and an "addict." She said, "Do whatever you're comfortable with." I told her I was starting to feel okay about the "alcoholic" part, but that the "addict" label still hurt. I also asked her how long her sweats, shakes, confusion and leg tremors had lasted. Three months, she said. Yuck!

I was in awe of the ease with which she shared her story. I hoped that the day would come when I would be just as comfortable sharing with the patients—just as I'm doing now. That same evening I started writing my autobiography, inspired by the life stories I'd already heard read out loud that were so moving in their honesty.

After about two weeks, things started to get better. Sleep came more easily. Especially after I was made "Granny" and helped two new arrivals get settled, I began to feel a part of the place and the process. I remember one of those new patients saying to me, "You make so much sense, I can't believe that you're a patient." It made me proud to hear that and to be able to help someone who was both anxious and angry about being in treatment.

Another sign of my growth was the time I sat in what's called the "hot seat," and my sisters sat around me and gave me feedback as to how they saw me as a person and the progress that I was making. The kid gloves came off, there was no pampering of "poor little Paula." What I heard was tough medicine. I was told to stop blaming others, particularly my parents, and to take responsibility for my life.

The counselors and other patients felt that my concern with appearances was interfering with my treatment and preventing me from getting in touch with my real, inner self. I was trying to hide behind a façade. They suggested I remove all my jewelry and put it into safekeeping in the Admissions Office. Malcolm smiled when I brought everything there, but he didn't say anything, just gave me the receipt.

The counselors and other patients also suggested I stop dressing up so fancy, and take off my makeup, including my mascara and false eyelashes.

Well, the thought of "having no face" scared the hell out of me. My mother's constant refrain, "You are ugly," tolled like a bell at a funeral service. I got an awful headache. I begged Claudia not to make me take off my makeup. She said that I didn't have to take it all off but reduce it to a minimum.

The next morning when I appeared in group I felt that I was naked before my enemies. But I was rewarded with a big round of applause! Josie and Laura hugged me and said that they were proud of me. The lesson that exercise conveyed has remained with me to this day. I came to understand how the *interior* woman is what truly counts in life's journey.

•   •   •

The group circle is a very important symbol and ritual in recovery. While sitting in the center of the circle is a trial by fire, both painful and cleansing, the center of the circle symbolizes wisdom and insight. Inevitably, while listening to the stories told by others who've gone through treatment, patients are struck by the degree to which other lives mirror their own.

As Paula continued with her story, she hoped to emphasize two key points for those listening: the importance of the community of women who together share the disease, and the importance—after leaving primary treatment—of following the prescribed plan for continued sobriety. Her description of her experience at Betty Ford as well as the portraits she drew of her sisters in treatment rang true to the patients who were gathered to hear her testimony.

◆   ◆   ◆

I had never heard of "Twelve Steps" before I came to the Betty Ford Center. But as I continued in treatment they began to be more and more important. After about a week, I was given a work sheet to begin my First Step process—"We admitted we were powerless over alcohol, that our lives had become unmanageable." It seemed like every day patients would be talking about their powerlessness over alcohol and drugs.

Before treatment I'd always thought I could control my use of prescription drugs and my drinking by just using a little willpower. Soon I was hearing that willpower had nothing to do with it.

I was confused, but as I listened to other women in the First Step discussion, I began to glimpse what was meant by powerlessness—a loss of control.

My counselor, Claudia's, First Step discussion helped me understand that my total preoccupation with alcohol and pills is what caused my loss of control and the unmanageability that had invaded my life. I became a prisoner to pills and alcohol. My whole life revolved around getting and using. That's the insanity of this disease. The pills and the booze were what at Betty Ford they called "an allergy of the body and an obsession of the mind." Even when the chemicals no longer worked for me, when they didn't make me feel good any more, I still had to have them.

Before I started work on my First Step assignment I went to my room and said a prayer: "God, please help me to get well and guide my words and thoughts as I complete these work sheets." Then I started writing, and it all seemed to flow so easily as the secrets poured out on the paper.

I wrote down examples of how the drugs and the alcohol affected me physically, emotionally, spiritually; how they affected my family and my friends. The shame came out as example after example spilled out onto the paper. How I lied to the doctors to get prescription re-fills; how I hid the pills and filled the liquor bottles with water, hoping nobody would realize how much I was consuming; taking pills and drinking alcohol when I was pregnant; trying to recollect how I'd gotten bruises all over my body; making late-night phone calls that I couldn't remember having placed the next morning.

I felt terribly ashamed.

There were so many examples of my crazy, destructive behavior. I recalled that one day I'd noticed an entry in my husband's day planner: "Check up on wife." I was petrified and angry at the same time. I knew that he would be checking on me, calling the doctors and pharmacists to see if I was getting pills from them.

He did call the pharmacist in Idaho to find out if he was the source. The pharmacist told him, "Is Paula being a naughty girl? Well, she's not getting the pills from me." That, of course, was a lie.

I dreaded the arrival in the mail of the pharmacist's monthly bill. One day I was nearby when Robert opened the envelope and saw the incriminating bill. "Jesus Christ, honey. Come in here."

When I entered his study, my heart pounding, he said, "My God, this bill is for eight hundred dollars. It can't be right!"

I must have sounded ridiculous when I said all I'd bought was some body lotion, some aspirin and a new bathroom scale. "What about the Tylenol Four, Percodan, Valium, Seconal and muscle relaxant?" he asked, with disgust in his voice.

"Honey," I alibied, "my back pain is so bad that I need those pills." But I put on a contrite face and said that I'd try to ease up on the pills and reduce the size of the pharmacy bill. At that moment, I thought I meant it. But really, it was a lie.

Reciting my First Step in front of the group was very hard, but a tremendous relief when it was over. It was a great cleansing, a catharsis. My peers gathered around me, thanked me for sharing and began telling me how they could relate to the stories I'd told. I gained another powerful insight into what it means to tell one's story and have others identify with it. One of the patients admitted, "I used to steal pills out of the medicine cabinets in the homes of friends that we were visiting." Another one said, "I thought I was the only one who played the pill game."

I wasn't alone and I wasn't rejected. Secrets weren't secrets anymore. Claudia smiled and said that we were healing each other by trading secrets and sharing examples.

To learn more about the disease and its effects, we often attended lectures given by experts. One in particular—about withdrawal—was a real eye-opener. My withdrawal symptoms included feeling jittery, anxious, depressed, weak, exhausted, experiencing numbness, heart palpitations, icy cold sweats, leg jerks and insomnia. The whole ball of wax.

I felt like I was going to die sometimes. It was a great relief to know that I was not crazy but going through withdrawal.

That particular lecture was also timely as it came on the same day when I thought of strangling Dr. West. I was more than two weeks into the program, and I believed I'd be on my way home in less than two weeks. I was devastated when Dr. West said that because of my long and difficult withdrawal they would be keeping me for six weeks instead of four.

I said, "Sorry, Dr. West. I won't be able to do that. But thanks anyway." I thought to myself, "There's no way they're going to keep me here another two weeks." Dr. West then asked gently, "What's so important that you have to get home to?" I told him that I had things to do, my family to take care of, Christmas shopping—any excuse that I could muster. It was like clinging to a life raft to avoid drowning. He looked at me and said it was important for me to stay another two weeks, and that I would still have plenty of time to prepare for Christmas.

It was the eighteenth of November, and now I wouldn't be discharged until the eighteenth of December. I looked at him with pleading eyes, careful not to show my anger and displeasure. I thought to myself, "He's a man. What does he know about Christmas shopping and the time needed to get things ready for the holidays?"

Of course, if I'd been honest with myself, I would have remembered the disasters that my previous Christmases had been, when I stumbled through the house in a fog. All that day (November 18) I thought to myself that I would *never* get out of this place. I wondered if I could keep going.

But then in group that evening, one of the patients who had suffered multiple relapses talked about how hard it is to keep sober after completing primary treatment. I got scared, and I didn't need a "feelings chart" to identify what I was afraid of. What would happen to me after December 18? Could I stay straight? All of a sudden staying two extra weeks didn't seem so bad after all.

One assignment, which at first I dreaded, but which gave me great pleasure when it was completed, was on the subject of assertiveness. It also helped me relate to some of my sisters in treatment, particularly the New Yorker who invaded the swamp the third week I was there. Her trademark was a black leather jumpsuit (she must have had a couple of them since she looked the same every day) and gold chains galore. She was an angry woman who pushed the buttons of practically everyone on the unit, including me. Whenever she joined a group at the coffee table, she'd start to argue and bully the others. Everyone thought she was obnoxious. I told Claudia about the situation and she told me that it was time for me to change roles, from "Doris Doormat" to "April Assertive." She assigned me the book *The Assertive Woman* to read.

Reading the book made me realize how poor my eye contact had been, how inappropriate some of my gestures were, how ineffectively I communicated. My peers helped with the assignment by telling me that I talked too fast and way too much—without really adding anything to the conversation. Josie, Patricia and I talked about it at the coffee table and we laughed about the names that the book assigned to different personalities. In addition to "Doris Doormat" and "April Assertive," there was "Agatha Aggressive" and "Iris Indirect." We gave what we thought were appropriate names to one another.

The real test of my newfound skills occurred when Claudia, who'd been listening to me complain about Lady Black Leather, suggested I give a book report on *The Assertive Woman* to the group, and then confront my roommate from the swamp. Needless to say, I wasn't thrilled about displaying for public consumption my newfound persona of "April Assertive." I was just getting comfortable with doing it privately. But somehow I found the courage to do it.

Of course Lady Black Leather wasn't the least bit happy being singled out. She was her usual argumentative and angry self and was offended when I related incidents of where she'd put me and others down. I told her exactly how I felt when she claimed that she wasn't an alcoholic like the rest of us sluts—*because all she ever drank was champagne!* When the session was over she stomped out of the room while my peers crowded around me, offering congratulations. Many of them said that they wouldn't have had the courage to do what I had done.

Lady Black Leather didn't talk to me for days. Finally, I said enough of that and when we were alone sat down with her in the swamp and suggested that, for the sake of our sobriety, we let by-gones be bygones. I told her I regretted that we had not settled our differences in private, but that being assertive and getting my feelings out rather than burying them was important to me. I also told her that while my fear of her anger had subsided, it was still there be-cause she was such a strong woman, and I admired that in her. She softened at that and told me she knew that her anger was a defense mechanism and that she had to be strong to survive. She believed that no one would like her if they got to know who she really was.

I thought it odd when I was told that I would be doing my Fifth Step on the fourth of December, given that I wasn't being discharged until the eighteenth. Usually the Fifth Step is completed the day be-fore discharge. Claudia said, though, that I was ready to do my Fourth and Fifth Steps. She gave me a Fourth Step guide and told me to write down an inventory of my strengths and weaknesses with examples of each.

I found the whole process very scary. I wasn't even sure what "inventory" meant. I wondered when I would have time to do the assignment, there was so much going on: completing assignments, auditing lectures, attending meetings, attending group, meditating, exercising . . . There never seemed to be a free moment.

I decided to go to my room, where I would have some quiet time to think and write things down. I just put pen to paper, and it all started to come out: examples of my shame and guilt (those were the biggies), my anger and resentments, my self-pity and selfishness. Dredging up all the guilt and resentments was draining, but defi-nitely worthwhile. We were told to spend a similar amount of time listing our assets. I whizzed through that part, unwilling to give my-self credit for much of anything.

One of my peers, I think it was Mary, said the Fifth Step was all about secrets. She remembered how she had gotten started in that terribly difficult department—someone told her that she should just kick off with the subject that she was most afraid to share with an-other human being. She said once she got through that it was a snap.

I decided to start my Fifth Step process by recounting the night-mare day in the "cave" when Robert walked into our bedroom and found me zonked, laying out my jewelry on the bed.

Sure enough, when I finished writing up my Fifth Step and walked outside and felt the sunshine on my face and looked up to the clear blue sky, I took what I think is the deepest breath I'd ever taken in my life. It went right down to my toes.

The circular path back to the hall reminded me that I had come full circle. It was amazing; I felt that I really didn't have to put one foot in front of the other and walk the way other folks were walking. I could just fly right over the trees! It was the greatest sense of well-being and freedom that I'd ever experienced. I couldn't help but con-trast it with the negative feelings that I'd had when I first arrived at the center.

A huge millstone had been removed from around my neck. I had just dropped the heavy boulders, those secrets that kept me sick. The title of one of the chapters in the Big Book kept coming into my mind: "Freedom from Bondage."

I remember skipping into the hall singing, "What a day this has been, what a rare mood I'm in." The gals immediately gathered around and asked, "How was it?" I told them I felt as pure as a newborn baby and that it was a wonderful catharsis. "Put everything down, write everything out and don't omit anything. It will get the monkey off your backs forever," I told them. I was now the expert.

"I just wish I could be this happy for the rest of my life," I said. I shared some of the most poignant parts with Josie, who was in my group and with whom I had become very close, and even made some suggestions to Lady Black Leather. She was a tough cookie, though, and continued to maintain that she was not an alcoholic. She claimed she didn't drink, even though she kept a case of expensive champagne under her bed in her fancy Manhattan co-op.

That night, encircled by the women of West Hall and under the gaze of a magnificent moon and brilliant stars, a fire consumed my Fifth Step. What a ritual! And I threw in my false eyelashes for good measure!! Then we did the hokeypokey and retired to the common room for pizza and Coke—Coca-Cola that is!

The night before my departure, I was sitting at the coffee table when my parents called. I was able to measure my progress by the way I handled my mother. She said things like "I know you've had lots of time to rest there," and "I know all about AA; when you come home, you'll sound like a preacher." I remember telling her that I would never preach to anybody and especially not to her, the person who already had all the answers to everything. I felt great about the straightforward way I asserted myself in our conversation and my responses to her. No more crying and emotional breakdowns. She got very quiet and handed the phone to my dad.

When the call was over, I sat down at the coffee table with some of my sisters in sobriety and told them about it. I told them how Mom was always putting down Dad's family as "those stupid German yodelers." I told them how Mom used to describe me as "nothing but a fat, stupid milkmaid."

Josie's response was, "It's important that you're able to tell your mother, 'I love you, Mom, but I hate your behavior.' That way you won't listen to the negatives she gives you, but you will be asserting yourself in a positive way." She said I should keep a copy of *Assertive*

Woman on my nightstand all the time and continue to be "April Assertive."

Dad had changed from those early years when he strapped me. He had become very loving and caring and told me when he got on the phone that night that I shouldn't pay any attention to my mother when she spoke like that. I remember about six months before I entered treatment in 1985, Robert and I sent him an airplane ticket to visit us in California. I recall every detail of when he walked off the plane. His face was bloated, battleship gray in color. He walked with a cane, and his baggy trousers looked like they might fall to the ground. His pants were so low that you could see the top of the crack in his behind. His stomach was huge.

Mom wouldn't come, and it was just as well. Robert and I were able to spend "quality time" with Dad. He told me how sorry he was for everything he'd done to hurt me. He apologized for Mom. He attempted to explain her behavior by saying, "She must have the devil in her." That was all he could bring himself to say about her.

Two weeks after I completed treatment, Dad committed suicide. I believe that before he shot himself, he wanted to make certain that I had completed treatment and would be all right.

I'm so thankful my father and I reconciled. But I was never able to win my mother's love or acceptance.

My discharge date was December 18, 1985. It's a day that I will always look back on with the fondest of memories. My treatment ended and my real recovery began the same day. Robert was coming to drive me home. The wild and wonderful women of West Hall celebrated my departure with a moving medallion ceremony. As my medallion was passed around the circle from woman to woman, each one shared how I had entered and affected their lives.

Almost everyone said something that touched me, but I remember what Michelle said in particular. Michelle had been in the unit two weeks and the best way that I can describe her is that she belonged to the hippie culture, with long, unkempt hair, no makeup, and she wore a baggy dress down to her ankles. She thanked me for being so honest and said she wished everybody would be like that. I considered it a real compliment, especially since I used to be such a chronic "people pleaser."

Actually, I thought Michelle was the most honest person in the unit. She wasn't afraid to speak her mind no matter what the reaction might be. I know I'm not the only one who will never forget the time in group when she lit into Miss Uppity, whom no one else had the courage to confront. She said, "Is it because you're from Dallas and married to a doctor that you feel superior to all of us? Truth is, you're no better than anyone else here. You're a phony and you're prejudiced and I don't give you much hope for recovery if you don't snap out of it." The fact that she said she admired *my* honesty filled me with pride.

But pride cometh before the fall. After Michelle spoke, Lady Black Leather said that she didn't hold out much hope for my recovery if I didn't get a little humility.

Finally the medallion came back to Claudia, my wonderful counselor, who clasped it in both hands and then brought it right up to her heart. She sighed and then started talking. As she did so she held the medallion in the palm of one hand and rubbed it with the other. I will never forget the gesture. She said such wonderful things. I can't remember a word, though, because there was so much love in her eyes that I was absolutely transfixed. I knew that I would be safe if she walked the journey with me.

Then came the call from Firestone that my husband was there, ready to pick me up. The rest was a whirlwind of activity. It was like a wedding scene. There were hugs and tears, last-minute autographs for my Big Book, invitations to visit, to attend AA meetings together, to exchange phone calls. They did everything but throw rice.

Someone put my luggage on a cart and started wheeling it out the door. I left the wonderful women of West Hall and followed the circular path to Firestone. Robert was waiting for me. I ran to him and hugged him as if I would never let go. I felt like a new bride.

I vowed to myself that I would never return as a patient. But I did.

♦ ♦ ♦

After she'd finished speaking, the women of Pocklington Hall gave Paula a standing ovation, and all of them came over to give her a hug. As was always the case with Paula, she teared up easily, but this time it was from the joy and happiness she felt in telling her story. Every time she did that, it strengthened her own recovery.

I'm afraid Paula's treatment story doesn't end there. It has another episode which deals with her "second coming" to the Betty Ford Center. Unfortunately, relapse is part of the disease of addiction.

6

Behavior Unbecoming a Lady

Claire went through treatment in 1984, two years after the center opened. She was assigned to McCallum Hall, the first residential unit to be opened on campus. When she arrived, McCallum was half male and half female, a tradition that was soon to change.

We left Claire Friday evening when she'd returned to Fisher Hall to continue telling her story to the patients. The women had gathered once again in the commons, better known as "the pit." Over the fireplace at the back of the pit is a statue of a woman called La Puebla. I'm particularly fond of that statue, which represents the woman of wisdom, a model for all the women who go through treatment.

These "pits" are the heart and nerve center of each hall, although much informal interaction goes on as well in the small kitchen and on the outdoor patios. In the early years of the Alumni Reunions, returning alumni were allowed to reenter their old halls and revisit the pits, the kitchen and the patios.

The stories and examples of powerlessness and unmanageability that were exchanged were the glue that bound their caring community together through the tough times and the good times after they left the Center to go home.

•   •   •

Current patients always enjoy listening to former patients who've come back to share their stories of tragedy and triumph. Claire, in particular, had a way of telling her story that made the patients laugh and cry, and filled them with hope. You could see everybody thinking, "If Claire could do it, there's no reason why I can't find my way."

Claire reintroduced herself in the usual fashion, "Hi! I'm Claire and I'm an alcoholic." All the members of the group shout out their response, in unison, "Hi, Claire!" She continued her story by recounting the circumstances of her coming to the center. How, over lunch, her friend had suggested a number of treatment centers in Georgia, Minnesota and California. She chose California because it was warm. Then, she uttered that line that's become rather famous at the Betty Ford Center, "I came for the weather and they gave me my life."

Claire

Lou Ann, my friend from AA, called the Betty Ford Center for me. Malcolm, the Admissions' officer, told her that I'd have to call myself to make the reservation. I did and after some preliminary questions, he told me it would be six weeks before a bed was available. My reaction to that was a mix of disappointment and relief. Sure, I needed help—but a few more weeks of drinking would help ease the prospect and pain of getting sober.

I firmed up my decision by alerting a couple of my friends that I was going to the Betty Ford Center and told them I was counting on them to make sure I was present and accounted for when the curtain went up for my big show! They were really happy for me and promised they wouldn't let me back out. Everybody but me knew that my drinking had become unmanageable and that I needed help.

Harold took me to the airport. At the stopover in Dallas I called Malcolm to let him know I was coming. He said that I wasn't expected until the next day and that he wouldn't have a bed for me that night. I told him to book me a room at the Marriott. To keep my nerve up, I had a couple of shots on the plane.

When I got to my room the TV wasn't working. What could a poor, lonely woman do but call room service and order two lamb chops and four scotches for my Last Supper? When I called Lou Ann to tell her what was going on, she said, "For God's sake, don't get snookered!"

The next morning one of the young workers at the Marriott drove me to the Betty Ford Center. Turns out he'd gotten sober at the center fourteen months earlier. That made me feel better.

My chaperone-in-recovery carried my bags into Firestone Hall, where I was greeted by Malcolm. Then a wonderful volunteer named Eddy searched my bags. I was a little put off by that but she did it in such a sensitive fashion, chatting all the while, that I didn't find it offensive. When she was finished her search-and-destroy mission for any alcohol or medications that I might have inadvertently (or purposely!) brought with me, she looked at me and said, "I haven't had my hug today."

That was my introduction to the splendid ritual of the hug, which is so commonplace among recovering people. When she told me that "Granny" would soon be there to fetch my bags and escort me to McCallum Hall, I didn't know what to expect. I was imagining an old white-haired lady barely able to walk. I later discovered that the person designated "Granny" was responsible for the good order of the unit.

As we left Firestone and walked to my hall, "Granny" told me that the girl I'd be rooming with had only arrived the day before. Lynn was my daughter Beth's age and we didn't hit it off. I found her to be very standoffish. I don't know what she thought of me but later, after I had been nicknamed "mother," she said in no uncertain terms, "You're not *my* mother!" For the most part I stayed away from her.

She was an early riser who liked to run every morning. That made it easier for me to pull myself together in the morning while she was out torturing herself to keep in shape.

The morning immediately after my arrival I witnessed a medallion ceremony. All the women and the staff sat or stood in a circle in the pit, so that everyone could see and hear. The counselor explained that the medallion would be passed around from one person to the next. She said that everyone should hold it for a moment, breathe his or her own energy into the medallion, and whoever wished could say something to the patient who was leaving. Then she gave the medallion to the person on her left.

I was deeply touched by the love and care that everyone in the group showed to the woman who'd just completed primary treatment. When the counselor spoke to her about what she had accomplished in treatment and what the future held in store for her, I experienced my first real ray of hope. I know that I was quite arrogant at that point because I was thinking if she could do it, I certainly could, too. I found out later that she'd been much worse off than I when she entered treatment.

Ray was my counselor, and he introduced me to my small group of women. I was more nervous at that moment than I'd ever been singing before a live audience. I didn't know what to expect, as I'd never been in group therapy before. He asked me to tell the group why I'd come to Betty Ford for treatment. I stumbled around and finally zeroed in on the incident with my daughter Cindy and how she found me so drunk that she wasn't able to tell me about the reconciliation with her former husband. The group listened attentively, nodding their heads as though they had had similar experiences.

It was a remarkable group of people with diverse backgrounds. As the days passed, I was absolutely fascinated by how such different women had such similar stories about their relationships with alcohol and drugs, and the devastating consequences. I wept when another woman shared her past experiences of being hurt as a child.

Ray was watching me and during one of the pauses asked, "Claire, why are you crying? Does Melanie's story bring up memories for you?" I wasn't able to answer him directly, but I said that I felt so sad for Melanie. Later I thought that her narration might have triggered memories of Beth and the father who abused her and the stepfather who neglected her.

The McCallum community helped me recover my laughter and sense of humor. Paul, a patient whom we called "the controller," had the task of assigning the times when the telephone could be used. There was only one telephone for the patients and some scheduling was necessary, otherwise it would have been chaotic. He was very meticulous about his assignment, which he took very seriously. Two others and I were assigned a particular half hour to use the phone; when one of the girls was late, Paul was fit to be tied. He went around ranting and raving, stamping his feet and acting so put out about a missed telephone time that it actually was very, very funny.

Al, a Hispanic man whom I liked, and I started to laugh—so hard that we put our arms around each other and sank to the floor. I said, "Isn't it good to laugh again?" I also thought to myself, "This is the first time in my adult life I've touched a guy without having to pay for it with sex."

My first job, or "therapeutic duty" as it's called at Betty Ford, was taking care of the laundry room. I had to clean the dryers, vacuum the floor and empty the lint boxes. Sometimes I also pitched in cleaning up the coffee room and patio. I had to set the tables in the dining hall just as I'd helped Mom set the table back in Illinois. She and I used to sing while we were doing it. Doing it at the center made me feel like I was part of a family. I hadn't felt that in a long, long time.

The first assignment Ray gave me was to engage in conversations with three of my peers as to how we got to the Betty Ford Center. We did that for three nights, and it was a great way to get to know each other. I remember I talked about sorrow a lot, and for that reason Ray assigned me to a grief group. There I discovered that I hadn't really achieved closure about the loss of Dad and Mom and my brother Ben, who died of causes related to alcoholism.

During my second week of group therapy I received not a "spiritual awakening" (quoting the Twelfth Step), but a "rude awakening." At the beginning of group each patient had to tell how he/she was feeling that morning. If any person was at a loss for a "feeling," there was a big chart on the wall that contained a whole list. When it came to my turn I would always say, "Well, I'm feeling fine."

After hearing this for ten consecutive days, a twenty-two-year-old hippie said, "Well, if you're always feeling so fine, what are you doing here?"

I just looked at him, smiled in a grandmotherly sort of way and wondered why he didn't have any respect for his elders. Beneath the smile, I was really intimidated. The next day when I again said, "Fine," the counselor had heard enough. "Claire," Ray said, "there's something phony about you. Every day you come to group and say 'fine.' Do you know what 'f-i-n-e' stands for? 'Fucked up, Insecure, Neurotic and Emotionally insecure.'"

I was shocked, shocked, shocked. I couldn't believe what had just happened and what Ray had said to me. I was furious that he'd talk to me that way. At the kitchen table that evening I was telling Al (my Hispanic friend) how angry I was. He smiled and said, "Well, now you have your feeling for tomorrow morning!"

That's when recovery started for me. I felt proud as punch the next morning when I looked Ray in the eye and told him that I was feeling angry and that if he used the "F" word in front of me again I would deck him. I'm short and weigh less than 100 pounds; Ray weighs twice as much and stands a foot taller—but I meant it!

As time went on, I started to feel a sense of hope. I had to read my "autobio," the story about my life with and without alcohol, to the group like everyone else. To my great relief, it was well received. There were a lot of questions about areas that I had skimmed over, but for the most part those who heard it thought that I had been honest.

One of the turning points for me was the lecture by Dr. West, the medical director, about alcoholism as a disease. Hearing that alcoholism was an illness was a tremendous eye-opener, as well as a relief for me. The word *alcoholic* had always conjured up an image of the drunk under the bridge with his bottle of booze in a paper bag.

Ray suggested I read a chapter titled "Women Suffer Too" in the Big Book. I underlined this passage: "I wasn't the only person in the world who felt and behaved like this! I wasn't mad or vicious—I was a sick person. I was suffering from an actual disease that had a name and symptoms like diabetes or cancer or TB, and a disease was respectable, not a moral stigma!" I've since discovered that a marvelous woman named Marty Mann wrote that chapter.

As the days and weeks passed, I got to know my peers better. They were a remarkable group of people. Paul ("the controller") used to fall asleep and snore during the relaxation exercises. He was probably exhausted, policing all those phone calls. I got the moniker "mother" because, as someone said, I was always looking after everyone like a mother hen. Al was "the Latino." Our group included two Anns— Annie from Washington and Ann from Denver. Annie was the fancy dresser, black suits and dresses and high heels, the whole nine yards, while the rest of us wore sweats. Annie had planned to fly in her maid the first week to do her ironing! Little did she know . . .

We cried and laughed a lot. I had enormous fun when I was assigned to throw a birthday party for one of the gals. That was ironic— my birthday was the day before Christmas, and I'd rarely had a birthday party. It would have interfered with the Yuletide celebration.

I had a great time setting up the games: Hide and Go Seek, Pin the

Tail on the Donkey, Drop the Hanky. In the midst of playing those games a new girl was being shown around McCallum. It must have looked like a scene out of Looney Tunes.

I remember shortly after that we all cried when the tall, skinny guy talked about how he'd been verbally abused by his boss in front of all his co-workers. That was the first time I saw someone punching a pillow and shouting at the same time. It was a way of releasing his pent-up anger.

Gradually I began to understand the way things worked. These chores were assigned to help us to get in touch with our feelings, particularly our anger and resentments. Only then could we change from self-defeating to responsible behavior and put an end to the triggers for our drinking and using.

There was one exercise that scared the heck out of me—the trust exercise. We each had a partner who stood behind us; then, without looking, we had to fall backwards, trusting that he/she would catch us before we hit the ground. It was one of the most important things that I had to learn—trusting the group and then myself.

But not everything was clear to me. For instance, let me tell you about Jean.

Most of the patients had visitors on Sundays, for lunch. We'd do what we could to dress up a bit, but nothing fancy, really. One Sunday the dining hall suddenly became quiet when one of our sisters, Jean, came into the room. Everyone was stunned. She looked like a Japanese kabuki dancer. Her face was covered with a white paste and she had on maroon lipstick. We couldn't believe that that was how she was going to greet her grown children when they arrived at one o'clock. She looked like the face of death.

Later, I asked Ray, my counselor, what he thought was going on. He said that she was still so ashamed of her drinking and loss of control that she had to wear a mask. Wearing all that makeup was her attempt to go into hiding on Sundays. It was tragic. During the week we were never allowed to hide from one another with sunglasses or anything that would mask our true selves from one another.

One day, the granny sent me to meet and accompany a British rock star to McCallum. I'd never heard of him, but because of our backgrounds we took to each other immediately. We would talk about our musical careers and the worlds we inhabited. We would reminisce and laugh about how it used to be in the old days in the music business. Then one day we were told that we couldn't walk the circle together in the morning. The staff saw that we were having too much fun together. At Betty Ford, you check your professional career at the door. The only "career" that bears discussing is your "career" of using and abusing!

I had ignored the consequences of my drinking, the elephant in the living room, for a long time. Working on the Fourth and Fifth Steps allowed me to take an inventory of my life, to highlight the assets and wipe clean the slate of liabilities. What I learned most is how I had hurt my daughters and myself with my drinking. Surrounded by my peers out on the patio, I threw papers into a fire on which I'd written out my Fourth Step. The fires of purgatory cleansed my spirit.

At the medallion ceremony the next day, I was proud and humble at the same time. Ray said that I came into treatment with my tail between my legs, full of shame and guilt. "Now," he said, "words cannot describe the progress you've made." I was proud of the progress, grateful for all the hugs, and humbled enough not to look for perfection any longer. I felt a tremendous sense of relief. At last I was no longer running away from things.

The medallion ceremony was on a Wednesday. My daughters had been in the Family Program since Monday. Ray told me I should come back to McCallum during the day on Thursday and Friday so that we could all leave together as a family on Friday. Somehow I sensed that Ray wanted me to stay longer. To be truthful, I could have—and probably should have—stayed another three months.

I was still shaky when I got home just before Thanksgiving, but thank God everyone was very supportive back in Kansas City. Then early in December Harold called and invited me to Las Vegas, where Frank Sinatra was doing his last hurrah. He said he had great tickets and a suite at the Desert Inn. I called my sponsor, Lou Ann, and told her about the invitation and how badly I wanted to see "ol' blue eyes." She listened, and finally said, "Okay. This is what you have to do. As soon as you get there, call up the AA Central Office to find out the times and places of meetings. You have to go to a meeting a day." I promised her I would.

The usual stretch limousine met us at the airport and took us to the Desert Inn. Everyone was happy to see us, as we were regulars. They carried our bags up to the suite with its sunken this and push-button that and I said to Harold, "I have to call the Central Office." He had a quick, astute response, "Catholics look for their churches; recovering people look for their meetings!"

The person on the other end of the line told me a meeting was about to start at a place called Turning Point on California Avenue. I hung up the phone, told Harold to go and have fun, went downstairs and asked the doorman to flag down a cab. When I told the doorman where I wanted to go he tried to talk me out of my mission. "You don't want to go *there*," he said, quite forcefully. "I do, too," I replied. "I'm meeting some friends there." I thought to myself, "Besides, it's none of your damned business!" He reluctantly gave the cabdriver the address and soon we were driving through the industrial part of Las Vegas.

We stopped at the address, and sure enough it looked like a Gypsy tearoom. The cabdriver eyed the place and insisted on escorting me in. On the right-hand side there was a bar with a coffee machine and sandwiches; to the left, a bunch of old chairs were lined up. On the walls were a lot of slogans, like "One day at a time."

I turned to him and said, "This is the place." He gave me his card and told me to give him a ring when I wanted to return to the hotel. My guess is that he knew what the place was all about.

I greeted the others, sat down, and, as is usually the case with AA meetings, time flew by. I was drinking some coffee, then looked at my watch and saw that I had been there an hour and a half. I asked where the phone was so I could call the driver to pick me up. One of the men said, "Don't bother with a cab, I'll take you. I'm parked out back." I said good-bye to everyone; they told me to come back.

When my Good Samaritan driver and I got outside, there was the biggest Harley-Davidson I'd ever seen. Before I could say I'd never ridden a motorcycle before, he strapped a helmet on me and helped me aboard. I said, "This is wonderful. Let's go!"

The ride back was exhilarating. I had the time of my life on the back of that motorcycle. When we arrived at the hotel, the doorman looked at me with his mouth open. Three hours earlier I'd arrived in a stretch limousine, and here I was now driving up on this big Harley-Davidson. But the best part of all was when my companion, a tall man with bulging biceps, dressed in leather, took out his card, gave it to me and said, "If any of these people give you any shit, just call me."

◆ ◆ ◆

Whenever Claire tells that story she gets a big laugh, and she certainly did tonight. I've heard the story many times and still enjoy it, especially the way Claire tells it.

Claire's one of those women I or anyone at the center can call upon in times of need—when, for example, a female patient needs to talk to somebody "outside" about remaining in treatment.

Current patients can always relate to Claire's stories. After all, they too trembled at having to deliver their "autobios" and working through their first AA Steps in front of the whole group. They too shared in the happiness of the medallion ceremonies. The rituals of burning "life's garbage" and chanting antidrug doggerel are alive in everybody's minds, as are the lectures and the grief groups.

The women in Fisher today are grateful that they don't have to coexist with men as Claire did. Despite her gregariousness, Claire had never been totally comfortable opening up before men. And needless to say, when Claire tells the story of a female patient ironing one of the male patient's shirts, today's women get angry!

It should also be noted that today there are special sessions devoted to topics like body image, relaxation therapy, gay and lesbian issues and the legacy of physical and/or sexual abuse.

◆   ◆   ◆

I now want to introduce you to the final woman whose story is recorded in these pages. I'm so happy that she accepted the invitation to tell her story because in one way she represents all those who've been through treatment at the Betty Ford Center. An active member of the Alumni Board, she helps organize the Alumni Reunions. Since she got sober at the center in 1986, she's attended every one of the annual reunions, including the twentieth. You can't miss Beatrice on our special weekends together; she's everywhere!

Beatrice

I grew up black, in Alabama. Segregation was still part of the fabric of life there as it was before, during and after the Civil Rights Act of 1965. My parents were hardworking middle-class people, and I was taught the importance of conducting myself as a young lady and to abide the ostracism imposed upon us by white society.

I was not allowed to drink at home. I started drinking in high school with my peers, but not a great deal. I don't suppose I was different than any other young girl who wanted attention and needed to have her own way.

In college, alcohol was part of the campus culture. I started my precollege in Alabama. One of my friends who attended Fisk University in Nashville urged me to transfer there to become more independent of my family, particularly my mother and grandmother, who she felt were pampering me. Fisk had already started its semester, so I enrolled at another college in the Nashville area and liked it so much that I decided not to transfer to Fisk at the end of the semester.

In my senior year, I was a dorm counselor in charge of the girls on my floor. There was a lot of drinking and some smoking of marijuana. On one occasion I went to a frat party where I drank some hard liquor on an empty stomach after taking some medication. When I returned to the dorm, a couple of the girls had to take me to my room, where I threw up in front of them. They cleaned me up and helped me to my bed. I was supposed to be an example to them and their caretaker, and here they were taking care of me. Actually, the incident broke down some of the barriers between us as I was now viewed as a human being and not just a cold resident assistant.

That same year, I started dating an engineering student, a relationship that was very important to me. During our time together one incident stands out vividly. I attended an important social gathering, got drunk and threw up in the ladies' room. One of his friends told him about it. He took me aside and said, "Ladies do not get drunk. If you want to be a real lady, you should know when you've had enough." Try as I might to bury that phrase, it continued to haunt me during all the years and decades I drank.

The summer after grad school I'd gotten into a lot of heavy drinking. On some mornings-after, I couldn't remember how I'd gotten home. What I do recall with a great deal of embarrassment were the times when I'd lose control and go on a rampage while drinking. Once when I was visiting the home of one of my girlfriends, my boyfriend called to tell me that he would be delayed in picking me up. I went into a rage and had to be physically restrained after I started throwing and breaking expensive glassware. My girlfriend was horrified and cried all the while she picked up the shards of glass, wondering, between sobs, how she was going to explain the mess to her parents.

When my boyfriend later decided to end the relationship, I remember (with horror) breaking into his apartment and taking scissors to his expensive suits and shirts.

For a while after college I had a job working in human resources. In a short time, I became a supervisor. I didn't drink with my coworkers but downed a lot of rum and Cokes with my friends. Then, in the fall of 1969, I started a career as a high school teacher. I was soon drinking with my colleagues on a regular basis.

While I loved teaching, I found myself stressed-out practically every day. There were no teachers' guides, no photocopy machines, and every night after preparing for the next day I'd chill out on cold duck (cheap champagne mixed with cheap burgundy wine) or rum and Coke—or both.

I had an affair with a prominent businessman but soon suspected that he was involved with another woman. When I told him I was pregnant and that he was the father of the baby, he refused to admit it. About a month before Audrey was born, he married someone else and I had to take him to court for child support. More than the money, I wanted to convince him through the blood tests that he was indeed the father. To this day I am waiting for him to apologize for what he put me through—his deceit, his marriage to another woman and his refusal to support our child until he was ordered to do so by the court.

By the time that happened, his wife had left him. But before she did, when she discovered that he'd fathered my child, she called me and asked if I needed anything. What I really needed was the father of the child, and she had him.

I continued drinking wine during the pregnancy. I was advised to do so by my doctor, who wanted to counter my anemia by building up my strength and my blood count. I still did some serious drinking on the holidays and special occasions and just before the contractions began I guzzled down some champagne. In my defense, in those days only a few doctors were knowledgeable about fetal alcohol syndrome.

I was emotionally derailed by my pregnancy. I knew that I'd hurt my family deeply by having a child out of wedlock. The old tapes were playing again in my head, "Behavior unbecoming a lady . . ."

I'll never forget a remark that I overheard at a party. Some people were concerned about my behavior and someone who knew me observed sarcastically, "Oh, that's Beatrice. She's just drunk again." I cringed. After all, "A lady never drinks too much . . ."

In those days, more than now, it was disgraceful for a woman to be seen staggering about drunk, slurring her speech or generally making a fool of herself. No one looked at the drunk woman as a victim of a disease, a person needing medical and spiritual help. She was simply a hussy, a disgrace to womanhood.

With Audrey's birth, my whole focus was directed toward being a good mother. She was a beautiful baby and since motherhood was a natural high for me, in those early months after her birth I managed to cut back on my drinking. But soon it started to escalate once again and even having a daughter to care for didn't serve as a brake. As she got older, though, I did attempt to conceal my drinking from her. I never thought it was affecting my daughter. Honestly, I didn't. But signals about the seriousness of my drinking soon started coming from lots of other people and places.

I was beginning to think like an alcoholic—I was preoccupied with alcohol most of my waking hours. I'd pour liquor into jars and then hide them around the house. One of my friends had a good laugh one night when I brought out a little mayonnaise jar and drank from it to brace myself for the evening. I'd bring miniature bottles with me to parties, go to the ladies' room and guzzle them, and then return and drink champagne "like a lady" with the others. My addictive, shadow self was slowly taking hold of my real and better self.

A friend called once when I was drinking heavily. She heard my slurred speech and decided to come to the apartment to help. There was so much booze in me that I was reeking of alcohol. She cooked something, made me eat it and stayed with me until I went to sleep. When I went to school the next morning, my eyes were bloodshot, my hair disheveled, my clothes wrinkled and the smell of alcohol seemed to ooze from my pores. The principal sent for me and asked me what was wrong. I said that I needed to go to the hospital. While they detoxed me, I was unable to sleep. All I could do was cry.

The psychiatrist who saw me there began the interview by stressing all my positives: I was a good mother and an excellent teacher, had a good education, was very attractive, had a lovely daughter, and had done much for the community. Then she dropped the bomb. "Why then, with all that going for you, would you want to take your own life?" I was stunned. Such a question was totally unexpected.

"Take my own life?" I exclaimed. "I don't want to take my own life."

"The reality," she continued softly, "is that if you continue to consume so much liquor you'll end up killing yourself." She then went on to explain how, chemically, the alcohol affected my whole system, including my brain. Listening to her smartened me up quite a bit. But at the same time I felt depressed and absolutely devastated.

There was a golf outing the next day and I told the doctor that I wanted to attend, that if I stayed in the hospital feeling trapped I would only get worse. So the doctor released me and I went golfing. I drank a little wine but that's all my fragile body could handle.

This incident at the hospital occurred about a year before I entered the Betty Ford Center. During that year little things about alcoholism kept coming up and knocking at the door of my consciousness. I'd be sitting in the waiting room waiting to see a doctor, would pick up a magazine and there would be an article about alcoholism or Betty Ford or a self-test to determine whether one was drinking too much. I remember seeing one article on the disease of alcoholism and how insurance would pay for its treatment. I cut that one out.

For the longest time I simply didn't understand what was going on with me. Once I was visiting a friend in the hospital who was recuperating from a terrible car accident in which he had totaled his new Volvo. He told me that he'd been driving while in a blackout. I asked him, "What's a blackout?" He said that's what happens when you wake up the next morning unable to remember what happened the night before. I thought for a while and then admitted, "That happens to me a lot."

I eventually went to talk with another doctor who listened to me and then advised that I choose a more expensive wine to drink with my dinner. "That way," he said, "when you're paying top dollar, you won't drink as much." That made eminent sense to me at the time. Looking back I can see clearly that it was a classic case of a doctor who just didn't "get it" when it comes to alcoholism.

But I took his advice and started buying wine at $17 a bottle. At dinner at my home one night a friend remarked on the expensive wine and suggested something much cheaper (a Gallo wine) that was equally good. I was only too happy to seize on her suggestion. After all, my budget was strained, since I was forever buying expensive wines—and still drinking to beat the band! It wasn't long before I was consuming several liter bottles of the Gallo on weekends.

I always thought that controlled drinking rather than total abstinence was the better and easier path for me. I can't count the number of times that I promised myself that I'd take only one drink—and then proceeded to consume a whole bottle. This inability to stop or drink moderately began to gnaw at me. It was only later when I became acquainted with the Big Book that I understood it was the insanity of the mental obsession that was plaguing me. I always thought that *next time* I'd be able to limit the number of drinks. Always *next time . . .*

One day I came home from school during summer session. It was stiflingly hot and I poured myself a rum and Coke and sat down to watch the soaps. My daughter was at summer camp. All of a sudden I started to cry for no reason at all. I felt depressed, alone, with a bottomless pit in my stomach. I thought that I couldn't go on feeling this way and that I needed to get away as far as possible and get some help. I called a friend who worked at the rehab program at a local hospital; she suggested I go to the Betty Ford Center. I then called my doctor, who said he was relieved I'd finally decided to do something; he recommended Northwestern Hospital, where they had a program for alcoholism. I said that was too close to home.

So I called the Betty Ford Center and was told that it would be six weeks before I could get in. But just a few days later the Admissions Office called and said they had an unexpected opening and that I'd have to be in Palm Springs the following Monday by twelve noon. I started to hem and haw saying that my daughter would be going back to school shortly and I didn't think I could leave at that time. They told me I had thirty minutes to make up my mind. Something clicked inside of me and forced me to call my travel agent at once. She was a friend of mine and when I said Palm Springs was my destination, she said, "Why in heavens would you want to go there in the summer? It's too darned hot!"

I told her I was going to the Betty Ford Center to be treated for alcoholism. "You?" she said. "Well, then I'd better go there, too, 'cause I don't think you drink too much. You just want to be with the stars." That was the furthest thing from my mind. When she asked when I wanted the return flight, I said I didn't know. So she left the return open. I called the Betty Ford Center and told them I'd be there Monday.

*   *   *

It's difficult for those who haven't been through treatment to imagine the feelings that engulf the patient the first day she enters the Betty Ford Center. The staff tries its best to alleviate the fear the woman feels. To appreciate this fear, try imagining moving to another city or changing jobs or getting married or getting divorced—and multiply it by ten!

From the very first contact, whether it be the gentle voice of an Admissions officer or the volunteer greeting arrivals at the airport, or the assignment of the "buddy" to help the newly arrived person become familiar with the hall and its expectations— from the very first moment a woman reaches out for help and arrives in the desert, she knows that she is welcome, that she is at a home away from home, that she has found a safe place. Friends made in treatment often remain friends for life.

Indeed, the core value of the Center is that it is a "caring" community—whatever it takes to make the patients feel that they belong, to feel cared for, to feel accepted, to feel at home. The first person who entered the center back in '82 later confessed to being "scared to death," the second to being "overwhelmed." A whole parade of women can identify with one of their peers who said, "I was so frightened, I could hardly speak. It took all of my strength and courage to stammer through some answers. But my roommate was so kind. She said that she had been through the same thing and understood exactly how I felt."

Beatrice's story is particularly poignant, not only because she was living in a hall populated by men and women, but, as she herself tells us, she was a black woman amongst a mostly Caucasian population.

Beatrice provides a very moving description of her first days in treatment.

*   *   *

It was a dreary day when I arrived at the Center, which is unusual for the desert, where people are used to continual sunshine. Although everyone was very friendly, both staff and patients, I felt alone and isolated, helpless and hopeless. It was excruciating being away from my daughter, Audrey, whom I'd left in the care of one of the neighbors. I was determined not to allow her to be involved in any of this. But then in one of the first conferences with my counselor I was urged to invite my daughter to the Family Program. Five minutes after the interview I was on the telephone with my travel agent to make arrangements for Audrey to come to the Center. She, of course, was overjoyed at the prospect of coming to Rancho Mirage, California, to be with me.

The color of one's skin compounds the anxiety. Being black in the midst of a predominantly white population adds a difficult dimension. It was like moving into a segregated neighborhood in Chicago. I wasn't certain what the reception might be. The Betty Ford Center wasn't Alabama, but I thought the chances were pretty good one or some of the patients might be from the Deep South. But I soon found that all the barriers of race, color and creed disappear in our common quest for sobriety. In fact, the disease of chemical dependency is the most democratic of all!

The collegial environment infused by the spirit of care and compassion has the power to remove the defensive barriers, the sense of isolation, the pessimism, the mistrust and the general sense of "not belonging." It gave me a sense of hope that something good would come out of this, a sense of trust that would gradually break down the defensive barriers that I'd built around me, and a sense of faith that the environment was safe and nurturing and that I truly did belong.

During my first couple of weeks in treatment I learned a lot about the how and why of the unmanageability that alcohol addiction had brought to my life. When I was first asked in the initial assessment whether I ever had the shakes I said no, and I meant it. But as I heard other women telling their stories I realized that the times I was "hyper-nervous," I was actually going through the detox process, and I was experiencing "the shakes." I learned about blackouts and how I would have absolutely no recollection of how I'd gotten home after a big night of drinking.

I began to remember and recount all the times that I had lied to others on the phone, telling them that I'd promise to do this or that, although I really had no intention of keeping my word or showing up. I wanted only to stay home and drink. I learned how when I was drinking, my anger could explode into such an uncontrollable rage that I would smash the windshield of my father's car, cut up my boyfriend's clothes or break the dishes at the family home of my friend.

What was even *more* frightening were the "not yets," those things that had not yet happened to me but almost certainly *would* happen if my drinking had continued to accelerate. I learned about those "not yets" as the other women told their stories to the group in the evenings. I remember Sharon crying as she told us how she'd dropped her baby after drinking too much and how they had to rush the infant to the hospital.

All the learning was great, but my real turning point came in the most unexpected way. At least to me it was unexpected; it certainly wasn't to the staff.

I'd tried to be a model patient and followed all the rules. When I got "caught" talking to another patient during the morning meditation walk around the lake, I took the reprimand with humility. I didn't know that was a no-no.

Things seemed to be going well. And then, in one of the group sessions, the counselors told us there were three people whom they felt they couldn't do anything for. They named the first two, and we were all waiting for the third. "Beatrice."

I was shocked and devastated. I honestly believed that I had been doing very well. When my counselor called me into her office that afternoon, she explained, "You act like you don't have a problem, as if everything's okay." She said on the surface I was doing everything that was expected of me, *except what was most important:* contributing to the group by sharing my own personal experiences. She pointed out to me that I hadn't really joined the circle of women.

After the hurt lessened and I reflected on what the counselor had said I realized that the privacy I cherished was traceable to my family culture—that we should keep our problems within the family, that they were no one else's business. Besides, being black in Alabama did not encourage sharing with people who looked down on us! We certainly couldn't expect any sympathy from them. Mom was always telling us there was no need to burden other people with our family and personal problems, "to wash our laundry in public" as she'd put it.

I remember writing in my journal how depressed I was after being told I was "withholding." I didn't realize that I was holding out. I had already acknowledged that I was powerless over alcohol and was faithful in doing all my assignments.

That group session was a turning point for me. It got me busy. Pat and Buddy, the mother hens, were especially helpful with their encouragement. I filled my journal with my true thoughts and feelings. I was opening up and not keeping anything back. Beatrice now became the sharer-bearer of good tidings.

I had to spend a lot of time on the Second and Third Steps, sharing with my peers and building up my trust level. I wrote out the Fourth Step, but it actually took me another year to do my Fifth Step. The Fourth Step inventory became a valuable tool for me, as it is for all recovering people. It makes us conscious of the behavior that precedes, accompanies or is consequent upon our drinking and using and sets up speed bumps that remind us that we might very well once again be accelerating into old patterns of behavior.

Even more important, the Fourth Step encourages us to search our souls for the underlying causes of our character defects: the fear, dishonesty and selfishness. We are urged particularly to catalog our resentments, the number-one enemy to our sobriety. For me this was particularly true regarding the man who fathered my daughter, Audrey. His behavior before and after her birth, his unwillingness to take any responsibility for his child and her welfare made me very angry and resentful. I needed time to sort this out before I worked on my Fifth Step.

I remember taking great comfort from lines written by Marty Mann in the Big Book. "Talking things over with [my friends], great floods of enlightenment showed me myself as I recall I was and I was like them. We all had hundreds of character traits, of fears and phobias, likes and dislikes, in common. Suddenly I could accept myself, faults and all, as I was—for weren't we all like that? And accepting, I felt a newer inner comfort, and the willingness and strength to do something about the traits I couldn't live with."

I remember one of the men in my group back home telling me that if you haven't done your Fifth Step, "then you're not in the goddamned program." Well, when I did finally work through my Fifth Step, I made a point of telling the guy who'd said that, just so I could prove to him that I was, in fact, in the goddamned program.

What that meant for me was the fulfillment of a set of promises: freedom from loneliness and isolation; a sense of communion and shared humanity with others; self-forgiveness and humility; closeness to my Creator; and the lifting of the alcoholic obsession. I could never have accomplished any of these things by myself.

There are a couple of people whom I remember very well because of incidents that occurred between us. There was one woman who had a daughter about the same age as mine who told me quite bluntly that she was jealous of all the attention I was receiving. She felt that the staff was bending over backwards to help me because I was black.

She also told me later that she was envious of me because her daughter lived with her husband while mine lived with me.

I became friendly with one of the men in the hall who was Italian and projected this godfather image in his manner of speech and the way he carried himself. He was a movie producer and he introduced me to his wife. A few days before I was leaving, I mentioned in passing that I would call him since occasionally I was in the Los Angeles area. I was shocked when he said that he wanted everyone to forget that they ever knew him. He must have seen how hurt I was because later he came to me to explain that he wasn't including me when he said that. He was paranoid about his career, and didn't want people to know that he was chemically dependent and had been through the Betty Ford Center.

The celebrities who come to the Center for healing represent less than 1 percent of the population. Mrs. Ford tells the story, a true one, about a young woman, a celebrity, who became very angry when the group began to focus on her. Anger is usually a substitute for fear. Announcing that she was not going to put up with it anymore, she walked out of the group and went directly to the pay phone where she called the toll-free number of one of the airlines.

She announced, "This is so-and-so, and I want a flight to New York tonight." The reservation operator who happened to have taken her call said, with genuine affection in her voice, "Oh, Miss so-and-so, I can't believe it's you. I'll get you booked in a minute, but I need to tell you that I've been in the AA program for almost eight weeks, really struggling, and when I found out you were at the Betty Ford Center, that gave me the hope I needed to keep going."

After a long pause, the patient said, "Thank you. And never mind the reservation. I won't need it after all." After hanging up the phone she took a few moments to compose herself. But she was unable to stifle the tears as she walked back to the group and announced, "I guess my Higher Power knows where I should be."

I love what Mrs. Ford has repeated many times: Every person who has the courage to come to the Center is a star in her or his own right, and is treated as such.

The medallion ceremony is one of my finest memories. I was filled with departure pains (I suppose one could call them "postpartum" pains) each and every time someone completed primary treatment. This was particularly true of those people with whom I'd become close. I didn't realize what their presence really meant to me until they were leaving. When I received my medallion, I shed an ocean of tears—of joy. So many people voiced such tender and loving blessings and messages of good fortune. I never knew how much I meant to others. They teased me about the big colorful earrings I wore every day. They said they looked forward to the different shapes and colors that I would display each time I appeared in group. Every once in a while I still read their comments, which they wrote on the inside cover of my Big Book.

The day I left the Betty Ford Center was so different from the day I arrived. In place of the gray, threatening skies, it was a glorious sun-filled day with not a cloud in the sky. I arrived gloomy, depressed and ashamed. I left with a bounce in my walk, my spirits high, and filled with pride in my own self-worth and goodness. I was so proud to be a member of that circle of women and to have discovered the sanctuary that is the Betty Ford Center.

7

Circles, Chants and Tibetan Chimes

I can't remember many of the details about my treatment at Long Beach. Most of the lectures, meetings and groups that I sat through were just a blur to me. I was bombarded with words and phrases that were a mystery to me: "surrender," "powerlessness," "let go and let God." But I listened and I was respectful. I went to the AA meetings every night. They provided me with more information on the Twelve Steps, which were to play an essential role in my recovery.

It is only with the passage of time that I can see how everything I was exposed to in treatment fit together: the Steps, the Big Book, the sisterhood of recovering people, the fact that we were all suffering from an illness. It was too much to absorb at one time, like cramming for an exam. Only after a while does the information that we have learned take on real meaning in our daily lives. We were being educated about alcoholism and we were being introduced to a community of fellow sufferers. But we had to work the program as soon as we left treatment. Then, over the course of several years of meetings and contacts with our sponsors, things gradually made sense, and with that further "spiritual awakening" I came to understand what it meant "to practice the principles" we had learned "in all our affairs."

What contributes to the transformation that takes place while a person is in treatment at the Betty Ford Center? I can recite a litany of things. There is the physical environment, which is so therapeutic, appealing to the women's sensibilities and healing the women's wounded souls. The majestic mountains, the incredible blue sky, the rich colors exhibited in the plants and flowers, the paintings in the halls, the solitude and the silence—all these had the power, as one woman wrote to me, "to penetrate one's soul and cause one to breathe deeply."

When Leonard Firestone and I cofounded this place in the desert, little did we realize what a spiritual oasis it would become for the thousands of people who were suffering from a spiritual thirst that alcohol was incapable of satisfying.

When we made the decision to separate the men and the women, it promoted a distinct sense of belonging. It is a sense of belonging nurtured by all the group meetings and all the sharing that goes on as patients tell stories of their drinking or using and hear warm and positive feedback from others. Through it all, the women finally comprehend what it means to be suffering from an illness, and that their lives don't end when they admit they were dependent on alcohol or other drugs. As a matter of fact, that's when their lives start to get better!

The most important practices and rituals that occur in the residential halls haven't really changed much over the years. Sharing stories and working steps remain the heart of the program. Just as it was for me at Long Beach, working through the First Step and the admission of powerlessness is essential. The women talk about their drinking and using and the wild and crazy things they did to try to hide it. They begin to identify with one another, and that's good. Some little thing might light a fire of illumination in their souls. Oftentimes they're able to say , "I'm not the worst. Look at her and what she did. She's going to make it, and by God, so am I."

As the years passed, it became widely known that women at the center are treated with dignity and respect, love and kindness. Alumni tell anyone and everyone who'll listen about the rituals associated with the halls, the good-bye groups, how they danced like dervishes, sang with gusto pretending to be the Von Trapp family, talked incessantly and laughed from deep within. They describe the burning rituals, the medallion ceremonies and finally the camaraderie felt by the "wonderful women of West" and the "Fisherettes" of Fisher Hall.

They never ceased speaking about the abiding circles and the chants and cheers. The chanters came and went, the words changed slightly, but the message remains the same:

We're the women of Fisher Hall
No more drugs or alcohol
No more guilt or shame at all
We are going to leave here—walking tall
Sound off—one, two Stay off—three, four
Sound off—one, two, three, four
No more!

Among our three women who went through Fisher—the angry Laurette, the docile Jacqueline and the pleasant but reserved Harriet—the contrasts are striking, the results unexpected and the healing journeys upon leaving the center totally different. Treatment is the purgatory where the woman must be cleansed of her addicted self. The transformation is not easy, and sometimes the confrontation with one's addicted nature is terribly painful.

No one returns alive from Dante's "Inferno." But from the hell of addiction, escape is always possible. But the price is demanding—the woman must purge herself of her addicted shadow, that person who has been her constant and most dependable lover for many years. It's a price that not everyone is willing to pay.

• • •

We last saw Harriet at the Saturday-morning Alumni Weekend chip and medallion ceremony. Her story had taken us with her to Georgia where we left her going through the Yellow Pages searching for help, finally deciding on Betty Ford. While she waited for a bed to open up, she maintained her resolve to get help via the bottle. Finally she got a call telling her to show up on a Monday in the middle of June. She later told me that one of the reasons she decided to reach out for help was that she didn't want to end up the subject of a newspaper story in Atlanta, describing a woebegone lady who drank herself to death in a disgusting-looking apartment!

Harriet

My neighbor Kathy helped me to catch my cat and promised to take care of him while I was gone. I had a 7 A.M. flight. I needed a few drinks when I got to the airport and then a few more on the plane to settle me down. I had to change planes in Los Angeles, and when I tried to phone the Betty Ford Center to tell them I'd be a little late, I had trouble getting coins out of my pocket. They kept dropping to the floor, and I couldn't figure out why. I was wearing jersey-knit pull-on pants with a matching top, and I thought I looked pretty darn good.

After I'd been at the center for a few days, I decided to wear the same outfit again. There was just one problem when I went to put the pants on—they were inside out. How the heck had *that* happened? I tried desperately to remember.

And then it hit me—during the entire trip from Atlanta, and during the whole hours-long admissions process at the center, *I was wearing my pants inside out!* I was mortified.

Now it made sense—*that's* why I kept fumbling for those coins at the pay phone, trying to get them out of my pocket. The pockets were hanging *outside*, but I had to access them from *inside!* No wonder people were looking at me a little funny when I checked in at the center. And here I thought I was looking so cool—my God, everybody must have known that I was a fall-down lush!

I'm laughing about it now, but I sure wasn't at the time!

The whole dumb thing was a metaphor for my life. Here I thought that nobody knew what was going on inside of me, that I was just one big tightly wound secret. But because my life was "inside out," *everybody knew!* As a matter of fact, people who really loved me had been telling me that for years.

When I arrived at the Palm Springs airport, I was quite drunk and pretty self-conscious about going to the Betty Ford Center. A man dressed in a white cotton jacket was nervously scanning all the incoming passengers, looking as though he was afraid he might miss someone. I had the feeling that he was looking for me, so I walked up to him and introduced myself. It was a small step but it was to be the first of many self-disclosures that would eventually lead to my being comfortable with people knowing who I really am and knowing about the illness I was suffering from.

I was grateful that Lucy, the woman I had originally talked to on the phone, was the one who greeted me at Admissions in the Firestone building and told me how glad she was that I had made it. She took me into a little room where she had me sit down. I was too unsteady to sort out the down payment which Tom, my stepbrother, had sent to me and which I had converted to cash. Bless her, Lucy counted the money for me. Turns out I was missing a hundred dollars, which was not surprising given the amount of alcohol that I'd consumed on the voyage.

Something other than alcohol was putting me at ease. It was the gracious, respectful manner in which I was being treated, most particularly by Lucy. Then someone accompanied me to Fisher Hall, which was directly across from Firestone. I was pretty well out of it.

I have trouble recalling many events from the first week, but the day after I arrived, something profound happened to me.

For years prior to my admission to the Center, I had had trouble sleeping. My psychiatrist had spent some time teaching me self-hypnosis, and I would create these visualizations for myself that would help me calm down and eventually fall asleep. The one that was the most effective was a fantasy that I conjured up that had me living in this beautiful private nursing home that was built in the 1930s. I would imagine myself walking down a grassy slope to a little lake where there was a bench on which I could sit and watch the ducks, with a full view of the mountains in the background. Not far from the bench was a large weeping willow tree, beautiful tall bushes and a field of flowers similar to those Dorothy encountered in *The Wizard of Oz*.

The morning after I arrived I dressed and went to the patio for a smoke before breakfast. I couldn't believe my eyes. There in front of me were the bench, the lake, the ducks, the weeping willows and the majestic mountains in the background. I'd never seen oleanders before but there they were, just as I'd pictured them in my visualization. I didn't tell anyone for quite some time lest they think that I was completely crazy and should be in a loony bin, not a treatment hospital.

But at that moment on that patio, every doubt and reservation that I'd had about getting help vanished. I knew that God had answered the prayers that I'd whispered while crouched on my knees beside my bed, surrounded by bottles.

During the first week it seemed like I had to repeat the same things to everyone who interviewed me—the nurse, the counselor, the psychologist, the chaplain, then the group. I thought to myself, "Don't they talk to each other? Why do I have to keep repeating this?" But I was really touched during the interview with the staff psychologist. When I talked about myself, she cried. That made me a little nervous, though, because I didn't think that I was really in such a bad way. But maybe I was! I wondered if it was time to start writing my obituary!

A young, blond California girl was assigned to be my "buddy" and gave me a perfunctory tour of Fisher and then hardly spoke to me ever again. She belonged to a clique of about four youngish women who hung out together and thought themselves better than the rest of us. The typical reaction of the rest of the women toward them was "Fuck you." After my experience with Miss Southern Cal, I made a point to take a personal interest in every newcomer to our hall. I would give each of them a Cook's tour of the campus, including the Serenity Room, which soon became one of my favorite spots. It was nice to hear them say afterwards that they thought I'd been assigned their buddy because I went out of my way to give them a personalized tour.

About a week into my stay a young woman from Indonesia arrived; she was having a terrible time. She couldn't stop crying. She thought she'd made an awful mistake. She was so determined to leave that she'd told her husband to stay a few extra days at a local hotel, so they could vamoose together. I gently reminded her that everyone, including me, shared the same doubts and feelings when they first arrived. I promised her that everything would get better and urged her just to do whatever she was asked to do. The next day she had stopped crying and told her husband that he could fly home.

A week later another newcomer was walking the hallways, crying. I said to the Indonesian woman, "Why don't you go talk to her and tell her about your first days here?" She did, and the crying stopped. I wasn't aware that what we were doing was practicing one of the key principles of Alcoholics Anonymous, one alcoholic helping another alcoholic, providing one-on-one support. It was part of the magical elixir of the place.

When I first saw the view from the patio and connected it with my relaxation dream, I knew that something serendipitous was happening, and it was bigger than me.

But not everything was peaches and cream. One of the major issues that my mother had with me was that I always did exactly what I wanted to do. And at Betty Ford, I resisted everything, even though I knew that what I was being asked to do was for my own good.

Finally, I decided to make a little game out of it. I'd say to myself, "Okay, I don't want to go to grief group or the Family Program because I don't need them, but I'll do it because it's bound to result in something good happening." And it always did. Though "resistance and rebellion" (as it's called in AA circles) dogged my every step at Betty Ford, it was obvious that something bigger than me was at work and play here.

In group I would listen very carefully to find something I had in common with another patient, no matter how different or obnoxious she was. This was a big step for me in understanding the commonality shared by women in general and by chemically dependent women in particular. It helped me grasp how important to recovery it is for women to identify with one another and to be able to say, "Look at all she's been through with her drinking and drugging. If she's able to turn things around, so can I." There was hope for me.

That first week I was unable to join the other women in walking the circular path around the perimeter of the grounds because I had intense pain in my legs. This was an exercise required by all after breakfast in the morning. Besides the physical benefits derived from it, walking the circle was very symbolic of the spiritual wholeness that all of us were seeking and which alcohol and drugs had stolen from us.

The medical director, Dr. West, assured the staff that the pains in my legs were not imagined, they were the result of my drinking. Instead of the walk, I sat in the kitchen and read the Big Book. I used a yellow marker to highlight everything that was important; later I noticed that I'd highlighted virtually every word in the whole book!

During those first days, though, nothing much was sinking in. I had too many layers of cotton candy in my head. The first time I knew that the fog was lifting was when I heard Del Sharbutt lecture in his mellifluous voice on Tuesday night at the AA meeting. I was completely alert. His remarks penetrated the cumulus clouds surrounding my brain. After the lecture, I went up to him and told him what his words had meant to me. He smiled in that wonderful, contagious way he had and then gave me a big hug.

As expected, my mother turned out to be a major distraction during treatment—"bad mommy" was still there no matter how hard I tried to separate myself from her, both emotionally and physically. The second week into treatment my stepbrother, Tom, called my counselor, Sharon, wondering if I could have a leave of absence to attend to some things in Atlanta. Apparently the stench in my apartment had gotten so bad that the manager called my mother. When the manager opened the door, my mother was mortified. Mom called the Board of Health and the Sheriff's Department and whomever else she could think of and ranted and raved about getting a restraining order to keep me from coming back to Atlanta because I was dangerous, insane. My mother gave all my furniture, paintings and everything else of value in my apartment to the Salvation Army.

I was pretty hysterical when I heard that Mom had gotten into the apartment, but gradually I settled down. Tom helped me calm down. My counselor, Sharon, said I had two choices. I could try to get super-involved myself, or I could turn it over to my stepbrother and, as the AA slogan says, "Let go, let God." After a night of fitful sleep I found myself in the "surrender" camp, and the next morning I sent a power-of-attorney form to Tom.

I even wrote my mother a letter thanking her for all the trouble that she had gone through in cleaning up my apartment. I had no intention of returning to Atlanta. Words from one of the lectures flashed in my mind: "If you don't go back, you're not 'running away.' You're simply 'running for your life.'"

I ended the letter, "God bless you." I couldn't quite manage "I love you."

Sharon asked me if I wanted to postpone my First Step presentation, given the emotional upheaval I was experiencing because of my mother. But I said no, I wanted to be finished with it. I had a lot to tell the group about my powerlessness when it came to alcohol and my life's unmanageability that resulted. I shared examples of my behavior related to my addiction, such as sleeping around with people at work, lying to my colleagues, making inappropriate phone calls to my ex-boyfriend, Chris, when I was drunk, endangering lives while driving my car drunk, living a life of isolation in my pigsty of an apartment. I shared with them the time I was a victim of "date rape," which never would have happened if I'd been sober. When I was finished, the circle of women closed in on me, embraced me, and I felt the first inklings of healing and hope.

While I was in the middle of all of this, sometimes calm and sometimes hysterical, the staff told me they thought I needed more time in treatment and that I should stay for the Extended Care Program. The patients in extended care had a separate table in the dining hall, which the other patients referred to unkindly as "the losers' table." But it wasn't being labeled a "loser" that bothered me so much as how I would pay for it. Sharon said that wasn't the issue. "Are you willing to stay?" she kept asking. I kept on replying, "I don't have the money for it." When I finally said I *would* stay she told me that my brother had already offered to pay for the extra time in treatment.

I wouldn't admit it to anybody, but I felt lonely and isolated. Neither my sister nor my mother would come to the Family Program, and given the nastiness of the relationship with my mother, the counselors didn't force the issue. As a matter of fact, they probably thought it a good idea that the family not come. I thought maybe Chris would come. I deluded myself into believing that our relationship wasn't over and he was still my significant other.

Every day I hoped Chris would call. When the phone rang in the unit, my heart would race with anticipation. Then my spirit would be crushed when I learned that the call wasn't for me.

Sunday afternoon was visiting time, and I would wander in and out of the dining hall where my peers would introduce me to their families. Then I would return to my room hoping that the next name called on the loudspeaker would be mine, with an announcement that Chris was here to see me. But it never happened.

Finally I received a loving letter from him, which nearly broke my heart. Had I not been at the center I would have drunk myself into oblivion. He wrote of his concern for me and his hope that I would get well. But he also wrote toward the end of the letter that he thought it best that he not come to Family and that he did not intend to see me again. He signed the letter, "Your friend, and regards, Chris." For days I was inconsolable and didn't feel that I could go on. Sharon was very solicitous during that time. She had talked to him by phone before he'd even written the letter, and knew what was coming.

The important thing was that I stayed and went to Extended Care. I remained in Fisher; six of us in Extended Care were assigned to three bedrooms. There was also a comfortable lounge area, filled with books dealing with women's issues. Books were my friends, and I loved to read. We had our own quiet patio with its own flower garden and a clear view of the mountains.

Dr. West, the medical director, delivered what turned out to be a very important lecture for me while I was still in primary care. It had to do with the physical effects of drinking. As he spoke, I realized that a lot of the mental and physical deterioration that I'd suffered was caused by my over-the-top consumption of alcohol.

Interestingly, although I knew I was pretty sick, I nevertheless wondered if I'd be able to stop drinking over the long haul. My body still craved the alcohol, I could tell.

One night, at a lecture, I asked a woman from the AA Central Office if she thought the craving would ever go away. She paused before she answered and then in a very nurturing way said, "I felt just like you are feeling now. When I went to the AA convention in San Diego, I asked my sponsor the exact same question, and she said, 'If you ask God for help and follow directions, the craving will go away. It may return but over the years it does so less frequently and with less power, and then at some point it is gone.'" I was very reassured by that.

I needed a longer stay at Betty Ford. It's as simple as that. Without it I would have taken a drink as soon as I got to the Palm Springs airport because of the emotional and mental stress I was undergoing as a result of my mother's machinations in Atlanta.

But there was another reason. After two weeks I was still toying with the idea that when I left treatment I could have a few drinks without getting into any trouble—and there'd be no need to tell anybody about it. That thought or temptation persisted for quite some time. It was only in Extended Care that I began to really grasp the concept of "powerlessness."

One of the alumni gave a talk in which she told us how she'd talked herself into believing she could go back post-treatment to drinking moderately without anyone knowing. But she didn't fool anyone. After the first drink she felt physically compelled to keep drinking, until she was back to her old ways. Her ticket back to treatment was being arrested for drunk driving and spending six hours in the Big House before her sister bailed her out.

I don't know how many times they told us in treatment, "Because of the physical allergy, you can't drink. Because of the mental obsession, you can't quit. That's what we call powerlessness." Oh, so true.

Certain sister patients in Extended Care remain in my mind. Letitia was one of the young Southern Cal gals from primary care. On her way to a halfway house she got out of the car driven by her father and was never seen or heard from again. Ann was an older woman who was very ill and had swollen feet, a large belly and yellow eyes. She hardly ever spoke. Ruth was a nurse; she was tiny, and we all watched out for her. The Indonesian woman stayed on for Extended Care, too. We all suffered together, and had fun together. It wasn't quite the "Ya-Ya Sisterhood," but it was close.

Why did we all have to stay on? Because primary care had just cracked the shell and the wounds were still open and raw. They needed to be assuaged and healed with the ointment of time. For me, the idea that I could really fundamentally change didn't sink in until Extended Care. Much of the credit for that goes to our counselor, Patty, who showed all of us great love, understood our problems, blended our personalities, made us angry when we felt sorry for ourselves and tended our wounds when we hurt so badly.

Everything wasn't sweetness and light with Patty. One day in particular she really pushed my anger button. We were in group and I was sounding off yet again about my mother, the awful things she'd done back in Atlanta, how was I going to get my clothes back, etc. When I finished my litany of sorrow I was crying again, hoping for sympathy and some positive therapeutic input from Patty.

But she ignored me completely, and started telling a story about her house burning down and how she'd lost everything. I was so mad at being slighted that I completely missed the point of why she was telling that story at that time. All I could think about was how dare she minimize my problems! My loss was much worse than hers!

She knew I was angry, but neither of us said anything.

It wasn't until the next morning that the light finally went on in my brain. Patty told that story to make the point that I'd managed to escape from a burning building—why the heck was I fixated on running back in to retrieve a bunch of knickknacks?

I went in to her office to tell I'd figured out the puzzle, and to thank her. She said she was pleased about two things: one, that I'd gotten angry, and two, that I was beginning to get my priorities right.

Grief group helped me enormously. The pastoral care counselor, Amy, had me write a letter to my father, evoking some of the sadness I felt when he died. I also included my frustration at not being able to win my mother's love. Amy had me read it in group, where all my peers shared my sorrow. They told their own stories about their wounded relationships with their mothers. It was very touching and strengthening. That night the patients stood around me as I burned the letter in the urn on the patio reserved for such ceremonies.

For the first time I was able to admit that the estrangement between my mother and me might never be resolved. I told myself, "If
Mom really doesn't love me, that's okay." But notice I still held on to
the "if." In bed that night I came upon a quotation from a Barbara
Kingsolver book that I shall treasure always: "The substance of grief
is not imaginary. Like the absence of air it can suffocate and kill." I
finally realized that my grief was pulling me under and that I would
drown in alcohol unless I could break through the surface and let the
cool clean air revive me.

The pace in Extended Care was much slower. Three times a week
we would go to a women's AA meeting. On Saturdays we would drive
together to a shopping mall. On Sundays we went to an AA meeting
at the Foundation for the Retarded, where we also did volunteer
work. In honor of a woman who was going back to "civilian life," we
went to the Ritz Carlton for tea. As I said, it was a leisurely pace: just
what we needed.

Gradually the message began to a sink in, a message I didn't really
grasp in primary care: I cannot drink again—*ever.* I must change my
self-defeating behavior. I must go to AA meetings.

Now, I know that doesn't sound complicated. And it isn't. But you
really have to pay attention to hear it. I thought about that as I listened to nature's sounds on our secluded patio. If you want to hear
that hummingbird, you have to block out all the other distracting
sounds.

◆　◆　◆

Harriet, who would be taking photos at the Saturday night banquet for the Alumni
Newsletter, hoped that Patty would be there. She owed a lot to Patty, as well as to all
the counselors and other patients who'd been at Fisher when she was there. One of the
great things about the reunion every year is that patients on the road to recovery have
the opportunity to see their counselors again. Some counselors who've retired make a
point of coming back for the festivities. Harriet would look for Patty, Laurette and

Jacqueline for Ann and Tom, Beatrice would search out Alan. Counselors play a very important role in treatment. Everyone who returns has a special story about their counselors, their eccentricities, but most important of all, their caring.

The counselors may have been tough-minded and critical of some of the patients' behaviors during treatment, but they always exhibit great understanding and compassion. There is a pithy phrase that says it all: "Been there, done that. Time to move on, forget the past and deal with the present." When patients hear that, they always come away relieved that another human being could easily and willingly identify with their unmanageability. The plaque outside the meditation room dedicated to Jerry Bohannon and the whole community of counselors is a fitting tribute to their care, competence and compassion.

I know that I am biased about counselors, in fact about the whole staff. I consider them the best clinicians in the world, and I say that every year at the annual Christmas party as well as at the Alumni Reunion.

•   •   •

Laurette's recovery illustrates well the importance of the counselor-patient relationship. When Laurette made the commitment to enter the Betty Ford Center, she had no idea what she was getting into. She thought it would be a thirty-day vacation, a much-needed rest, a chance to lose some weight, a time to quit using alcohol and drugs so post-treatment she could moderate her intake. She was disabused of this idea the moment she walked into Firestone Hall.

Laurette

What was I bringing to the center, besides a radio and some good novels? Well, my baggage also contained a big-league attitude of defiance and defensiveness. My face was frozen in anger, a mask of hostility—but really that was a façade for the covert fear that lurked within.

My anger level notched up even higher when a staff member started to search my bags and take away contraband. Even though it was really nothing like it, I said it reminded me of the strip search when I was thrown into jail. I told the staff I thought this was a lousy way to start things off if they wanted to make friends with me! I said if I'd known this was part of the routine I never would have come. I wrote in my evaluation that they ought to mend their ways!

I lied to the shrink about my sexual orientation because the fact that I'm a lesbian was shameful to me. My mother had forbidden me to talk about it or ever mention the *l* word. I was rude and hostile when introduced to my roommate. It's not that I didn't like her for any particular reason; at that point I didn't like *anybody!* It didn't help that she was well-off; I couldn't understand why rich people would have problems with alcohol and drugs. Couldn't they just buy a cure?

I really didn't have a clue about the disease.

I slept most of the time during the first week. When a meeting started, a patient would be sent to come get me. No luck. So then a staff person would be sent to cajole me out of bed. I'd reluctantly get up. But after we'd gathered in a circle and recited some mysterious mumbo jumbo, I'd go back to bed. A little while later someone would come to rouse me again. Each time it happened, I got angrier and expressed that anger in no uncertain terms.

The first time another patient in group said she loved me I looked at her like she was a weirdo and told her to fuck off. For heaven's sake, even my mother didn't love me, I sure as hell didn't expect a stranger to love me! Hearing that love shit in group made me want to barf. Likewise, the first time someone tried to hug me, I almost hit her. From that point on, the women were told they had to ask my permission if they wanted to use the *l* word with me, or wanted to hug me. Naturally, nobody ever asked for permission because the last thing anybody wanted to do was make nicey-nicey with the bitch in the corner.

I went to every group they had: self-esteem, body image, grief, others I can't remember. If I didn't like what I was hearing, I'd walk out, usually leaving an obscene comment in my wake. My anger allowed me to keep people at a safe distance. Heck, I even *looked* mean.

I could live without caffeinated coffee in the mornings, I could live without the phone, but I could *not* live without my anger. I hated the place, through and through.

I despised the counselors. After all, they were the authority figures. I reserved most of the hostility for my own counselor, Ann. In front of the other patients, I'd make fun of the way she dressed. I called her the fat bitch in cowboy boots. (I didn't realize at the time that she was pregnant; much later when I was on the road to recovery and heard that she'd lost her baby, I felt devastated at my cruelty.) One time, after a guy lectured to us, Ann asked me what I thought of it. All I said was, "Macho fucking asshole." She smiled and told me the guy was her husband. Of course, I'd already known that. And she knew that I'd already known that.

We were like two bulls in an arena. No, I realize now that I was the raging bull, always charging toward the red flag; she was the gifted matador, playing with my emotions. She pierced my thick hide with deft strokes. I often felt the sting, but because of her care and compassion, she never drew blood.

Finally, the staff had had it with me. Most of them thought I was hopeless and should be shown the door. My attitude and behavior were taking a toll on the other patients.

◆   ◆   ◆

Later, when Laurette came to work for me, she told me a few of the highlights of her treatment stay. The staff put up with a lot because of the advocacy and pleadings of her counselor, Ann. Because of her own background, Ann could see right into the depths of Laurette's wounds. In all her years of counseling, Ann had never seen a patient who'd built up such high walls of defense and denial. As a result of her advocacy role, Ann was in conflict with the rest of the staff about Laurette many, many times. Everyone was complaining about her. Ann protested that making Laurette go to so many group sessions was counterproductive; she needed to focus completely on her chemical dependency.

The staff treatment team told Ann that her relationship with Laurette had become codependent, that she was too involved with Laurette. They wondered how far they could let Laurette stretch boundaries before it caused a real upheaval in Fisher. For Ann's part, she thought that peer interaction would finally bring Laurette around; but the peers weren't getting anywhere and were beginning to complain that the staff was letting Laurette get away with murder.

·   ·   ·

After my first roommate completed treatment, another woman was assigned to my room. She was young, immature and a lesbian. The staff suspected some sexual activity, which was against the rules. If that was the case, both of us ought to have been discharged. But the staff decided to give us the benefit of the doubt, and she was assigned to another room. Shortly thereafter she was told to leave the center.

The other patients were upset; they saw me as public enemy number one and the bigger pain in the ass, yet the other woman had gotten the boot. The hall was in an uproar, and hardly anyone could focus on their assignments and the reasons they were there. The staff tried to put the incident to good use and told the women to write in their journals all their feelings about the past few days.

Having read all that vitriol, the staff called me into the office, where they were sitting in a semicircle. I was told to sit facing them. I acted really cool as I sauntered to the chair, but I was thinking, "Oh boy, here it comes." A couple of things that were said are branded on my memory. One of the counselors sarcastically described me as

needing to look "hip, slick and cool" and said I had a walk and swag-
ger like a "gangbanger." Well, I've had a lot worse said about me, but
there was something about that comment and the way it was uttered
that made me suddenly feel ashamed of my phoniness. I look back
on that moment as a sort of spiritual awakening, one of those "Holy
Cow!" moments that come out of nowhere. Did I *really* look like a
gangbanger?

The staff did most of the talking, all of them citing reasons why
I should be asked to leave. I was completely surprised when toward
the end of the session they told me I was being given one more
chance—with one big condition attached. I'd immediately be asked
to leave if I didn't do *everything* Ann told me to do.

That was my moment of truth. For whatever reason, I suddenly
realized that I didn't want to be tossed out of the center. I swallowed
my pride and, after a few moments of silence, agreed to the condition. I felt an even greater release than I did when I was let out of
prison. When I left prison I took my addictive self with me, and she
in turn became my jailer. With this unexpected, unconditional surrender I had just taken my first step toward leaving my addictive self
behind bars.

For several minutes, nothing was said. Finally Ann asked me to go
tell the group in Fisher what had happened. When everyone had
gathered in the pit, I made what felt like a confession. I told them
what had happened between my roommate and me and about the
contract that I had made with the staff.

I cannot explain this sudden change of heart. It was simply another of the many transformative experiences that routinely occur at
the Betty Ford Center. After two weeks of hell, and bondage to my
anger, that moment was when I began to bond with my sister patients. They listened respectfully and welcomed me back into the hall
and into the community. I couldn't believe that they still liked me as

much as they did after the dreadful two-week-long performance I'd delivered.

When it came time the next day to tell my autobio to the group, I was almost physically sick. I dug deep down; so deep, in fact, that I wasn't even conscious of what I was pulling out of myself—all that fetid, rotten stuff that was poisoning my whole soul. It was as if a big molar had been extracted, and when my tongue explored this big empty cavity, I wondered how it would be filled up again. It was frightening and unnerving.

I finally had to get up and leave the group. I was crying so hard that I was shaking. All that day other patients kept looking for me, coming to my room or out to the patio, to tell me how much they cared for me. It was like they'd adopted an abandoned child. I didn't know what to do with that. The bonding continued. We had different stories but they all played on the same theme. We could identify with one another, tell one another that we'd been there and that there was hope.

Even more poignant was the exercise where half the group sat in a circle and the other half stood behind us, one on one. The women standing whispered into the ears of those sitting one nice thing that they would have liked to have heard from their mothers, and then it was repeated from person to person. Once again, I started to cry and couldn't stop. Imagine, this tough macho bitch—hip, slick and cool—couldn't continue and had to get up and leave. I was upset for days.

The bonding with my peers got stronger. I no longer felt isolated. An eighty-year-old woman loved me to death, and the Jewish princess wanted to hug me every time she saw me. I still wasn't totally ready for that, and my hugs were pretty stiff and formal. But I was learning.

The day after I told my story, I had to go over to Firestone to see the nurse about something. Instead of following the circular path, I walked straight across the lawn. Sitting on the bench under the tree was this enormous guy. As I got closer to him, I said, "Hi, how are you doing?" I had never greeted anyone on campus before. I was hostile to everybody.

When I said "Hi" to that man sitting on the bench, he looked up and I saw that he had no nose. Sniffing coke, I surmised, as I walked passed him. I thought no more about it. A couple of days later he stopped me on my way into the dining hall in Firestone and thanked me for being so friendly. He had just checked into the Betty Ford Center that day and my greeting helped him know he was at the right place with the right people. I thought to myself: "For someone to think of me as being friendly, I must *really* be changing!"

My trust relationship with my counselor, Ann, was a gradual process with some rough edges. Occasionally I would fall into my previous behavior of pushing the envelope with her, daring her to challenge me. But she never took the bait, and I began to suspect that she really cared for me and most important of all that she was really there for me. I found myself liking her and looking forward to talking with her. She helped me look at my lesbianism in a positive manner, and we actually started a group at the center for people with gay and lesbian issues. Being in Ann's continuing-care groups after I left the center gave me added strength and confidence.

After things got sorted out two weeks into my treatment, I was given two assignments that required responsibility. "The announcer" was the person who had to gather everybody together for group; I was pretty good at that. As "granny," I had to make sure that everybody performed their "therapeutic tasks." These included making their beds and keeping both their own and the common rooms clean and orderly. In the beginning it was a fiasco. The person who had been granny gave me zero instructions.

Naturally, I did nothing. Things started to get messy. One of the techs told me I wasn't taking my responsibility as granny seriously. That made me angry. The next day at the community meeting I confronted all my peers, told them we all had to get our cleaning-up act together. I used some pretty colorful language, I'm sure. This in-your-face method was probably unorthodox, but it worked. When it came time for the next granny to take over, I took the initiative and told the tech that we needed to type out a sheet of instructions with the granny's responsibilities. Otherwise, how did they expect to run a clean and orderly ship?

The grief group was very difficult for me. Geneva, the pastoral counselor, had us sit in a circle in her office. She would then sound a Tibetan chime to bless the space and to encourage us to center ourselves. She explained that the chime represented the element of air whose sound floats above and surrounds all in the circle. The chime is then used to mark the beginning and the end of each person's sharing time. Some members of the group wrote closure letters to those they had lost through death, divorce or separation of one sort or another. This grief ritual is intended as a gentle process of giving everyone the time they need to share their pain and loss. I was asked if I wanted to write a letter to my grandmother, but I refused. I couldn't do it. It was too hard. Each time that Tibetan chime sounded, it sent shivers through me.

During one of the grief group sessions, a woman read a letter to her brother. It was as though I had written that letter. Geneva, who was so perceptive, saw how it upset me and asked me what was going on. I was quiet for a long time and finally said that Marsha's letter had brought up a lot of the same feelings of abandonment that I had. Because of that letter I felt a special connection with Marsha from that point on. We became good friends.

Sandra was another woman with whom I became very close, probably because she was so angry with everyone and everything. I could identify with her and was able to see myself in everything that she did and said. It was like a slow-motion replay of my own first weeks in Fisher Hall when no one could reason with me. But unlike me, Sandra was unable to turn it around, and I felt so bad for her when she was asked to leave. "There but for the grace of God go I," I thought.

Then it was time for me to go. Suddenly I dreaded leaving the Betty Ford Center. I had bonded with some wonderful people, established solid friendships, so different from my drinking friends. I was frightened at the prospect of losing these women who accepted me without seeking anything in return.

My medallion ceremony was very emotional. The entire hall, staff and patients alike, gathered in a circle in the large common room. Ann explained the meaning of the medallion ceremony as a ritual of passage and then gave the symbolic object to the patient on her left who took it and held it in the palm of her hand and either said something or just passed it on. My peers said so many wonderful things about me that I was embarrassed. I kept thinking while they spoke one after the other, "I don't deserve this." I almost wanted them to take back the nice things they were saying about me since I might screw it up after I left treatment—and then what would they think!

Finally, after what seemed an eternity, the medallion came back to Ann, who looked at me and said, among other things, that I had been dealt a bad deck of cards but that somehow I still had managed to draw an inside straight. She contrasted my present behavior with who I was when I first arrived. Everybody laughed. Then she paused and said, "I know you don't like to hear this, but I'm going to say it anyway, and I'm going to say it without your permission. I love you."

Then she came over, gave me the longest hug I'd ever allowed anyone to give me, and gave me my medallion. What she was offering to me was all that I had ever wanted from anyone. I knew that she meant every word she was saying.

Everything was so very new to me that when I tried to respond, I couldn't. Nothing would come out. Finally, I managed a quiet murmur, to Ann and to everybody: "Thank you."

Tears were streaming down my cheeks. The place erupted into applause, and I felt so proud to be part of that wonderful group of women from Fisher Hall. As everyone hugged me they said they loved me without asking my permission. I didn't stop them, and although I didn't reciprocate by saying anything—I couldn't—I let them know silently that I loved them all to death.

I left the Betty Ford Center uncertain about the exact meaning and implications of the Twelve Steps, and without ever opening the Big Book. We were supposed to read the first 165 pages but I had read *Time* and whatever other magazines appealed to me from the contraband that one of the girls concealed in her room instead.

Nevertheless, I was convinced that something spiritual had happened to me. I didn't believe in the God thing so I chose the staff and my peers as my higher power. I tuned out the talk about abstinence and believed that my spiritual transformation would translate into my being able to handle my liquor better. The message about my powerlessness had not yet quite sunk in. But the power of the group had.

I was supposed to leave early in the morning, but I kept delaying my departure. Finally at noon I managed to force myself to depart. As unbelievable as it may sound, I really didn't want to go.

8

Christmas Past, Christmas Present

A t this point, two statements need to be made: Not every story has a happy ending, and appearances can be deceiving.

The disease of addiction to alcohol and other drugs is both cunning and manipulative. Not everyone who goes through treatment is ready to give up the chemicals that brought him or her down. Despite experiencing truly awful things because of their drinking or using, some women believe they can return to "normal" drinking or using after they leave treatment.

The addictive shadow, which is so powerful and seductive, can sneak up on the real self in a variety of stealthy and sinister ways. Some women who come to treatment never really intended to totally stop consuming alcohol or doing drugs, but only to learn how to "control" their intake. Some women who come to treatment have every intention of staying sober, but when they get back home they return to patterns of behavior that will inevitably lead them to start using/abusing all over again. Some women fail to follow through on their aftercare plan, which includes guidelines like finding a sponsor and going to a whole bunch of Twelve Step meetings.

Some women, I'm afraid, are just going through the motions both during and after treatment. Such was the case with Jacqueline. For her, treatment was simply a brief interlude.

For years after the intervention was staged on her, Jacqueline compared herself to Joan of Arc, who was burned at the stake for her "transgressions"; Jacqueline felt she'd been persecuted because she drank a little too much.

After she completed treatment at Betty Ford, her life soon turned into a nightmare all over again. But I'll let Jacqueline continue her story, which left off with her describing the "funeral cortege" on its way to the center, and her feelings of abandonment.

Jacqueline

The point and value of treatment passed me by completely. I became the most compliant and accommodating of clients. I walked around always smiling, I had no problems, and everything was fine and great. I would repeat that I was grateful for the intervention, as treatment was exactly what I needed. I was told to read the Big Book—and obediently I read it; to keep a journal—and I kept it; to participate in all the activities—and I didn't miss a one. I wanted to stand out as the model patient.

But it was all a sham. Deep within my heart I never considered myself a patient because I never accepted the reason for my being there—that alcoholism was an illness and I was powerless over it. I had this wonderful gift of looking people in the eye, daring them to accuse me of the opposite of what I said. My counselor, Ann, intuited that I had zero authenticity when it came to dealing with my alcoholism.

My treatment plan made note of my propensity for people pleasing and my need to look good on the outside. Appearances were everything to me. To combat this, the staff made me "granny" for a week. Ordinarily, "granny" confronts those patients who don't complete their chores. But of course that wasn't my style. Instead of confronting them, I would clean up for them!

One of the patients was using her wheelchair to garner attention and sympathy. She really didn't need it, and the staff insisted she leave it behind when she left the hall. Then she started coming to me, pleading with me to wheel her around the campus, which I would. Eventually the staff called me on it and told me that I was an enabler—I was willing to take care of everybody else, but not myself.

Naturally, my peers liked me a lot and indeed I did everything to make myself eminently likeable. The fact that I failed, after many promises, to keep in touch with any of them post-treatment confirms that I had been going through the motions and that my treatment had been doomed to failure. During my Fifth Step I spent a great deal of time blaming my father but never really got to the point where I really understood how his drinking had affected me. I told the stories about my father leaving me and my brothers in the truck while he drank in the bar, but I never was able to come to terms with it—although I certainly pretended that I had. At my medallion ceremony, Ann said she was afraid for my recovery, as everything had appeared too easy. Ann knew that I was just going through the motions.

I remember very clearly what I continued to conceal from my peers and my counselor. All during treatment I kept asking myself how I could possibly discontinue my drinking—forever. I really had fooled myself into thinking that someday I'd be able to drink just like everyone else. But for a while I'd have to act out my role as a person in recovery and go through the motions.

The notion of "one day at a time" might be for others but it wasn't for me. Even though I knew in my heart of hearts that there was a connection between my father's drinking and my drinking, I somehow half convinced myself that (1) alcoholism wasn't really a disease and (2) that there wasn't any genetic connection in the drinking department between father and daughter. I had a very touching letter from my father in which he wrote how awful he felt that the only thing that he ever gave me was his alcoholism. But I wasn't ready to hear that and was unwilling to accept that sort of legacy.

I started thinking it was pretty cool to be at the Betty Ford Center. My "celebrity status" was enhanced the second Sunday of my stay in treatment. It was my birthday, and forty people came to visit. I was pleased with the attention and basked in the love and acceptance that their visit demonstrated. It was my thirty-fifth birthday, and it augured a new birth and a new life. My discharge date was just before Christmas—that, too, signaled a new birth. But it never came to pass. I never accepted the reality that I was an alcoholic. In recovery terms, I never did "get it" while I was in treatment.

When Michael picked me up the morning of December 24 I wasn't exactly in a joyful mood. I had the Christmas blues, and I was even resentful that I wouldn't be around for the traditional Christmas Eve tree-trimming in Firestone Hall. All the patients participated, and it was always a lot of fun—sometimes a certain former president of the United States even turned up with his wife (and some Secret Service agents) to help serve ice cream and coffee, which were offered after a movie.

The trip home was hardly cheerful, and the conversation was stilted and strained. When we got home, there were presents under the tree for the girls and for me. Michael had bought me a beautiful necklace with five diamonds, in honor of the Fifth Step. A singing group stopped at our door to sing Christmas carols. Michael invited them in for hot chocolate. All the while, my resentment continued to smolder. I was upset that more hadn't been made of my return and that I wasn't the center of attention. Didn't Michael know who I was? A celebrity, just released from the Betty Ford Center!

Christmas Day was awful. I fixed a pretty meager dinner; there were only the four of us. The atmosphere was heavy with unspoken recriminations. There were long periods of silence. Michael was walking on eggshells, constantly worried that I'd throw the intervention back in his face. Now that Mom was "fixed," everything was supposed to be fine—just one big happy family.

But things aren't fixed that easily. A family isn't like an erector set, where the parts neatly fit together. Relationships have to be reworked and rediscovered, and reentry is a difficult time. In my case everyone was reticent, our behavior was tentative and awkward and emotions were left dangling. The girls were wonderful, but Michael didn't know how to act with the return of the conquering heroine. I felt the resentments stirring within me for what I misjudged to be his central role in the intervention. I held him responsible for the fact that I couldn't drink. We were strangers to each other during the day and aliens during the night. It was the perfect setup for what was to happen.

The day after Christmas, Michael went to work, the girls went to visit friends and I sat around with nothing to do but think—which soon became "stinking thinking." I didn't know what to do with myself. I felt so alone, restless and uneasy. That sense of "discomfort" that the Big Book speaks about seized me. At Betty Ford I'd used quiet time to read and meditate, to nourish my spirit. Now the only thing I nourished was resentment—enemy number one of the alcoholic—about the intervention. My "burning at the stake" had happened so quickly that I'd never had the chance to have my last drink. Twisted logic, I know. But that's how this alcoholic was thinking.

They told me I'd had my last drink. That wasn't my decision. I kept thinking, "If I'd known my last drink was my last drink, I would have had one more." Boiling resentment coupled with the terrible craving to have *just one more* was unbearable. After a few hours of such "stinking thinking," I was worn down and obsessed with the notion that one or two drinks wouldn't hurt. I was also convincing myself that nobody but me would be the wiser if I had a few drinks and kept going to meetings, acting as though nothing had happened.

After this exhausting wrestling match with my dark side, I was vulnerable, feeling sorry for myself and angry with my husband. I blocked out everything I had learned and drove immediately to the liquor store and bought two miniature bottles of vodka, which I gulped down as soon as I got to the car. It provided the ease, comfort and pleasure that I so desperately needed and temporarily blocked the shame and guilt that would soon start all over again. When I got home Michael was there and he sensed that something had happened. Over the years he had cultivated a keen sense for the behavior associated with my drinking. But he didn't say anything.

If it's true that good and bad things come in threes, that day was an inglorious triple-header for me. First the obsession and the overwhelming urge, then the vodka and Michael, and finally that evening my first session in the aftercare program that I had pledged to continue for a year. Only forty-eight hours after leaving treatment and I was drinking again. I thought I could fake my way through the session without being discovered. But during the break the counselor, Tom, took me aside and asked me if I'd been drinking. I acted indignant and without blinking my innocent eyes said, "Of course not. I mean, I just got out of treatment, for heaven's sake!"

Then I took the offensive and asked, "What makes you think that?" He said Michael had called and said that I'd been acting funny and wondered if I'd been drinking. Michael also said he thought he'd detected alcohol on my breath. I was furious with my husband and told Tom that Michael was absolutely mistaken. He asked again, "Are you sure you haven't been drinking?" I lied again. "Tom, I just finished treatment at the Betty Ford Center. How could I possibly have a drink two days later? Do you think I'm that stupid?" Tom finally ended the conversation by saying, "If you *are* drinking, you'll have to live with the consequences."

I convinced myself that I'd gotten away with it. That was the beginning of a pattern of deceit that was to last for the next three years.

Michael's phone call to Tom infuriated me and only increased the tension at home. Unlike my usual passive-aggressive behavior, this time I let him know exactly what I thought.

I went to AA meetings every morning at 6 A.M. I thought that if I did all the things I was supposed to do—attend aftercare and AA meetings—then no one would ever suspect me of drinking. The reality was that my addictive self had not been banished and her presence became even more compelling and seductive. I was soon back performing the tragicomic stunt of sneaking drinks while bent over under the dashboard of my car.

Memories of my time at the Betty Ford Center seemed like a long-ago dream, almost like scenes from a previous life. All the good resolutions quickly vanished. I picked up where I had left off before I went to treatment. I yelled at the kids and generally made life miserable for them. I reached the height of cruelty with Michael when, after one particularly nasty screaming session, I told him I knew he was behind the intervention and that I would never forgive him for it. As soon as I yelled it, I knew I'd gone too far. He simply said, "I have forgiven you for all the terrible things that you said and did when you were drinking." I had had my petty revenge, but I had also crushed his spirit.

I don't know exactly what expectations Michael had when I returned from treatment. But they were never realized. He'd gone through the Family Program, and he learned that he wasn't to blame for my drinking. But for a long time he was unable to grasp something else that he *should* have learned at Family Program: He could not keep me sober. No matter what he did, no matter how hard he tried, he couldn't keep me from drinking. I had to do that for myself. And I wasn't ready.

Life was cold at our house. It was supposed to be one big happy family as a result of my receiving treatment. But it wasn't. I was the same old Jacqueline.

Michael, bless him, continued in aftercare for a whole year, while I continued to live the big lie: going to meetings and seeing a counselor twice a week for three and a half years at $50 a session. She would drive me crazy talking about my inner child. I usually drank before I went there to anesthetize myself for the session, rinsed my mouth with Listerine and doused myself with plenty of perfume. I didn't feel the need to stop because the same tune danced through my brain: "If I do everything that everybody expects of me, then nobody'll suspect a thing."

But Michael was suspicious and soon the repetitive pattern of drinking behavior took on an eerie déjà vu quality. A shadow stood on the edge of my consciousness whispering that I had been through all this before.

In January of 1993, I was taking down the Christmas decorations at the home of one of our neighbors. The husband had been diagnosed with a massive brain tumor, and I told the wife I'd take care of things while she was away caring for her husband. The place where the Christmas decorations were stored also happened to be their liquor cabinet.

It should have taken a day to take down the decorations and put them away. Of course I stretched it out to a week, in the process drinking every drop of alcohol in that cabinet. Then I filled up the bottles with the cheap replacement booze I bought.

I was smashed the last day I played this little charade, and Michael decided we should all go to McDonald's. I was acting in such a bizarre manner that he kept asking me what was wrong. When we got home he took the girls to my friend Karen's. When he returned he was very angry and started yelling, accusing me of drinking. I screamed back that I hadn't been drinking and to stop nagging me. I then picked up a basket of clothes and started for the laundry room. He grabbed my arm to turn me around to face him. I tried to pull away, slipped, and as I fell my chin hit the edge of the doorway. Just like last time, I started to bleed profusely.

It was the same script and the same characters. Karen returned with the kids, saw the blood and said the wound needed stitches. On the way to the hospital, she asked if I had been drinking. I said, very calmly, "Of course not. I've been to the Betty Ford Center."

"Well," she said, "something is going on." I told her I was having an "out-of-body experience." That was the pathetic line that I used for the next several months with my husband, our friends and the counselor whom I'd been seeing since I finished treatment. Really, of course, the only extrasensory experiences I was having were blackouts!

When I returned from the hospital with my chin swollen and patched up, Michael called my supervisor to tell her that I was unable to be on call that weekend. Despite all he'd learned in the family and aftercare programs, he was very protective of me, still believing me when I told him that I wasn't drinking. Had I turned up at the hospital inebriated, I would have been fired.

Some months after that sorry incident a few of my co-workers at the hospital suspected that I was drinking again. They thought they smelled it on my breath from the night before. Oftentimes my behavior was suspicious if not inappropriate. The night of my birthday I drank a great deal, and the following day I was called into the Human Resources office. There the director and my supervisor confronted me and asked whether or not I had been drinking. "Of course not," I said, feigning anger and indignation. But I was trembling inside and doing a quick review of my past behavior, wondering if there had been anything that they could put their finger on. After an embarrassing silence they told me to absent myself from work the rest of the day and the following day until they figured out what to do.

I started to cry and make a scene. I shouted, "How can you do this to me? If you suspect I've been drinking, why not do a blood test?" One of the stipulations for continuing work at the hospital was that random tests would be conducted, yet that hadn't happened to me since my discharge from Betty Ford. I reminded them that I'd been going to a counselor all that time and that there was a possibility I was having out-of-body experiences. That distracted them, and they looked at each other nervously.

The director, now embarrassed, decided that I should see a neurologist; he decided I should have an MRI that afternoon. This was by far the worst thing that could have happened to me. I was extremely claustrophobic and even the thought of being confined in that large machine made my skin crawl. I needed a drink, but there wasn't time to go home. This is what my initial "extrasensory experience" nonsense had led to. I thought I was going to die as I was slowly rolled into that forbidding dungeon. No human may have known for sure that I was drinking—but God knew, and this was my penance.

From then on, I knew that I had to watch my drinking because the hospital staff was getting suspicious. Initially, I cut back—but I was incapable of stopping altogether. Gradually I lapsed into my previous pattern. Even though my job was in jeopardy, I couldn't live without alcohol.

Then the worst and the best thing happened to me. I was arrested for drunk driving. In a funny way it could be described as an "out-of-body experience" because the whole scene played itself out in slow motion.

I'll never forget the day. It was January 12, 1994. My parents were visiting. When they left to go to my sister's house, I proceeded to get drunk. Michael called from the hospital for a ride home; he'd loaned his car to my sister. The baby-sitter, who probably knew that I'd been drinking, told me to leave the girls at home with her—even though she'd finished work for the day and should have been on her way.

I was about a mile and a half from home, slowing down for a red light, but not slowing down enough. When the light turned green, I plowed right into the car in front of me. It frightened the life out of me—mostly because I knew I'd been drinking.

Both of us moved to the side of the road. We got out of our cars, checked the bumpers. I thought I could bluff my way out of it; most of the damage had been done to my car. We started to exchange telephone numbers and insurance information. In the meantime, a woman who had witnessed the accident pulled up behind us and came over to see if she could be of any help.

The witness then returned to her car and proceeded to call the sheriff's department. She told them it appeared that I was drunk and was preparing to leave the scene of the accident. They told her to take the keys from my car and said they'd come immediately.

I was trying to act normal, but wanted to get out of there as quickly as possible. I couldn't move my car, though. I was sandwiched between the other two cars. The woman who had seen the accident was conferring with the man whose vehicle I'd hit. They came over and told me that I couldn't leave until the sheriff came. He then reached through the window, turned off the ignition and took the keys. I was terrified, riveted to the seat of the car with my hands clenching the wheel.

The police were there within minutes. Not one but three cars pulled up with their red lights swirling, making me dizzier than I already was. They wrote out an accident report and then had the cars moved to the entrance of a nearby country club so that we'd be off the street. There they gave me the sobriety tests. I tried holding my breath when they told me to breathe into the Breathalyzer. The officer sighed and said I'd better comply, there was no escaping the inevitable. My blood alcohol count was .18, way over the legal limit. They were going to have to take me to the county jail.

I remember my total panic when I was put in the squad car and driven to jail. I was handcuffed, seated in the back of the police car with no handle on the inside of the door and with a metal screen between the front seat and myself. It was the claustrophobic thing all over again.

I heard myself asking them over and over again, "Do you know who I am?" and saying, "I have not been drinking."

The officers had heard it all before and simply responded, "Yes, ma'am."

When I got to the jail they took my necklaces, my rings and other jewelry. Then they put me in a private cell after they relieved me of my shoelaces. The officer on duty was a friend of mine, and I thought she would see to it that I'd be released immediately. She kept warning me not to tell anyone that we knew each other.

I was allowed one phone call, which she said she would make for me. I asked her to call Michael. He had been fretting for some time, having no idea where I was. He got a ride home with someone else.

Of course, he was absolutely furious when he heard that I was in jail, and he refused to come get me. He told the jailer to keep me there. She said that they could only hold me for six hours. He hung up. Sometime later my sister Donna came to get me. When we got home I fully expected that my clothes would be in the front yard, but they weren't. It was late, and the house was as quiet as a funeral parlor. I went upstairs, got undressed, went to bed and stayed awake until the alarm went off in the morning. I got up, took a shower, dressed and was putting on my face when Michael interrupted me and said, "What do you think you're doing? You're not going to work today. You're a mess and you reek of alcohol." He called the hospital and told my supervisor that I was sick.

I was sick all right, and everyone could see it but me.

It was one of the worst days of my life. My parents were there, and they were very quiet. The silence among us was like a concrete wall. No one knew what to say. I tried to make myself busy but I wasn't used to being home. Next to my drinking, my work had been my life. Sometime during the day the director of the department called to ask if I would be at work tomorrow. I said that of course I would. She asked me to stop by Human Resources on the way in.

My feelings of anxiety were compounded. I wondered if they knew. Later that afternoon, when my neighbor, Karen, came to visit, I found out that they did.

Turns out the man I ran into was the husband of a nurse who worked at the hospital. He told her; she told my supervisor. I felt like my life was over. The only thing I could think of was how badly I needed a drink.

The next morning as I entered the Human Resources office, I was petrified. The director asked me to be seated, shuffled the papers in front of her and then looked at me. "You know, Jacqueline, one of the conditions for returning to work after treatment at the Betty Ford Center was that you would not drink or use other mood-altering chemicals." After a long pause she asked, "Do you deny that you have been drinking?" I said that I didn't deny it, but that it was my first relapse since leaving treatment.

She paused for a while and then told me that I could either take a leave of absence or I would be suspended without pay until the hospital decided on a course of action. With that, I was abruptly dismissed. The "course of action" turned out to be a choice of either going to the outpatient program at the Betty Ford Center for six weeks or to the inpatient program at Charter Hospital for eight to ten days. I chose Charter because my driver's license had been taken away and because I would be away from my girls for a relatively short time.

At Charter, the lies continued. I swore that the drunken-driving incident had been my first and only relapse. I continued to babble about "out-of-body experiences." After eight days I was discharged and was put on Prozac. I had no intention of giving up alcohol.

When I got home, I added vanilla extract to my drug smorgasbord. It contained 70 percent alcohol. The vanilla extract, together with the Indural that I'd already been taking, plus the newly prescribed Prozac, proved to be a lethal combination and almost did me in.

I continued that regimen through February and March, graduating to the twenty-ounce bottle of vanilla extract so that I would always have enough on hand.

On April 12, my mother was visiting again. She went out for a walk, during which she always said the Catholic rosary. She came back into the house at the precise moment when I was drinking from the twenty-ounce bottle. I was caught like a naughty child, not with the proverbial hand in the cookie jar, but with my lips kissing the mouth of my clandestine lover.

My mother was furious, accusing me of lying. She threatened, "If I have to testify in court so that Michael gets the girls, I will. I won't have them being raised by an alcoholic. You'll wind up killing them and yourself." I was wounded by her remark and I needed to get in the last venomous words, so I said, "It was okay that *we* were raised by an alcoholic." My mother blanched and turned her face from me.

Even in my alcoholic stupor, I realized that I had gone too far. In my angriest moments I had never said anything like that to her before.

Later, when I took my mother to the airport, I told her that I would never drink again. I also asked her whom she was talking to on the phone just before we left. She said she'd called Richard, an old friend and cattle rancher from South Dakota, who happened to be in my AA group. She said she called him to express her concern about me and wondered if he could be of help. She told him the family seemed to be getting nowhere even though they had been responsible for the previous intervention. I didn't say anything, but Richard's name must have remained in my subconscious when I needed someone to turn to a few hours later.

No sooner had I dropped mother off than I drove like a cowgirl to the store, bought the vanilla extract and rushed home. My mother said that she was going to call from the airport in half an hour and that she expected me to be there. I flew through the front door, frightening the baby-sitter who, to my great relief, told me that no one had called. The baby-sitter left and I proceeded to finish off the twenty-ounce bottle which I had already been drinking in the car. It was four in the afternoon.

Then—and to this day I cannot explain it—for some reason I knew the insanity could not continue. It was one of those lucid moments that no one can explain. Maybe it had something to do with my mother mentioning losing the children. I couldn't bear the thought of losing my girls.

Richard's name came to mind. I liked him. We had similar backgrounds, spoke the range language and seemed to have something in common at the meetings we attended. I called him and asked if we could meet for breakfast the following morning. He said he'd be glad to and asked if something was wrong. He was playing it cool since he was already suspicious because of my mother's phone call. He picked up that I was drunk. I said I think I have a problem. The die was cast. I had hit my physical, mental and spiritual bottom. He proceeded to call Ann, who had been my counselor during treatment. She immediately called Michael.

By the time he returned home, I had passed out on the couch. I had almost overdosed. My respiration rate was down to about five a minute. Michael panicked, carried me to the car and took me to Ann's house, where he asked what he should do. He was beside himself. He told me later that part of him wanted me just to croak and be done with it. The other part begged God not to let anything happen to me. Ann and her husband took pity on him, gave him some coffee and advised him to take me home and put me to bed. They said they'd deal with it first thing in the morning.

For me it was a real "out-of-body experience." While waiting in the car, I got sick and almost passed out from the heat.

Michael took me home and put me to bed. I woke up about three in the morning feeling just awful, physically and emotionally. I went to the girls' room, where I lay down next to Anna. Michael, who'd been sleeping in the guest room, came looking for me about an hour later. When he found me in the girls' room he woke me and whispered harshly, "You have no right to be in here." I looked at him and started to quietly weep. He took me by the hand and led me into our bedroom, where we both sat down on the edge of the bed.

He got up to leave, but I reached out and pulled him down next to me. I could see the tears in his eyes. We just looked at each another, holding hands. Finally, he broke the silence. "I'm going to ask you one question. Were you drinking yesterday?"

Up to that point, while I knew that people had their suspicions, I'd never admitted to anyone that I'd been drinking, not a friend, not a stranger, in or out of group. But at that moment I knew I had to come clean.

"Yes," I said. "I've been drinking ever since I left the Betty Ford Center." He sat there for a few moments, took me in his arms and stammered through his tears, "Thank you for the truth. I thought I'd been going crazy."

After a while, he looked at me and asked, "What are we going to do?"

"I'm going to call Ann, as soon as it's light," I said.

I'd been going to Ann's aftercare group since returning from Charter. Often I'd been drinking before the meetings, and Ann knew it. In fact, she suspected that I'd been drinking for a long time.

For several months I'd been seeing another therapist, to whom I'd been talking about "out-of-body experiences" and whatever else popped into my mind. After our sessions she'd call Ann to brief her on her observations. After listening patiently Ann would say simply, "Jacqueline is drinking. That's all there is to it." Ann had been through five treatment experiences herself before beginning her real recovery, so she could smell a rat from a long way away.

Whenever Ann confronted me about my drinking, I'd look her right in the eye and say, "Ann, that's history. Since treatment I haven't touched a drop." Ann would counter, "I hope when you're ready you'll come see me."

Besides, my behavior was becoming more and more erratic. At the end of Ann's group I would hold my breath while we were in the circle saying the serenity prayer, hoping that the others wouldn't detect any alcohol on my breath.

I called Ann that morning after Michael and I had our emotional but honest conversation and told her what had been going on for the past three and a half years. Of course, she already knew. She simply asked me what I was willing to do. I said, "Anything. Whatever you tell me to do." After some moments she said that I needed to go to Alina Lodge in New Jersey where the treatment program took at least three months. I said I was ready to do it, although when I heard "three months" my stomach took a nosedive. She said she'd make arrangements to have me detoxed at the Betty Ford Center before I left for Alina Lodge.

◆   ◆   ◆

On Monday, Jacqueline went to the Betty Ford Center to be detoxed. It took four days. Then she transferred to Alina Lodge.

In the early nineties we started an Extended Care program at the center for women like Jacqueline who needed more time and a slower pace in treatment. But after six months we made the decision to concentrate on primary care and send our patients to other extended-care programs if they needed them.

Alina Lodge offered extended treatment. Ann had gone there, and she knew that a three-month stay was the exception at Alina. Most women stayed for at least six months. Jacqueline's counselor, Ann, went through five cycles of treatment before she ended up at the Lodge. She was there for nine months, and in fact that's the average length of treatment there.

Women are reluctant to seek treatment because of the shame and the stigma at-

tached to being an alcoholic. Mothers have an added burden. They are reluctant because of their children. One of the main reasons women leave treatment before completing their program is because of the concern they have for the children they left at home. It is not uncommon for women to leave the center after having spoken with their little ones on the phone.

Patients at Alina Lodge are not allowed to talk with members of their family by phone. Jacqueline told me later that she was convinced that if she had spoken to Emily and Anna and they had started to cry, she would have been out of there that day. Jacqueline also told me that some days at the lodge the pain was bottomless and she would rebel inwardly against being there. She'd wake up and think if she could just make it to lunch, then she would leave; if she could just make it to Sunday, then she would leave on Monday. Of course, having made it to noon, having made it to Sunday, she'd feel different, and she'd stay. One day at a time, as they say. In her case, one hour at a time!

Ann told Jacqueline that she had to tell the girls that she was going away. Jacqueline thought about this and then asked Ann if she would tell them for her. Ann refused and told her to do it right away so that her children would have time to process what they were being told. Even children need that time. On Friday, Jacqueline sat her girls down and said that Mommy had something to tell them. Emily was six and a half; Anna had just turned five. They looked so small and innocent, and Jacqueline felt terribly guilty for having deprived them of a sober mom for so long. She told them that Mommy was sick and would have to go away for a while; that sometimes Mommy was not a nice person when she yelled at them. The girls cried and cried. Anna promised that they would be good if Mommy didn't go away. Jacqueline thought her heart would break. But she knew that more than her heart would break if she lost them to alcohol.

◆   ◆   ◆

On Monday morning I walked the girls to school. I'd already alerted the teachers that I had a problem with alcohol and that I would be going away for quite some time. I knelt down to hug Anna and Emily. They were crying and I was crying. The teachers held their little hands as I turned and walked away from them. I was afraid to look back. It was the last time I saw them or talked to them until nine months later.

It was significant that this was the day after Easter. The pain that I was enduring and would continue to endure was a prelude to my own spiritual resurrection.

I think it was that scene more than anything else that made me realize how spiritually bankrupt I had become because of alcohol. During my drinking days I still did the whole Catholic thing: I attended Mass, went to confession and prayed to God not to let me drink that day. My mother even gave me a rosary—the same day I drove her to the airport, promised never to drink again, then raced to the store to buy my precious vanilla extract! At the time that gucky stuff was infinitely more important to me than a thousand rosaries!

To this day I cannot abide the flavor of vanilla.

But none of my pious practices and pledges worked to stop the drinking and arrest the illness. I didn't think much of it at the time but my recovery actually began during Holy Week, which is so symbolic of death and resurrection. What started that week for me was the death throes of my shadow self and the rise of my real self. Had I continued to drink, I would have self-destructed.

After three months at the lodge, I knew it wasn't time yet to leave. Very few patients were ready after three months. Alina Lodge got the hard cases that needed the elixir of time.

Meanwhile, Michael did everything with the girls that we would have done as a family. He was both Mom and Dad to them. He took them on vacation just as we had planned. They celebrated my birthday without me, and he told them we would have another party when I came home. He told them we'd have another child when I came home.

He told me later that Anna once said to him, "You wouldn't lie to me, would you Daddy?" Michael replied, "Of course I wouldn't. What made you think that?"

"Mommy hasn't called since the day she left. I think maybe Mommy's dead."

Michael swept her up in his arms in a bear hug and reassured her that I was alive, and getting better.

Having gone through the Family Program at the Betty Ford Center, Michael adamantly refused to go through a similar program at the lodge. He told me that *this is about you.* But Mary Kay, my counselor, called him and asked him to reconsider. She told him she was concerned that while I was always in a good mood and doing all the right things, I was not letting my anger surface.

"Jacqueline seems to be going through the motions," she said.

Something snapped in Michael when he heard this. All the anger that the spouse feels after years of putting up with alcoholic behavior erupted. He poured his bitter thoughts out in a letter to Mary Kay. "You're supposed to be the professionals," he wrote. "What kind of staff are you if you can't get at the truth with her?"

Again, he refused to come to the program.

He then wrote to me, still angry, warning that I'd better not be playing games with the staff while he was in debt up to his eyeballs, and he and the children were eating macaroni and cheese every day. "My heart knows or hopes that you are doing your best," he wrote, "but you need to level with the staff." When I read the letter I got so mad I went slightly ballistic myself, slamming doors, yelling at my sister patients and screaming at my counselor. Michael's letter was like vinegar being poured into my open wounds. I seized on his reference to macaroni and cheese and told anybody and everybody who'd listen that it was time for my husband to get in touch with a divorce lawyer.

Mary Kay waited a few days until my anger had dissipated before she called me into her office, sat me down, smiled and said, "Jacqueline, now you can start to get better."

What the Lodge had given me was time to get in touch with my feelings, to experience and express them when I was sober. I didn't fall apart, reach for a drink and proceed to get drunk and bury the anger or the hurt. I couldn't! I started to look at things in a whole different light. My recovery was about *me*.

Then Mary Kay gave me an assignment to write out how my anger was affecting me physically, emotionally and spiritually. That was the beginning of my Fourth Step.

· · ·

Jacqueline was taken totally by surprise when she was told that she would be going home for Christmas. She'd resigned herself to being at the lodge over the holidays.

Part of the treatment process at Alina Lodge is to allow patients—after they've completed their initial long stay—to return home for several weeks, usually two, and then return for two weeks. After a few rounds of this they return home for three months, and then return for a final week. Experience has taught them that that kind of "toe in the water" schedule allows the patient to test the waters of life without alcohol, to test the waters without being caught in a riptide of unexpected emotions and events that can pull them under and drown them, without warning.

When panic sets in it's so easy to forget everything that's been learned about reaching for a life preserver or swimming away from danger. At the Betty Ford Center we really emphasize that recovery begins the moment you leave the center, on your journey home. Treatment gives you the tools to get well. It's up to you to use those tools, beginning when you get to the airport and see the bar filled with jovial drinkers, and when the flight attendant walks down the aisle and casually offers a choice of drinks.

Do you fully comprehend that you can never imbibe again? That there's no way you can "experiment," no way you can just have "a little something" because, after all, you've learned how to "control" this nasty little "habit" you've acquired?

Temptation, temptation, temptation. When you're in recovery, you can't give in to it!

Jacqueline was given three weeks to celebrate the Christmas season with her family. If the Christmas after her first treatment experience was a full-scale disaster, this Christmas was filled with magical moments and became a high point in her life.

Jacqueline recorded the highlights in her journal:

As I departed Alina Lodge I asked God to grant me strength, honesty, openness and willingness. I believed with all my heart that I could do this.

I was sad telling my friends I was leaving, but as I closed that door, ten more doors opened up, and one of them was the door to my home!

The freedom that came with my growth at the lodge was wonderful, especially when I realized that I didn't have to be the person I was before. My good friend Beth left the same day I did. We're looking forward to exchanging experiences when we come back in three weeks.

When we got to Newark Airport I was a little frightened and grateful that the driver, Catherine, who was also one of the nurses at the Lodge, offered to stay with me. We arrived there in plenty of time and we talked about a lot of things, including what had happened to my good friend Pam. She'd been asked to leave. In fact, over the last two weeks, nine people had been kicked out and another two had left against the wishes of the staff. I remember saying to Catherine how strange and sad it is that so often our family and friends want recovery for us more than we do.

As I thought of Pam, I thought, "There but for the grace of God go I."

When they called my flight, Catherine gave me a big hug and reminded me to call the Lodge when I arrived in Los Angeles, on my way to Palm Springs. After the plane took off, I cherished a feeling of joy and quiet excitement within me. For nearly nine months I'd been anticipating this moment, returning home sober and free, free and sober.

At the same time, I kept thinking to myself, "Did this really happen, or am I going to wake up after this five-hour flight and discover that it was all a dream?"

In Los Angeles I made the required telephone call, took my carry-on bag and proceeded to the concourse where I would catch the small Delta plane that would arrive in Palm Springs at 11 P.M.

As we approached the Palm Springs airport I prayed that the girls would be there, but then thought it would be too late, since they had school the following day and the airport was a good forty-five minute drive from our house in Banning. I had plunked myself down in the front row, so I could get off as quickly as possible. As I walked down the ramp I had to breathe deeply and stop myself from running.

Then I saw them. Emily, Anna and Michael. The girls had their Christmas pajamas on and new tennis shoes that Michael had bought for them that day. At first the girls didn't recognize me. Michael hadn't told them I was coming home. He said they were coming to the airport to meet a friend.

I lost it and started to cry. When they finally recognized that it was Mommy, their eyes and their faces lit up, they ran to me and I knelt down, pulled them into my arms and squeezed them for what seemed like an eternity. They were holding on to me as tightly as they could. Emily looked at Michael and said, "Daddy, why didn't you tell us that Mommy was coming?"

When I stood up to embrace Michael, we were all crying—tears of joy. The excitement was overwhelming, beyond my wildest expectations. In the car the girls didn't stop chattering and asking questions all the way home. Every once in a while Michael would reach for my hand, and I would squeeze his.

The thought kept repeating itself in my head: "At last, we are a family."

To wake up in my own bed was a wonderful feeling. I wanted to get up with everybody else and take the girls to school, but I was so emotionally exhausted that I slept right through. The girls had wanted to stay home from school because (who can blame them?) they were afraid that I wouldn't be there when they got home. At dinner that night Anna said that I was the best Christmas present they could have. Michael was somewhat tentative and apprehensive (who can blame him?) but I felt that with continuing recovery we would heal as a family.

My first full day at home was also my fortieth birthday, and the start of a new life for me. I felt whole spiritually and physically. To celebrate, I had a massage. Michael had given me a gift certificate for one the previous Christmas, but I was in no condition to use or enjoy it. What a treat!

Then he took me out to dinner, and I had macaroni and cheese. Just kidding! I had steak and lobster. I thanked God for the celebration of life.

Being with the girls once again was more than ample reward for the nine months of painful separation. It was like a nine-month pregnancy, only this time I was giving birth to my real self, which needed the milk of constant love. It was so good to feel the love and warmth of the girls. On Tuesday, before they got out of school for the Christmas holidays, I went with Emily on a field trip. I was so proud of her, and she was so pleased that I was able to go.

I can't erase the mean episodes from my drinking years. But perhaps the memory of them will fade and drift away like a cirrus cloud as Emily and Anna continue to experience my love for them. They have both grown into such beautiful young girls, so innocent yet so wise.

On Wednesday night I attended Emily's Christmas play. She was wonderful, reciting all her parts without a hitch. The next day was her Christmas party. I made cookies and allowed her to decorate her own gingerbread house, which in itself was a great improvement for me. No need to control! Friday I helped Anna prepare for her

Christmas party, and we had a lot of fun together. She was so happy and proud when she won the musical-chairs contest.

We did a lot of walking, and the kids were great about it. Don't forget, I didn't have a driver's license! One day we walked all the way from school to the grocery store to the house and then back to the school—probably five miles in all. (My license was restored a week after I returned home, with the stipulation that I attend the Alcohol Awareness Program at the Eisenhower Medical Center. The punishment fit the crime, and I was only too happy to return to the campus where my healing journey had begun.)

I remember one thing especially after I began to drive again. The day before Christmas, Anna and I were out shopping. It was raining. Anna said, "Mommy, be careful. It's raining, and I don't want you to cut yourself like you did last time."

Bless her, she remembered that it was raining the night I cut my chin and had to go to the hospital. I grabbed her and gave her another big hug. I think I almost squeezed the life out of my two little girls during the three weeks I was home.

My DUI fine was $1,500. I had to pay it before I got my license back. I beat Michael to the punch by saying that paying the fine meant we had to endure a lot more macaroni and cheese dinners!

I attended AA meetings every day, sometimes twice a day, and my friends were genuinely glad to see me. No judgments, just acceptance and understanding. I really enjoyed the women's AA meetings and especially one on "feelings are valid." It was a small but very personal sharing group of neat women. I had to laugh when one of the ladies said, "I know the men will pat my ass but you women will save it!"

I tried so hard to keep it simple, and it appears that each day I accomplished that.

Christmas was special, and everything wonderful that happened helped to bury the memories of the previous one. The girls and I went to an afternoon Mass, and it was wonderful to be able to attend it sober without alcohol in my system. Christmas Eve dinner was at my sister Donna's, and all during the meal I cast glances at her. She'd done so much for me. Once her eyes met mine, and I could see that they were full of love and gratitude for the changed me. She also had to be wondering if this time my recovery would really "take."

The next morning the girls were up by 6 A.M. to open their gifts. They were so excited, still in their pajamas, unwrapping the presents. My heart was so filled with love for them and I was so grateful for the joy they brought us. I had worked so hard for the last nine months at Alina Lodge, being ruthlessly honest with myself. But it was *so* worth it.

Michael was an essential part of that package deal.

The day was filled with lots of phone calls and good wishes. I fixed dinner and Donna, along with dear Karen and her husband, Craig, came to dine with us. It was a wonderful celebration with family and friends. The contrast with the previous Christmas was overwhelming, this one happily defined by the absence of both alcohol and the craving for it.

The day after Christmas was a busy day packing for my return to Alina Lodge, cleaning the house and doing some shopping. It was great to have the girls running in and out with their friends and wanting to be with me. I had group that evening. Ann, my counselor from the Betty Ford Center, was there and we celebrated the anniversary of her recovery. She is someone special in my life. The Lodge is in both our hearts and is a key part of the wonderful bond that we share. Our lives started at Alina Lodge.

When I had to wake the girls the next morning, I was feeling sad. I'd told the girls when I first came home that I'd be going back to the Lodge for a checkup and said that I'd only be gone for a week. We sat down and looked at a calendar and measured off the days that equaled a week.

They were feeling my absence even before I left. I was glad they had friends to play with the next couple of days before they returned to school. My little babies were in my heart.

The scene at the airport was heart wrenching. I still cry when I think about it. The little one didn't want to let go of me. She grabbed my leg and kept clinging to it and crying that she wanted to go with me. We sat down and took out the calendar and once again counted the days until I'd return. I showed them the postcards that I would send every day of the week.

Just before I boarded the flight they asked me to throw kisses to the moon.

There's no denying that my daughters have felt the consequences of my drinking. But they are so forgiving. Their conditions for forgiveness are much less stringent than those of adults.

I remember how in my drinking days, I used to get this scary sensation in my chest, heart and throat whenever I would hear or read chapter 5 in the Big Book about those who are constitutionally incapable of being honest with themselves about their drinking. That same sensation would arise whenever the craving returned to have a drink. One of the most significant signs of my recovery was that I wasn't feeling that sensation any longer. It stopped when I called Ann and told her I finally understood that the lies had to stop, that I'd finally do what I had to do.

*   *   *

After another week at Alina Lodge, Jacqueline returned home once again. One of the things that helped her recovery immensely was something important that was written into her aftercare plan. She was told that when she returned home she had to fit herself into Michael's and the girls' schedules. They were not to change their routine to fit hers. Just as she had to change to deal with her alcoholism, so she had to change to get the family dynamic working again. She had to break out of the straitjacket of her self-centeredness.

Now when I talk to families and patients at the Center, I tell them that when someone comes home sober from treatment it's bound to take some time to adjust to the new behaviors and relationships. You all have to give each other time and space.

III
PARADISO

What It's Like Now

The experience of this sweet life.

THE DIVINE COMEDY

9

"Cunning, Baffling and Powerful"

The Saturday-night banquet is the capstone of our annual Alumni Weekend. A thousand people come together for a rollicking "sober celebration." A stand-up comedian (usually someone in recovery) entertains and reminds us all that sometimes you just have to laugh at all the crazy things that happen when people are using and abusing.

Every year the alumni present me with a volume of memories—letters or notes written by the alumni in appreciation of the role the center played in their getting into recovery. The volume is really an oversized scrapbook, with a beautiful dark blue leather binding.

Among the many people attending the twentieth-anniversary banquet, Claire and Paula and her husband, Robert, are sharing a table with Beatrice. They've been friends for a long time. Claire completed treatment in 1984; Paula finished her first round in 1985; Beatrice left the center in 1986.

At a nearby table I notice Harriet and her husband, Jacqueline and Michael and Laurette and her significant other. In a sense they belong to another generation of Betty Ford alumni, all having gone through treatment in the nineties. Jacqueline and Laurette often attend the same AA meetings, and Harriet volunteers in the alumni office.

.   .   .

I have a particular relationship with Laurette, which is related to that stage of her re-
covery described by the Big Book as "What we are like now." She told me that when
she finished treatment she left uncertain about the meaning of the Twelve Steps and
without ever having opened the Big Book. Nonetheless she was convinced that some-
thing spiritual had happened to her. She didn't believe in "the God thing," so she chose
the staff and her peers as her higher power. She tuned out the talk about abstinence
and believed that her spiritual transformation would show up in her ability to han-
dle liquor better. The message about "powerlessness" had not yet quite sunk in. But
the message about the power of the group had sunk in.

We last left Laurette at that part of her story where she was reluctant to leave the
center on her day of discharge, and in fact delayed her departure until noon. She had
found something at the Betty Ford Center that she did not want to lose. Afraid that
she might, she really didn't want to go.

Laurette

I started going to AA meetings the same day I left the Center. At my
first meeting someone said to me, "We've been waiting for you." It
really blew me away, that people in the community had been watching me and had been aware of my problem.

Some days I went to two meetings. I'd sit in the back and not say
a thing. Unless someone directly asked me a question, I wouldn't
share anything and usually blew him or her off with some remark
like, "It's all a lot of bullshit." I was still very angry and defensive and
took it personally when someone asked me anything, misinterpreting
the offering of help as an attempt to pick on me.

I may have been uneducated in the ways of recovery, but I was certainly inquisitive. I would do my own research to see if there was

something of value to what was being said—and then I'd do it my own way. That's what I did with cooking, and I turned out to be very good at it. But sobriety was not the same thing. It was hard for me. I hung in there and did my best to get through the day. I'd go to the 7 A.M. meetings with all these "high bottom drunks" who'd pretend to be so cheerful and smiling with a full set of enamel white teeth. I'd remark caustically, "How the fuck can you be so happy at seven in the morning?"

Establishing new relationships was very difficult for me. I was lonely and it wasn't fun to be with me, unlike when I was using. I saw less and less of my old gang, but I didn't fill the void with people I'd met in recovery. I didn't like any of those people.

I was lost, in a netherworld between my using life and my recovery life. I spent a lot of time on my own; there wasn't much for me to do after work.

The breakthrough happened when I came upon a newcomers' group in Palm Desert. They were young, and it seemed as though every one of them was just as angry as me. The meetings were rowdy; there was a lot of verbal sparring. A number of the counselors from the Betty Ford Center went to those newcomers' meetings. That's when I learned that those counselors didn't just *tell* people to go to meetings and stay sober; they did it themselves, to maintain their sobriety.

I met my first sponsor at a gay and lesbian meeting. I didn't actually ask her to be my sponsor; I was too stubborn and above-it-all to do that; another woman in the group asked on my behalf. That first sponsor confided in me that she also found it difficult to share and at first hated it. But she said I had to call her every day. I thought that was a lot of bullshit, but she said that she wouldn't sponsor me unless I did. So I'd call her and we'd have this inane conversation. Usually what I'd say was along the lines of, "You told me to call you so that's what I'm doing and I have nothing to say." Then I'd hang up. We were a perfect fit—neither of us liked to open up. I was still defiant.

Fortunately, another part of my discharge plan called for me to attend a Continuing Care group with Ann, my counselor from the Center. I did that for five years. That's where I broke my silence and gradually learned to share with others. It was a mixed group and people didn't care if you were lesbian, gay or straight. I guess one of the hardest things for me to do was to come out and say that I was a lesbian. After about a year, I began to really appreciate the concern and love they had for me. No one gave a damn about my sexuality. They just loved me for who I am.

Eventually I started to feel a little too comfortable in that group. Ann tried to wean me off it by saying that it was time to strike out on my own.

I can't thank Ann enough. She helped me so much to help myself. At one time in her life she was much like me, so she was able to direct me in a positive way and in the right direction with love and understanding. Even when I pushed her to her limits, she never abandoned me; she just loved me more. She gave me the strength to do things that I never thought I could do, and whenever I think of our battles I have to smile—except for that one awful time years earlier when I called Ann a fat bitch when she was pregnant, and when she subsequently miscarried. I felt so ashamed and told her how contrite I was for my behavior. But she was just her usual warm, loving self and told me that she understood. She had been there and done that, she said.

A few months after treatment I was once again diagnosed with cancer, this time in my right breast. The recommendation was another modified mastectomy and reconstructive surgery. I shrugged and thought that having lost the one, losing the other wouldn't be a big deal. As I look back, it seems that both times I was suffering so much from the aftereffects of using chemicals that the loss of something so important, so sacred to a woman, had little impact on me.

Ann was a great help in getting me through that tough time. When I was discharged from the hospital, the doctor refused to give me a prescription for more painkillers. He said that I was leaving the hospital with enough medication and since I was "a druggie" I shouldn't have any more. When the small supply of medication ran out, the pain was almost unbearable. I thought he was the cruelest doctor in the world.

At the same time, the urge had returned and I definitely wanted the drugs. I turned to my old buddy, Vicodin. I continued to use that even after the pain was gone. My behavior changed, and no one except Ann became suspicious. I finally told her what was happening, and she urged me to tell the group.

That's when I began to understand a little more about the meaning and power of the group. No one judged me, and everyone could sympathize with the strength of my "craving" and the "drug seeking" concealed in my legitimate need for medication.

The group helped me come to the decision to remove all the drugs from my home. Ann and I took the pills and flushed them down the toilet.

Part of me wanted to do those drugs so badly. Truth to tell, part of me was blaming Ann—if I hadn't been through treatment and in recovery, I could have gobbled down those drugs! I was pissed at everyone and mostly at myself for having chosen the path to recovery.

In the meantime, I had returned to work at the restaurant after my discharge from treatment. I had some wonderful friends there who had stood by me when I was at my worst. While I was at the Center they baked me some chocolates and sent them to me. I wasn't allowed to keep them because they contained a little alcohol. They couldn't understand what the problem was with a little alcohol. But I appreciated the gesture. These people had been so good and so supportive of me that when I did leave I remember feeling the need to make it right with them, to make amends for any injuries or hurt that I had caused.

Eventually I started to feel that working at the restaurant no longer felt right. I was no longer comfortable in that environment. It was then that the unexpected happened.

One night when I got home from the restaurant my roommate was gesturing wildly for me to come to the phone. She was mouthing the words, "Betty Ford is on the phone." I thought she was playing a joke on me. I said, "Knock it off," grabbed the phone out of her hand, put it to my mouth and ear and said brusquely, "Who is this?"

The person at the other end asked, "Is this Laurette?" and continued, "This is Betty Ford."

It *was* Betty Ford! For once I kept my mouth shut as I thought to myself, "Is she checking up on me? Does she call everyone who goes through the center?"

Then she asked if I would like to interview for a job as a chef for the Ford family. I said something to the effect that I would like to do that very much. I was careful not to interject any four-letter words. The cook at the Betty Ford Center had recommended me, and the Fords got my phone number from her.

When I told my friends at the hotel, they were genuinely excited for me and offered to help prepare me for the interview. The only other time I'd been interviewed was at the hotel. My roommate took me shopping, helped me buy proper clothes and a leather briefcase.

Wearing my new wardrobe, I felt so out of place and like such a phony. I kept asking why I couldn't just go in my chef's uniform.

The interview was at the Fords' home. I remember sitting on the couch waiting for Mrs. Ford, wondering what I was doing there. I thought I had little chance of getting the job. Once again it seemed like I was jumping into something with no idea of what the result would be. Once again, my life would never be the same.

I really didn't know very much about Mrs. Ford, except that she had started the center. Once a month she gives a lecture to the patients, but either I didn't go to the lecture or I blocked it out.

Mrs. Ford's manner put me at ease immediately. She had a gentle voice and calm presence. I really don't remember much of the conversation, but I know that I never felt any judgment coming from her then or all the time I knew her. She asked me a number of questions, mostly about my experience cooking and baking, and then asked if I wanted to meet her husband. I said yes. After we were introduced and had some idle conversation he said I probably wasn't even born when he was president. I said that I wasn't *that* young. But if the truth were told, I really didn't know that much about the Nixon-Ford years. There were huge gaps in my education, which took place for the most part in the streets, not in classrooms.

◆　◆　◆

Rosalie, one of the excellent chefs at the Betty Ford Center, had told me about Laurette and her cooking talents. She was very highly thought of at the Italian restaurant, where Jerry and I occasionally dined. When we met for the interview she was shy and nervous. We made no mention of her being a patient at the Betty Ford Center until she brought it up in passing much later when she felt comfortable talking about some of the things that happened there.

My assistant—who'd talked to her for a few minutes before I met her—said Laurette had some rough edges but looked like a good prospect. I took to her immediately. After the interview I saw a few more people but in my mind I kept returning to Laurette as my first choice.

◆　◆　◆

I left the interview pretty hyped up and very much wanting the job. Just going through the interview was a big boost for my self-steem. I was restless and looking to move on to other things. Everyone was rooting for me, people in the program and the staff at Tuscany's. I was really disappointed when I didn't hear from Mrs. Ford the first week, and then after the second week I thought that someone else had gotten the job.

Then to my surprise and delight, Mrs. Ford finally called to ask if I was still interested in working for them. When I hung up the phone after saying yes and thanking her for the opportunity, I experienced a great rush of joy and satisfaction. I'd accomplished something meaningful without alcohol or drugs. It was the first of many new and wonderful experiences that would come with my sobriety.

It was around Thanksgiving when I went to cook for the Fords. I was still struggling with sobriety. The Ford family spends Christmas in Vail, Colorado, and I was expected to accompany them. That was a particularly difficult time for me. They were exceedingly kind, putting me into ski school and outfitting me with the proper clothes and equipment so I could enjoy the slopes when I wasn't working. It took me a while to acclimatize to the cold weather. They had to dress me so I wouldn't freeze to death.

I had a hard time adjusting to my surroundings. Even though the Fords had a big family and wanted me to feel a part of it, I felt very much alone. The people I was closest to were back in Rancho Mirage. I felt pretty shaky without my support groups. I'd been sober less than a year.

When we returned to the desert in January I threw myself into the job, determined to be the best cook that I could be. But I made too many demands on myself. Because of time pressures, I stopped going to meetings and then I got a prescription for a mood-altering muscle relaxant.

I knew that I wasn't working the program and I finally fessed up to Ann. She had me tell everyone in my aftercare group. Ann then urged me to talk to Mrs. Ford. That meeting with Mrs. Ford was one of my most memorable life events.

• • •

When Laurette asked me for a few moments of my time to speak with me, I really had no idea what was on her mind. I took her into my private study where we sat down on the couch. She was very nervous and said she didn't know where to start. I told her to take her time. Then quietly she told me about her relapse and ended by saying that she didn't think that the job was for her. I think she was surprised when I didn't look horrified or act disappointed.

At that moment I simply felt love for her, and accepted her. When no judgment was forthcoming, I heard a deep sigh and her relief was palpable. I certainly didn't tell her that what she'd done could be lightly dismissed, but I talked about the insidious nature of the illness and how powerful it is. I shared some of my own story with her and ended by saying that if I could do anything at all to help her, all she had to do was ask.

When Laurette suggested that she probably shouldn't work for us anymore, I said she should give it one more month before making any final decision.

• • •

This was really weird for me. I was almost blown away by Mrs. Ford's nonjudgmental manner. She accepted me and didn't make me feel like a terrible person. I gave it a month and then ended up staying with them for six wonderful years.

That conversation changed forever my negative attitude toward "high bottom drunks" and made me realize that it doesn't make any difference whether one is wealthy or poor, powerful or homeless— an alcoholic is an alcoholic.

I finally understood that alcoholism is the most democratic of all diseases. It can afflict anyone, no matter what their position in society. As a result of that conversation with Mrs. Ford, my life began to change.

Shortly afterward, I attended a meeting where the speaker was sharing her grief experiences. She had lost her husband and teenage son to a drunken driver. A few weeks after that her daughter had committed suicide. I was dying to know why that woman was sitting there with us and not out drinking.

I started going to that meeting with those old farts, and I would sit there and listen. I got Linda back, my old sponsor. She opened my eyes to the spiritual part of the program. She made me raise my hand at meetings and insisted that I read the Big Book with her. I started doing some of the service things at the meetings, like making coffee. She suggested I go out to breakfast with the group after the meetings. I resisted that for a while. Where in the Big Book, I wondered, does it say you have to go to breakfast with your group!

Then one day it came to me, after two years and two relapses. There was a simple formula: The more I participated in the program, the more I became a part of it; the more I stood outside in the cold, the more distanced I was from it.

It wasn't like I'd never heard that before. People probably said it a hundred times at the meetings I attended. But suddenly it was a great revelation. It finally dawned on me that it wasn't just a question of survival—I had to learn to live with my disease and be willing to change. I would find happiness and contentment by being honest and by believing in a power greater than myself.

My life is so different now. The change that's taken place is deep inside me. A lot of people think that change is something external, but it's the inside stuff that counts.

I find that I'm no longer living without purpose. *My purpose is to stay sober and to help other alcoholics.* I believe that with all my heart and soul. I go to five meetings a week because I feel I have to. Another member of the fellowship once said to me that he needed to go to only one meeting a week. I told him I'm probably the same—it's just that I'm not sure which one it is! So I go to all five of them!!

All my relationships have changed. AA has turned strangers into friends, unplanned situations into great memories. I am feeling better about myself and I find that, to the best of my ability, I am caring about people and they are caring about me. I gradually shed all my drinking buddies, as I no longer had anything in common with them. I felt sad, but that was another life that I left behind. All my real friends are in the program. I still consider the Fellowship my Higher Power.

This has become a "one day at a time" program for me. "Progress, not perfection" is what I strive for. I thank my Higher Power for that because I am far from perfect, and never claim to be. I try to do everything to the best of my ability. Some days I do better than others, and that's okay. If I have a bad day, there's always tomorrow. I learned that I never have to make the journey alone, unless I choose otherwise. I now take responsibility for my behavior and the state of my well-being. I'm continually reminded by my friends that I don't have to do a lifetime of amends and repairs in one day.

I've been angry all my life, and it's scary how it bubbles up at the most unexpected moments. One day I went for a hike in the beautiful desert mountains with my partner accompanied by my dog. On a hill just beyond us were two guys with their two pit bull dogs. When those dogs saw us they came racing down the hill, barking and snarling like crazy. I was really frightened, and yelled to the two young men that their dogs should be on a chain. A lot of good that did. The pit bulls were on us in no time and started attacking my dog, snarling and biting. I kept punching and kicking them and finally threw myself on my dog to protect him. In the meantime, the guys came running down the hill as fast as they could, pulled their dogs off us and leashed them. At first I was frightened, but that was replaced with rage and I started screaming at them with all the foul language that I could muster. My partner was trying to calm me down. They grabbed the dogs and got out of there as fast as they could.

I went to the police when I got home. They said unless I could provide names and addresses, there was nowhere to start and nothing they could do. I had the same old feeling about having no one to look out for me. Who would replace my mother and grandmother? I felt so helpless and vulnerable.

The next day a friend came into the restaurant where I worked. I was still angry. As we talked and he shared some of his wisdom I began to feel better. The friend was Tom, my counselor, Ann's, husband, the man I once called a "macho asshole." I now love him and find that we think very much alike. We share many of the same angry feelings that need appropriate channels of expression.

Recently I was run off the road by some punk kids and almost had an accident. I was so pissed and so tired of being pushed around that I roared after them in my new Jeep. When I caught up with them, they gave me the finger. That made it worse. I threw a glass of water at them and intended to run them off the road. Then I began thinking that if I didn't stop I was going to hurt somebody. That tempered the road rage.

My anger is still there, but it's different now. I can get angry without drinking or using. My sobriety helps me to live life on life's terms. The road incident is a metaphor for life in general: People are going to cut you off all the time.

•   •   •

When I finished my brief talk at the banquet, I happened to look in Laurette's direction and nodded to her before I sat down. She left our household after six years, and Jerry and I were very sad about her departure. It was a difficult decision for her, and she felt very down about it. But she felt it was time for her to move on and do other things.

Not only was she like family to us, but she and I were able to identify with each other in many ways. Her double mastectomy and reconstructive surgery was another wound that she and I shared. She was grateful that I helped her get in touch with some of the deep feelings that accompanied such a loss. I tried to always be sensitive about both her struggles with chemical dependency and her wholeness as a woman.

I was sincere when I referred to her as a close friend of the family, and I know it makes Laurette feel proud whenever she hears that I have said that to others.

I saw Paula sitting at the table next to Laurette's and waved to her as I settled in at my own table. I remembered when, years before, Paula and her husband, Robert, stood at the dais with me at the anniversary banquet. Paula was one of the principal speakers. It was a proud moment for her. For years she had been respected and viewed by many as an exemplary model of recovery, faithfully working the program, sponsoring people and helping in the Alumni Office.

Not long after that banquet she had her relapse, and when she met me her second time through treatment she thought she would die of shame and embarrassment. I was in the dining hall having lunch with the patients. On this particular day I just happened to be standing in the food line with my tray right behind Paula. It was her second day in treatment. She sensed my presence, but she was so ashamed that she couldn't turn and say hello. I took the initiative, tapped her lightly on the shoulder, and said, "Well, Paula, is the food still good?"

When she turned I could see the relief gradually spread over her face. She was probably waiting for me to express some surprise at seeing her at the center again. She had told others that she felt that she had let me down. What Paula did not grasp was that I understood clearly that relapse was a part of the disease of addiction.

When I finished treatment at Long Beach my counselor made it very clear to me that recovery began the day I set foot outside of the safe environment of the treatment center. Treatment is only the prelude, the place where we are provided the tools to live a life without chemicals. At the Betty Ford Center the counselors continue to stress the importance of the aftercare plan, now called the "continuing care" plan. The plan highlights attendance at AA meetings, participation in an aftercare group and possession of a relapse prevention plan. There are also recommendations for counseling in areas that needed further attention.

The center also makes every effort to provide an alumni contact where the patient is returning. That's a great help. Besides belonging to the same caring community and their familiarity with the treatment process at the Betty Ford Center, these contacts are able to share their own positive and negative experiences of coming home and trying to adjust to a totally new way of life.

I remember we were cautioned before leaving treatment about how our alcoholism and drug addiction—in other words, our addictive selves—can come in through the back door when we're not looking. Laurette, Paula and Jacqueline all had that experience. Our addictive natures are so manipulative. The passage from the Big Book says it all: "Remember that we deal with alcohol [and drugs]—cunning, baffling and powerful." This is especially true for people who get hooked on mood-altering prescription drugs as Paula and I did; cross-addiction is particularly baffling.

My dear friend Dr. James West, who has been with me since the opening of the Betty Ford Center and still lectures on alcohol and drugs, is very helpful in alerting patients to the dangers of cross-addiction. How many times in treatment do the counselors hear the newcomers protesting that they would abstain from pot but were unwilling to give up beer because they didn't consider their drinking to be a problem?

It works the other way, too. Paula, who after a time got heavily into prescription drugs once again for her pain, thought that she had maintained her sobriety because she didn't touch alcohol. Paula and I both had to learn that all mood-altering drugs—including alcohol—are a problem once we lose control over any one drug. The real problem is the game we play in our minds that we can somehow "control" our drinking or using. That's part of the insane thinking that accompanies the disease. I'm afraid not everyone understands that.

Paula's story is a good example of what I'm talking about, this "fool's paradise" of thinking somehow we can use willpower to "control" our drinking or using. We last saw Paula when she was saying good-bye to her sister Fisherettes.

Paula

When I left the Betty Ford Center in December of 1985, I was bound and determined that my life of addiction was over. Robert and I talked all the way home. He and Vicky had decorated the whole house for my homecoming. The lights were on, the tree was lit up and Christmas music was playing. I thought of the song "I'll Be Home for Christmas." It was wonderful to be safe at home.

At the same time, I was frightened. I'd asked Robert to get rid of all the alcohol in the house, but many of the pills were still there.

Before we got out of the car I said I had a request. "I want you to walk around the house with me and collect all the pills and flush them down the toilet." I was afraid that if I did it alone I might decide to save a few just in case. He smiled, gave me a kiss and we walked in the house together.

Vicky, waiting just inside the door, gave me the longest hug and then said, "Welcome home, Mom. I missed you."

Before Robert and I even sat down we began our "search-and-destroy mission," having explained to Vicky what was up. I went through all the cupboards, drawers and medicine cabinets. I found pills in my bathrobe and in my purses. There was one big black purse in which it was easy to hide hundreds of pills. That bag and a number of others I took out to the garbage bin. I found one brown glass bottle, which had a CALCIUM label on it but which was simply another convenient repository for my pills.

While I was at the Betty Ford Center I learned what it meant to "work the program": don't drink or use, go to meetings, read the Big Book and live one day at a time. I was determined to become the perfect recovering person. Robert was supportive—even oversupportive. He hovered about, attentive to my every need. He offered to take me to all my meetings and wait for me until I finished.

We had been cautioned that the family dynamic changes quite radically after treatment. The addictive self is supposedly left at the center; the real Paula would once again enter the family circle. We were reminded, however, that the addictive Paula would always be lurking in the dark alleys of the unconscious. Robert and Vicky went through the Family Program and knew that old behaviors had to change. This was true particularly with Robert and me.

Vicky seemed to have learned the lessons of the Family Program better than us. From the beginning she stood back and let me find my own way. But she was so loving and supportive. When I returned to the Betty Ford Center to get my three-month chip, there was a card on the seat of my car congratulating me, signed simply, "With love." When I got back to the house after receiving my six-month chip there were flowers and a beautiful card from Vicky waiting on my bed.

The first Christmas home after treatment was scary. In the past Christmas had always been a time of drinking, socially for others, excessively for me. In addition, my eldest daughter, Nancy, was going to be home for the holidays. My alcoholism had, over the years, driven a deep wedge between the two of us. She supported me in getting help, but she was, understandably, still wary of me after I finished treatment.

I tried to set the tone for the holidays when I announced at our Christmas Eve dinner that I had not made the fabulous rum Bundt cake this year and intended to end the custom. Applause mingled with laughter, and Nancy said, "Thank God, Mom, we all hated it!" And I always thought everybody loved it! I was surprised, but I shouldn't have been. As the years went by and I got sicker and sicker with my disease, I kept adding major amounts of heated rum to the concoction.

I experienced highs and lows, mountains and valleys. The level playing field promised by the prophetic counselors was still a long way off.

While I was in treatment I got letters and phone calls from my father. Despite our rocky relationship in the past and his verbal and physical abuse of me, I still loved him and he loved me very much.

His letters were sprinkled with comments that he knew how painful withdrawal was for me, that I should take courage, everything would work out, and that he was sorry for his past behavior toward me.

Dad was an alcoholic and had been addicted to pills, and I suppose that left me with a genetic predisposition toward both. He also said that I should disregard my mother's malice toward me because she didn't know any better and she was a sick lady. But Dad had changed. He was so happy that I was getting treatment and could look forward to a new life.

When Robert and I returned home from Indio, where we'd just bought a place so I could be close to the Betty Ford Center, Vicky was waiting for us at the door. I sensed that something was wrong. She was quiet, and her face was absolutely white. I panicked and asked her what the matter was. She hugged me, started to cry and said, "I have something terrible to tell you. Grandpa is dead. He shot himself."

For a moment, I couldn't breathe. Time stood still.

I thought I had to be brave and take charge. "Let's go inside and say a prayer," I said. "Please God, hold him in your hands and walk me through this sober."

I didn't reach into my purse for a pill or run to the cupboard for a drink. I led us in prayer. Proud? You betcha!

I called my mother early the next morning and told her I'd be there that day. In her perfect hurtful and put-down way, she replied, "No need to hurry. Your sisters are here already. Everything's under control and the funeral isn't until the day after tomorrow." Translation: Your presence is of no consequence and you'll just be in the way.

Somehow I managed an April Assertive moment and announced Vicky and I were coming that same day and that Robert would fly in tomorrow. But the legacy of hurt still stung.

The last time I'd spoken with Mom was on Christmas Day. I'll never forget that call. I may try to, but I can't. I'd called to wish them a blessed Christmas and a happy New Year. Dad answered the phone. After we'd exchanged greetings, I asked if Mom was there. I heard her say in the background that she didn't want to talk to me. When she did pick up the phone, though, she said in that spiteful voice of hers, "What do you want now? I can't talk with you, we're late."

When Dad came back on he said, "Don't pay any attention to her. She's just out of sorts and doesn't mean anything by it." Easy to say, impossible to do. How could I not pay any attention to her? She was my mother and she had invaded every secret and safe nook and cranny of my life.

I hoped that the tools and armor I'd acquired at the Betty Ford Center would work their magic and shield me from her cruel words and behavior.

My sister Judy, at whose home we were staying, met us at the airport. When we got to the house, Mom couldn't resist. "I told you you didn't have to come," she said.

But I had steeled myself to be impervious to her put-downs. The sorrow that I was feeling about Dad's death also helped to make me numb to her rantings.

When we got to the funeral parlor, I discovered that the readings and the music had already been arranged. When I asked that the Lord's Prayer somehow be included in the service, you'd think that I had asked her to bring Lazarus back to life. She coldly reminded me that everything had already been arranged.

"God," she said, "you're just causing trouble again."

The morning of the funeral I went to the florist and bought a little bouquet of fresh yellow-centered daisies—my favorite. The casket was open and I took Dad's hands and tucked the daisies under them, and told him that I loved him. My mother came up behind me and hissed, "You're holding things up. See, they're waiting to close the casket, and there are people you still haven't met." I looked at her and reminded her this wasn't a social occasion. That made her even angrier and she told me to go to the next room and sit down so the services could start.

Mom sat next to Judy; I sat between Judy and Denise. When I started to sob, Mom leaned across and said angrily, "Will you please pull yourself together and take a deep breath. You're an embarrassment to all of us."

I continued to cry and I remember it was Dad's sister behind me who leaned forward and patted my arm as a gesture of sympathy and understanding, something that I received from neither my sisters nor my mother.

Without having Vicky and Robert there—and without my month of treatment under my belt—I would have been a complete basket case.

Even with the trauma of losing Dad, I was busy attending meetings, making friends with others in recovery, getting a sponsor, driving to the Betty Ford Center every Friday to attend an aftercare session and helping Joan, the alumni manager. Sometimes I was going to several meetings in a single day. My urge to use was still very strong in the beginning. When I went shopping, I rushed through the pharmacy section so the pills wouldn't jump off the shelves into my cart.

During my first meeting with my sponsor she asked me to tell her my story, which I did. When I was finished with my sorrowful saga, she said, "Oh my God, you were *much* worse off than me!" I didn't know whether to feel flattered or shattered.

For a long time things went well. Then, surreptitiously, my addictive dark side began whispering in the background.

At one point my back had gotten so bad that I was confined to bed for three months. I would have AA meetings in my room. Both my sponsor and my psychologist (both in recovery) urged me take a modest number of painkillers. Some of my AA friends told me there are times when it's okay to do that.

Finally I went to my doctor and told him that I needed some medications. He gave me a prescription for Damason P. I took half a pill every twelve hours. That seemed reasonable and controllable. The pills took the pain away, made me feel good and gave me energy. Occasionally, when I remembered that it was pills that had resulted in my needing treatment, I would try to cut them out altogether. My cunning and addictive self also suggested that since I wasn't using alcohol, everything was okay.

This on-again, off-again relationship with pills went on for some time. I thought I had control over it. But I hit a great big cement wall at my sister Judy's wedding in the fall of 1992. From that moment on, it was downhill all the way to the bottom.

Robert and I flew out to the wedding. When we arrived, my mother looked at me and turned away. She wouldn't speak to me.

At the reception, there was no place for Robert and me at the tables that had been reserved for the family. By the time we wandered from table to table and discovered that, all the other tables in the hall had filled up. It was humiliating, standing in the middle of the hall, forcing a smile as though nothing was wrong, but having nowhere to sit.

We finally found two places at a table—outside on the patio. I was mortified. Robert said, "This is the coldest goddamn family I know. I don't want anything more to do with them." I felt my insides were being cut to tiny shreds. But somehow I managed to put up a good front at the reception, greeting people with a fake smile.

Doris Doormat had returned. I sobbed practically the whole night while Robert tried to comfort me. I didn't care what happened to me.

That incident really triggered my return to drugs. Despite my thoughts to the contrary, I hadn't really gotten over the deep resentment I felt toward my mother. Those negative feelings surfaced with a vengeance. The debacle at the wedding made the emotional pain unbearable and added to the intense physical pain that I was beginning to suffer once again. My intake of pills increased dramatically. I blamed it on the physical pain, but the truth is I wanted to deaden the emotional and spiritual turmoil as well.

The frustration I felt because my mother wouldn't treat me like a human being depressed me. I didn't care anymore, about my sobriety, about my future. My addictive self really took over and reminded me how easy it is to get rid of the pain. The old mantra that my mother had drilled into me when I was growing up—"You're worthless, you're no good"—returned with a vengeance.

I'd come a long way since I completed primary treatment. I'd become Ms. AA. People looked up to me. I began to give little talks. I was on the Alumni Board of the Betty Ford Center. I sponsored a lot of women (too many, in fact). I was the go-to person when it came to maintaining sobriety.

But there was a price to pay for all this. I thought I had to be perfect for all the people who were seeking me out and coming to me for my advice. Trying to behave perfectly all the time was an awful burden. I put too much effort into solving other people's problems and didn't have enough time left for my own.

Then, as my use of prescription drugs increased, so did my guilt and shame. I didn't even realize when I crossed the line and my addictive self took over completely once again.

I went to my meetings, but they became more difficult than ever for me to attend because of the lethargy that the pills induced and because of the guilt I felt for being on the meds. Paranoia set in. I felt that people were watching me and I found myself avoiding their eyes. Whenever my sponsor called it felt like she was checking up on me.

She knew I was on pills. She'd encouraged me to take them. While I resented her calls, I nonetheless waited for them. I was so lethargic in the morning that it would take me hours to get dressed. I could hear Mom's voice and laughter in my skull: "You ugly, worthless little thing."

The illness of addiction is insidious. It seemed like the more pills I took the more pain I felt. Sometimes they helped, but oftentimes they seemed to cause spasms and provided no relief. The drugs were wreaking havoc on my nervous system. The more pills, the more pain. The more pain, the more pills. Around and around it went. I was taking fifteen to twenty pills a day, sometimes thirty. My health deteriorated at a rapid clip. I quit my walking and back exercises. Once again, I fled to the safety of my room, searching for the respite the bed and induced sleep could provide.

I'd promise myself to get clean the next day, when I'd feel better. But that "next day" never came. I had severe burning in my esophagus and stomach. My heart would throb and thump, and I was certain that I was going to have a heart attack. I was chain-smoking, going through a pack and a half of cigarettes a day. I felt pain, real or imagined, in my liver and gallbladder. I worried about my lungs and couldn't remember the last time that I was able to breathe deeply. The pain pills seemed to be shutting down my respiratory system.

Worst of all, I wasn't working the Steps, and my spiritual life had deteriorated along with my body. I was dishonest with people and began telling them that I was "fine" when they asked me how I felt. My "God-consciousness" died and I didn't feel His presence in my life anymore. My candle reminded me of my prayers, but the prayers became a chore and when I did recite them it seemed like an exercise in futility and nothingness. I bought all kinds of meditation books, but I scanned them like a zombie.

Robert and my daughters started staring at me the same way I remembered from the last chapter of my life before treatment. I felt so ashamed and tried so hard to act normal. But the harder I tried, the more uptight and unnatural I became. It was like I was on a merry-go-round. Robert would get the bills from the pharmacy and ask how this was possible. Talk about déjà vu. I felt like a naughty little girl.

I tried to tell myself that I didn't care. But the guilt and shame wouldn't disappear.

My real self and spirit seemed to die within me. I felt no joy, only depression and fear. I couldn't laugh and seemed to be crying all the time. Before, when my daughters or grandchildren came or called, I would get so excited and I would wear myself out caring for them. But now it became a chore to call them, and I didn't want them to visit me and see the mess I was in. Then I felt guilty and sad.

Nothing Robert did pleased me. He knew what was happening because he was grounded in Al-Anon. Nevertheless, he couldn't help but get angry with me. When he returned home from work he'd give me that look of disgust that I'd seen many years earlier. He'd say, "I want to help, but I know that I am powerless over your illness." At the time, the words seemed so cold. He seemed so remote and robotic.

My previous pattern of behavior repeated itself. Instead of answering him, I would retire to my room where I could be alone. I would close the shutters, take the phone off the hook and wouldn't answer the doorbell. This time, instead of cutting things up, I was into "dying" things, usually purple, to go with my lavender robe with its burgundy trim.

I was angry, with myself for the mess I'd managed to get myself into, and with others, because I was the object of their pity. The addicted Paula had blocked out the illness and its progression.

But a stubborn remnant remained of my recovery. It wouldn't let go. It haunted me.

As I moved deeper into the cave of my self-pity I kept hearing, even if faintly, the word *fine* and my counselor Ray's definition of it: "Fucked up, Insecure, Neurotic and Emotionally insecure." It was like a radar ping that kept bouncing back from the center. I finally told my doctor, who had been so patient with me during these dark days, that I needed help and that I was going to telephone the Betty Ford Center. I said that I might need a letter from him. He said, "Gladly. And, Paula, you are one of the most courageous women I know."

My healing journey had been sidetracked, and it took all the courage I could muster to begin again.

The flight into Palm Springs was turbulent. I prayed, "Please, God, let me die, but let everyone else live." The first night, Friday, Robert and I stayed in a nice hotel in Indian Wells, near the center (I wasn't supposed to check in until Monday). Due to a reservation mix-up, I had to switch to another hotel on Saturday, after Robert had flown back home. The second hotel was a dump, dingy and drab. It was a perfect complement to my melancholy and depressed mood. I took out my pills and put them beside the bathroom sink. I kept staring at them, thinking it would be easy to take every one of them and end it all.

At that moment my brain turned on and I decided to call Josie, one of the women I'd gone through treatment with and with whom I'd kept in touch all these years. I told her where I was, that I was checking back into the Betty Ford Center Monday, and added, "Josie, I feel horrible and I don't know if I'm going to survive. I'm looking at these pills thinking that maybe the best thing to do is just take them all and end the agony."

She'd been through the same thing and recognized that what I was saying was a desperate cry for help. "I'll be right over," she said. When I met her at the door, she embraced me for the longest time, then looked around the room, and said, "Let's get out of here and go for a ride." We drove to her house, talking and crying the whole way. We drank pots of coffee. I stayed at her house that night.

◆ ◆ ◆

Paula told me that her second time through treatment was very difficult. She considered it a small blessing and a good omen that she had not been assigned to the "swamp" in Dupont Hall. She dreaded running into people who'd recognize her as someone who'd been here before. Like all of us, she didn't want to be branded "a failure."

When she met Dr. West again, she cried as he hugged her and said that everything would be all right. One of the worst moments was when someone asked her if she was the lady who'd spoken at the Alumni Banquet the previous November. She was so hurt.

◆ ◆ ◆

The first Friday at Betty Ford, I went to the AA meeting on campus. Several people who saw me there assumed I was on the panel of people in recovery who'd come to share with the patients. My heart was heavy with shame. I felt I'd let a lot of people down. I shared a little about my relapse, and I felt relieved that everybody now knew about it.

At the meeting the second Friday, my old "swamp" roommate Gwen was the speaker. I don't know if the others saw the shock on her face when she saw me, but I couldn't miss it. I guess I was expecting it. But after the meeting she came up to me, hugged me and said things that were very supportive. The shame wasn't so bad that time, and I guess I was starting to comprehend that relapse is a part of the disease.

I was also starting to comprehend that I was fooling myself if I thought my sobriety was A-okay as long as I didn't drink alcohol. I had fooled myself into believing that I could keep my pill-taking "under control." I didn't realize what a "fool's paradise" that ultimately led to.

Having to list the consequences of my drug use was a very helpful assignment. It made me realize how my addictive personality had fooled me. I would add the words *seductive* and *manipulative* to those adjectives from the Big Book, *cunning, baffling* and *powerful.* I learned that sobriety means abstinence from *all* mood-altering chemicals.

Probably the most important assignment I had, besides doing the first three Steps again, was to write an "anger letter" to my mother and share it in group. The staff, as before, felt that relationship was my most formidable trigger for relapse and that I had to dig deeply to get in touch with the anger involved in that relationship.

I'd been taught as a child that it was wrong to show anger. As a matter of fact, a show of temper resulted in physical punishment. Then I read a book my counselor assigned me, *Insights on Releasing Anger,* and learned that suppressing anger leads to self-pity, which leads to resentment, which in turn leads to drinking and using. If we keep anger inside, we become more and more preoccupied with that other person in our thoughts. That's exactly what happened with my mother.

I assumed I would read my "anger letter" in group, but that's not what happened. Rose, the counselor, had me talk instead to a chair, visualizing that my mother was in it. I had to take off my makeup before I started, which symbolized removing my mask and getting in touch with the real me. For a while I was very self-conscious, but gradually I opened up. I yelled and pointed my finger, cried, got angry and stamped my feet. It was a powerful experience. It made me realize how much power I had given to my mother and how cruel and abusive she was to me.

Although I didn't notice it at the time, everyone in the group cried with and for me. I couldn't see them as I was so focused on Mom's face in the chair.

When Vicky came to visit on a Sunday just before or just after that group session (I don't remember the time frame), she spoke to me about Mom. She said Mom had always been mean to me, always putting and pulling me down. She said in her mind my mother was dead.

Vicky then repeated something that had taken me a long time to learn: "Mom, you've got us; we're your family, we all love you so much. All your friends love you, too, so please don't ever go near your mother again. Dad should have kept you away from her."

◆　◆　◆

During her second stay in treatment, something happened that hit Paula really hard—and that has played a huge role in maintaining her sobriety.

It had to do with the memories of her roommate Sheila. Sheila had a lot of physical pain, just like Paula. The last day they were in the Jacuzzi together, talking about their use of painkillers and the plans they had to deal with the physical pain after they left treatment.

Paula remembers how proud Sheila was of her little five-year-old girl. Her medallion ceremony was very moving, and Paula escorted her to Firestone the morning she was leaving.

Three days later in full group the staff announced that Sheila had been found dead in her apartment. There was a long, heavy silence, broken by sobs. Paula's heart almost broke for Sheila and her little girl. No one spoke, but the message was clear: "There but for the grace of God go I."

10

Completing the Healing Circle

Addiction takes a terrible toll on family life, and specifically on children. They are truly the innocent victims of this disease.

Almost since the day the Betty Ford Center opened, attention has been paid to the special needs of children. In the mid-1980s we began a formal Children's Program. This is for young people age seven to twelve who are not themselves addicted to alcohol or other drugs, but who live in a family in which addiction is present. It's a four-day program; the kids learn about the disease, they learn that it is not their fault, they learn coping skills. The program has been so successful in Rancho Mirage that in 1999 we established a Children's Program in Dallas.

For the past several years we've invited children who've gone through the Children's Program to attend the Alumni Banquet. It's exhilarating to see their sparkling faces and their eyes dancing with pleasure at the food—especially the desserts. There's also something special about watching them get bored as the scheduled events go on and on and they get up from their places to wander about the ballroom. Sometimes their chaperones take them to another room where they can watch videos and play rather than listening to speeches and comedy routines. By the time the dancing starts, the kids are usually ready to head home.

• • •

I watched Emily and Anna as they searched the ballroom looking for their parents, Jacqueline and Michael. After they were reunited, Jacqueline and Michael hoisted Emily and Anna onto their laps, where they were content to snuggle and be quiet. I could see the parents looking at each other, and their eyes spoke of gratitude and love for the mending of their family circle.

Jacqueline

I'm embarrassed when I recall how cold life was at our home when I returned that first time from the Betty Ford Center. It was supposed to be a big happy family post-treatment, but it wasn't. It was the same old Jacqueline. At the dining room table Michael and I would speak through the girls. "Emily, ask Daddy if he's going out tonight," or "Anna, ask Mommy if she's going to her AA meeting tonight."

I continued to yell at the girls when something went wrong. One time Emily dropped a tray of ice cubes as she was taking them out of the refrigerator. She looked at me with her eyes wide, frightened and fearing the worst. I screamed at her to get to her room and stay there until I told her to come out.

When I finally remembered where she was, I went to get her. I found her in her room, holding her teddy bear, still shaking. I sat on the bed, pulled her gently toward me, and as I rocked her I whispered that I loved her. Eventually her sobbing subsided. I thought to myself, "What's wrong with me that I'm acting this way toward my little girls?" But then I'd rationalize my cruelty by thinking they were still young and had a long time to put it behind them.

Of course, I was dead wrong.

What Michael and I didn't realize is that recovery is so much different for kids. Their fears, hopes and dreams are their very own, not ours. They, like Michael and me, have been through a lot, are survivors and have their own agenda.

Both Michael and I were a bit skeptical about the recommendation from Ann, my counselor from the Center (here she is again!; like Marley's ghost in *A Christmas Carol*, she pops up everywhere!), that Emily and Anna attend the Center's Children's Program. After all, we all seemed to be doing quite well since my return from Alina Lodge. I'd just celebrated my fifth year of sobriety, Michael was still attending group sessions, maturing more with every passing day, and we had more honesty in the household than most people could hope for in a lifetime.

But still, Emily and Anna's issues had not been specifically addressed. When we asked them if they'd like to attend the Children's Program at Betty Ford, they got excited and quickly said yes. Now they would have the opportunity to see where their mother's miracle had occurred, and learn more about the disease.

The program runs Thursday through Sunday. For the first two days the kids are on their own; parents don't attend until Saturday.

On Thursday night, Michael and I shamelessly pumped the girls for information, but they didn't share much. Emily said something, though, about "ghosts in the graveyard"; Michael and I looked at each other, thinking "What could *that* possibly have to do with recovery?"

Over the years, though, we'd learned to trust the process, so that's what we did. But it wasn't easy.

When Saturday came, the four of us got into the transportation van and headed to the center. In the Cork Pavilion we were ushered into a conference room with other parents, all of whom were subdued. The kids were excited as heck. Jerry Moe, the director of the Children's Program (about whom the girls wouldn't stop raving), explained what the children had been doing during the first two days and what was in store for us. When he referenced a "confrontation" between child and parent, we did a double-take. Just the word made me uneasy. But Jerry kept reassuring us that our children loved us very much.

When the hour of reckoning came, Michael and I were very nervous.

Ground rules were established. We parents were to sit facing our children, listening to what they had to say. We were not permitted to make any comments at any time. I flashed on the worst-case scenario—that a child of mine would rip us to shreds and publicly humiliate us because we had been such terrible parents.

Emily went first. She told us how afraid she'd been when I left for treatment. She said she was angry because I'd lied to her. But, she said, she was proud of me for getting help. She felt that sometimes Daddy was too hard on her, expected too much of her. She wished he wasn't away so much and could spend more time with her.

Anna, my little trouper, was hurt that I'd missed the family vacation while in treatment, and had lied to her. She was upset with Michael because he never told her I was drinking and that that's what caused me to act the way I did.

The feeling of safety and security that Jerry Moe had nurtured in and among the kids in that room, their direct honesty in speaking about their hurt and disappointments, floored Michael and me and all the parents.

Sunday is parents' day, and the same rules held. We got the chance to express to the girls how we appreciated what they had told us and to thank them for being so honest. Then we told them how much we loved them and responded to their requests not to lie and to spend more time with them. Tears flowed freely and abundantly.

At the closing ceremony, which was very moving, each young person received a medallion. You should have seen their eyes sparkle.

Now the family circle was really closed and, once again, the Betty Ford Center had become a sanctuary of healing for the whole family—not just the alcoholic and spouse but for the children as well.

•   •   •

Back at the Alumni Reunion, Jacqueline and Michael decided that their children had had enough for one evening and told them to say good-bye to Laurette and Harriet, who were sitting at their table. I saw the parents make their way to Jerry Moe and tell him they were taking the kids home.

They were really going home. Not just to that place where you eat and sleep and ride the merry-go-round called denial. But home, honest-to-goodness home.

Speaking of home, I think one of the two most important results of my own recovery are that my home has become a place where my sons and daughter really enjoy coming together again. Also, my husband and I are no longer separated by a third party, namely my addicted self. When I was drinking and using, Jerry knew that I'd drifted away from the family, but didn't know what to do about it. He was used to the political world, where tough situations could be resolved through a give-and-take process.

By approving of the intervention he signaled his willingness to become engaged in a journey that was completely unfamiliar to him. He did it both for my sake and that of the rest of the family. It was an entirely different and more difficult way of expressing his love for me. My husband used to be running all the time from place to place, solo. Since my recovery, we run from place to place together, giving talks and attending meetings.

When we were planning the Betty Ford Center, Leonard Firestone, Dr. Cruse and I thought that we ought to wait awhile before starting a formal Family Program. But John Schwarzlose was adamant that the Family Program begin on day one. He was right, and he prevailed.

The healing journey has to include the whole family. When a person is in the throes of addiction, you can't have a true family, because one person is missing all the time. You can't have true recovery unless the entire family participates in the recovery process. Family members have to know what the illness is all about, that they are not responsible for the alcoholic's behavior and that they need to stop enabling the alcoholic/addict.

Working at recovery is a lifelong process for both the recovering person and her/his family. After the family's week in Rancho Mirage is over, family members have to plug in to something like Al-Anon and the support it provides.

I had succumbed to the intellectual temptation of separating my problem with alcoholism from my relationship with my children, in particular my daughter, Susan. I tried to believe that my alcoholic behavior didn't impact her—or the other members of my family—at all. It was something that I was doing to myself. I was oblivious to the harm that it was causing the people who loved me the most.

After suffering many years from the hurt inflicted on them by an addict/alcoholic's behavior, many family members are offended when they're asked to attend the Family Program. "We've already given at the office" is often the attitude. "How much more suffering do you want us to put up with?"

＊ ＊ ＊

The stories of Claire, Paula, Beatrice and Jacqueline speak volumes about the misdirected journeys that relationships take when impacted by chemical dependency.

Claire

Since I'd heard that my daughters, Beth and Cindy, were coming to the Family Program, I'd been one anxious cat on a hot tin roof. The girls started the program Monday; my medallion ceremony was scheduled for two days later, Wednesday. My counselor, Ray, suggested I stay in the desert through the end of the week so we could go back home together.

The girls stayed at different motels, Cindy at the spartan Embassy Suites on Highway 111, Beth at the upscale Rancho Las Palmas on

Bob Hope Drive. Even though Beth had practically raised Cindy when she was a baby, they were no longer close. Beth resented all the attention my husband David had given to Cindy.

We weren't allowed to formally visit during the Family Program, although we'd bump into each other in the dining hall. During one of those brief—almost clandestine—conversations, my daughters asked me with whom I was going to stay when I finished treatment on Wednesday.

I viewed this as my first sanity and sobriety test. I copped out and quickly said, "I'm still in treatment. You girls will have to decide that."

Then I ran off to my counselor, Ray, in a panic and asked him what I should do, forgetting everything I'd learned about "turning it over." I wanted him to solve my problem for me.

As it turned out, I stayed in Beth's hotel suite Wednesday through Saturday. When the girls had finished for the day, the three of us would stay up most of the night, talking about what we'd learned, comparing notes about other families, deciding that as difficult as things had been we weren't nearly as bad off as some of those other families.

As we talked and our feelings emerged, we began to understand what had been going on, how the disease affected the whole family, and how it served us no purpose to keep quiet and keep secrets. I told them how much I loved them and how grateful I was that each one had confronted me with love and tenderness.

My month in treatment and what they learned in that wonderful Family Program eventually saved our whole family.

Our healing journey, however, had just begun.

Back in Kansas City, Cindy was living nearby. She'd come to the house and she would have a beer with my companion and house-keeper. Occasionally she would come to an open AA meeting with me.

One night I asked Cindy if she'd like to come to a meeting at which I was scheduled to present my story. "But, Mom," she said, "it's not an open meeting." I said it would be okay this one time. "After all, you're my daughter." She agreed.

After the meeting I introduced Cindy to some of my friends. One of them asked her point-blank, "Are you in the program too?" Cindy glanced at me, turned to the woman and said, simply, "Yes."

You could have knocked me over with a feather. Cindy looked at me and after a moment said, "Mom, I'm two months old." She said when she came home from the Family Program two months earlier she couldn't stop thinking about what she'd learned. She concluded that she also had a problem with alcohol, and began going to meetings for beginners.

Cindy's candor caused the tears to burst forth and marked the moment when the real recovery dialogue began. I'd been sober for about a year, and I was so pleased and proud when she asked me to go to meetings with her. We were able to talk like we'd never talked before, about all kinds of things, including my sadness about the lost years with her father.

Five or so years into sobriety I remember saying to her that I felt I'd never really made amends with her. She said, "Mom, every day you're sober you're making amends with me."

I have every reason to believe that alcoholism is passed on genetically from one generation to the next. Beth was also a victim of the illness, but her situation incubated a little longer than Cindy's. She'd been left out of David's will and she felt that hurt deeply. I tried to make up for it in every way I could.

A few years after I'd completed treatment, Beth and her husband moved nearby to start a little business. I soon discovered that they were both heavily into drugs and that her husband turned ugly when he was using.

I managed to get them both into treatment, but recovery didn't last very long for either of them. They had been drinking and using for such a long time that when they came up for air after treatment they hardly knew each another. Apparently they didn't like the real selves they saw in the two-way mirror; they liked their addicted selves better. Soon after treatment, they returned to the cocoon of their chemicals.

Then a couple of years later, Beth called and told me she couldn't take it anymore. I brought her to my home, and she slept for three days. She stayed with me for two years until she went off on her own. She's been sober ever since.

◆　◆　◆

In the early years of the Betty Ford Center, patients interacted with members of other families, but never with their own. Gradually, however, the staff thought it would be more beneficial if the patient did interact with members of her/his own family, under the careful direction of professional staff.

Paula was involved in a family conference that was rich and rewarding. Her recollection of what happened reveals that each family conference has interesting twists and turns.

Paula

During my third week in treatment, the first time 'round, one of the counselors gave a lecture on the dynamics within a family when one or more of its members are alcoholic or addicted to some other drug. I was able to "cast" all the characters in the family drama. My husband was "the enabler." Nancy was "the heroine" and Vicky was "the lost child." I was also able to see the role my family played in the tragedy brought about by my destructive downward spiral.

What made the family conference particularly effective for me were the Sunday visits with Robert and Vicky before we met with Claudia, my counselor. I'd come a long way since I'd talked with Robert the first week and begged him to take me home.

He and Vicky came to visit the second Sunday I was at the center. I couldn't believe how my heart was pounding waiting for the call from Firestone that they were here. I rushed over to greet them with tears and laughter. They were probably a little embarrassed when I hugged them so tightly and for so long. When I managed to compose myself, I brought them over to West Hall, introduced them to my sisters, pointed out the refrigerator that was always full of snacks and proudly showed them the "swamp" and my bed in the corner. We went outside, walked the perimeter of the lake, fed some of the ducks, and then sat on one of the benches and talked—about everything.

Each time they visited, I shared a little nugget of wisdom that I had learned during the previous week. I'm sure I sounded a little condescending and euphoric that first Sunday as I chatted on and on about what I had learned and how important it was for all of us to express our feelings to one another. I told them I knew I could make it with their support.

The following Sunday was another great day. I opened up more and told Robert and Vicky about the $180 that I had secretly hoarded every two weeks to send to the pharmacist for 500 Tylenol #4 codeine pills. They didn't seem surprised. Vicky already knew about the little white box that came in the mail; Robert suspected the link with the pharmacist when he couldn't balance the household books. We decided that by saving all the money that I regularly spent on drugs and physical therapy, we would buy a condo in Cathedral City to be near the Betty Ford Center.

For the first time, we were dealing with the anger and the hurt that we had suppressed over the years. I was horrified when Vicky told me of a time when I had passed out on her. I had no memory of it. She saw that I was terribly upset and ashamed and as she hugged me she said, "Mom, that's in the past. Forget it." I saw my quiet little daughter starting to reveal her own feelings as though we were really talking to each other for the first time in our adult lives.

One Sunday I said, "I never want to go back to all that pain and misery. I don't think I could take it again." Vicky looked at me and said, "I couldn't either, Mom. It was hard for us, too." I managed to conceal my hurt. I was glad that she was comfortable expressing what she felt. My guilt had lessened somewhat during the weeks that I was in treatment, and I didn't automatically cry at the first hint of hurt feelings.

The family conference was scheduled for Friday afternoon, the day that Robert and Vicky finished the Family Program. I had told them the previous Sunday to say whatever needed to come out. Despite the bravado, I was scared and knew that I'd probably cry. They, along with Nancy, were the people I truly loved most in my life. It hurt me deeply to know how much I had hurt them by my drinking and using.

Every night when Vicky and Robert got back to the motel during the Family Program, they discussed what they'd learned that day, and worked on their assignments. It was a special time they had together. One of Vicky's assignments was to write down ten reasons why she was angry and resentful toward me.

When the time for the conference arrived, we were all nervous and very tense. Claudia, the counselor, explained the expectations: We were to be open and honest with each other, saying exactly what we felt; there was to be no blaming; we were to listen without interruption.

Claudia suggested Vicky begin with her "ten reasons" assignment.

I thought that I saw Vicky flinch a little, and I could see that it pained her to recite what she'd written out. But, little trouper that she is, she started the session. Out came the ten reasons, beginning with,

"(1) Mom, I resent you because of your drinking, (2) Mom, I resent you because of your pills, (3) Mom, I resent you because you were drunk, (4) Mom, I resent you and was crushed because you had our dog put down when you were drunk . . ."

I started to interrupt and explain that I wasn't drunk when I had Niko, our beloved dog, put down, but Claudia gently reminded me that I had to wait until Vicky finished. I don't remember the rest of Vicky's resentments.

The tears started pouring down my cheeks and I remember thinking how much of a grind it must have been for Vicky to come home from school day after day wondering who was going to come into the kitchen to greet her, the sober mom she loved or the shadow that she hated. I knew that it would take a long time for me to completely regain her trust, but I was determined to make it work. I was crying, Vicky was crying and shaking. I reached over to put my hand on hers to comfort her but Claudia gently removed it and reminded me that each person had to be allowed to experience and process their hurt on their own.

When Vicky finished, Claudia let us be silent for a long time. Then she asked Vicky if she had anything else to say. My daughter looked at me and said, "I love you, Mom."

Then Claudia asked me if I wanted to say anything to Vicky. I was still crying and Claudia told me to take deep breaths. Finally I managed to explain to Vicky that I hadn't been drunk when I took Niko to the vet. It was when I got home—still suffering from the trauma of holding him and then watching him being put down—and went next door to give Niko's little food and water dishes to the neighbor that I began to drink to wash away my misery. By the time Vicky came home, I was good and drunk. She had reason to be resentful.

When the session concluded, Claudia allowed us to hug each other. Soon thereafter, Vicky was excused from the conference.

Then it was Robert's turn. My resentment toward Robert had been building all week, nourished by a suspicion that he'd been having an affair. The seeds of suspicion were planted during one of the lectures. The topic was the Ninth Step of AA: "Make direct amends to such people (we had harmed) wherever possible, except when to do so would injure them or others." As an example, the speaker cited someone who was having an affair. For some reason I looked over at Robert and at that exact moment I saw his chin quivering. He had taken off his glasses and was wiping his eyes with a handkerchief. I said to myself, "Oh my God, he's been having an affair." I was terribly distraught.

Immediately after the lecture I went to Claudia and told her about my suspicions. I said that I had to bring it up in the family conference; I couldn't live with this.

When we were alone Claudia asked me to begin. I turned to Robert and told him that I'd seen his reaction when the speaker mentioned extramarital affairs. He was stunned and looked at me for a while before he said, "I was acting that way because I thought *you* were having an affair." It was my turn to be shocked. I said, "Are you out of your mind? I have *never* had an affair." We both started to cry and laugh at the same time.

To steal the title of a Graham Greene novel, that was "the end of the affair"!

It was a great relief to Robert to learn that he hadn't been going crazy, that there was a reason why my actions were so wacko—*I was sick!* The five hundred pills reminded him of the five hundred ways he tried to rationalize to himself and to others what was going on as I became more and more erratic. As he spoke I knew he'd be supportive of my recovery and would no longer be an enabler. I knew that he'd administer "tough love" when I needed it. He learned how to do that in the Family Program.

When the conference was over, we all hugged for a long time. I said I was one lucky lady and that the happiest days of our lives were still to come.

The next time I saw Claudia, I thanked her for conducting the conference in such a masterful way. I said, "I wish I could express the thanks and love I feel in my heart for you and all that you've done for us. You saved both my life and my family."

One of the blessings I received during the two extra weeks that Dr. West imposed on me was having the opportunity of participating in the Family Program while I was still a patient. I was able to sit and listen to the family's side of things. It shed light on how Robert, Nancy and Vicky must have felt about my behavior. I knew that our lives had to be healthier and more fulfilling. There were times when I first got home when we were all walking on eggshells. I thanked God for my AA group and my sponsor, which helped me keep me on track.

◆   ◆   ◆

I can really identify with Paula, Jacqueline and Claire, whose daughters were hurt by their mothers' drinking. My daughter, Susan, was the one who suffered most from my illness. As a young woman, she didn't know what was wrong with me and tried in every way to please me and to make things right. When I started to get well and become actively involved in the family again, Susan was at first resentful, which is typical for the family of an alcoholic. Susan had been at my side through my breast cancer and at other difficult times of my life. For all the years I was incapacitated, "out of it," she had been my caretaker. Now here I was on the path of recovery, receiving an enormous amount of attention; she was relegated to the role of daughter who had to listen to her mother. It took a while to adjust.

◆   ◆   ◆

The same could be said of the relationship between Beatrice and her daughter, Audrey. Audrey began the Family Program the day Beatrice was discharged, so she missed the

family conference just as Claire had. Like Claire and her daughters, Beatrice and
Audrey did their own processing in the evenings after Audrey had spent the day at the
center, listening to the experiences of other families.

Beatrice

It's not easy to describe how excruciatingly difficult it was being away
from my daughter when I was at the center. When I flew to Rancho
Mirage, I left Audrey in the care of one of the neighbors. I didn't
want my daughter to get involved in my problem. But early on during treatment my counselor urged me to have Audrey attend the
Family Program. Much to my surprise, she was overjoyed at the
prospect of coming to the Betty Ford Center to be with me.

Audrey arrived on Saturday to begin the Family Program on
Monday, Labor Day, the day of my discharge. I was worried about
her staying at Rancho Las Palmas by herself for two days—after all,
she was only twelve. But the truth is, while I was distracted by my affair with alcohol, she'd grown up into a mature young lady.

During those post-discharge days when I stayed on in the desert
while Audrey was attending the Family Program, I spent a lot of time
wandering around, wondering how Audrey was doing and flashing
back on my life.

What I *didn't* do was pay any attention to my own program! Here
I'd been given all the tools necessary for a successful recovery, and I
wasn't using them. I didn't go to a single meeting that whole week. I
made up for it, though, when I got back to Chicago. My Betty Ford
alumni contact went with me every day to a meeting.

At night, Audrey and I would talk about the bad old times. I listened
to her and was amazed at how concerned about, and protective of, me
she'd been. I had a pediatrician friend across the street whose place had

become a second home for Audrey. She'd go there when I wasn't home, or when I was home in bed, claiming to be sick, but in reality too drunk to function. She'd always call to ask, "Are you okay, Mom?"

I couldn't hold back the tears when she reminded me of the time there was no fruit juice in the house. She saw me pouring some wine for myself and said, "Here we don't have money for juice, but you've got money for that stuff." It hurt especially because I remembered the incident all too vividly. So often she ended up in her room eating alone and watching television, while I'd be in my bedroom watching TV, but drinking rather than eating.

I was there, but I wasn't really *there*.

The Family Program was our lifesaver. Audrey learned about the illness, she learned that she wasn't responsible for my behavior, and that she shouldn't feel guilty about it. Probably the most important thing she learned was that she couldn't change me. Still, to this day, she tells me when she thinks I should go to a meeting—and I tell her when I think she needs to go to Al-Anon. We have a new life together.

•   •   •

For Jacqueline and Michael, the "family program" dynamic evolved a little differently. The last stage of it occurred at Alena Lodge.

Jacqueline

Michael had gone through the Family Program while I was at the Betty Ford Center. He learned that he didn't cause me to drink and couldn't force me stop. But for a long time he was unable to grasp the fact that there was nothing he could do to keep me sober.

I don't know what expectations Michael had when I returned from my first round of treatment, but they were never realized. He had never lived with the Jacqueline who did not drink.

When I went to Alena Lodge, Michael adamantly refused to attend their Family Program. He told me that *this is about you.*

And then one Sunday in October when I was lounging in my room, a staff member knocked on the door, told me to get dressed and come to the dining hall. Who was waiting for me there but my husband! Michael got up, came to me and held me for a long, long time. He'd agreed to come, but only for two and a half days. After seven months of separation, I was so happy to see him I would have been content with two and a half hours!

We began the family conference that night. Both of us recognized the need to reestablish the trust necessary for our relationship to survive and grow. We spoke of "regaining" the trust, but I wondered how much trust had really been there from the beginning, given my drinking.

The issue that weighed most heavily on him was my dishonesty. While intellectually he could understand that it was the disease that had caused me to tell all those lies, emotionally the hurt was deep. Other issues included my chronic people-pleasing and his perceived need to "fix" me. Because he couldn't help me maintain my sobriety, he considered himself a failure.

More in sorrow than in anger. There were no shouting matches or fireworks during our time together at the Lodge, just a lot of sadness and heaviness. He was really hurt when I talked about the awful way I'd treated the girls. He was oblivious to my meanness, and it pained him deeply.

I still get cold inside when I remember screaming at them and thinking they wouldn't remember any of this when they grew older. Oh, how drink deludes us and keeps us unaware of consequences!

Michael and I had been married for fifteen years, yet we really didn't know each other, since I'd been drinking all that time. I'll never forget Michael saying during his short stay at the Lodge that I'd become a much softer person.

The contrast between the homecoming after my first treatment experience and after my second is stark, like night and day. When I left Betty Ford the day before Christmas, I was so truculent and haughty. I was the conquering heroine, expecting everyone to curtsy to me. I was irritated when Michael invited those Christmas carolers in for hot chocolate. For heaven's sake—hot chocolate for them and no drinks for me! What's going on here! Doesn't he know who I am and what I've been through? The family is supposed to revolve around *me.*

The second homecoming was quite a different matter. What helped immensely was the caveat written into my aftercare plan that when I returned I was to fit into Michael's and the girls' schedules. They were not to change their daily routine and habits. Just as I had to change to deal with my alcoholism, so I had to change to fit into the family dynamic and not force the dynamic to fit my routine.

When we went to bed that first night home we talked (which we didn't do the first time around), and he told me what the morning routine would be for the girls. He told me what time he'd be home from work. I asked him what time he'd like to have dinner and what he'd like to eat. We've continued to eat at the same time ever since. I cook what everybody wants, not what I somehow manage to throw together in an alcoholic haze. We made the decision that I wouldn't go back to work, so I'd be at home when the girls come back from school.

I had finally come home.

. . .

In my book, A Glad Awakening, *I dedicate a whole chapter to the healing of the family and how wellness spreads from one family member to another. My son Mike* remembers a talk I gave at Wake Forest University where he was a member of the faculty. He says my presentation represented for him the "complete circle of healing" for our family. He recalled how sick I'd been, and here I was providing a message of hope for others who were struggling with the same disease.

I cannot match the words he used in describing the experience: "What she was doing was in a very personal way articulating how the healing of a person involves the body, the mind and the spirit. Hers was a message of 'holistic healing.' She related some of her own pilgrimage, her own struggles, how she had hit bottom, been brought back again. And that it was not only a medical or physical transformation as she got off the drugs and felt better; it was also an emotional and spiritual experience. She was able to love herself again, able to love her family again, able to experience, in a spiritual way, God's love for her and His acceptance."

I started this chapter with the metaphor of coming home; I will end with it as well. The phrase "coming home" is particularly poignant in depicting the return of the recovering woman to the household and family she had left behind. In treatment we are told to leave our shadow selves behind so our real selves can once again return to the family circle. However, we are reminded that our addictive selves will always be lurking in the dark alleys of our subconscious, never so dangerous as when we forget about their presence and their ability to resurface.

Returning home, the recovering woman becomes the object of much scrutiny, sometimes suspicion. At first there is an awkwardness and artificiality about the family dynamic, in everybody's behavior toward one another. Uncomfortable is probably the best word to describe what everybody feels at first. Feelings are mixed, offers of help are suspect, gestures of solicitude misconstrued. The transition to the point where the whole family is in recovery is gradual.

11

Chanting Odes to Recovery

I t happens every year. The Alumni Reunion weekend comes to an end so very quickly. Saturday night's joyous banquet yields to Sunday's farewell brunch—with nary a hangover in sight! (One of the many blessings of recovery!)

It was time for everybody to leave their home away from home. There are always groans and moans that the weekend is too short and the opportunities to mingle too few. I identify with the participants' joy at seeing familiar faces and forging new sober friendships; I also am sensitive to the sadness we feel about the absence of those we knew in treatment who have not returned.

But as the Betty Ford Center alumni prepare to leave Sunday, nothing can dampen the feelings of hope and confidence in their recovery that the weekend instills and reinforces.

Once again this Sunday morning we have been blessed with a beautiful day, plenty of sunshine and a clear blue sky. The cooks outdid themselves in preparing the traditional brunch that is served in the dining hall between nine-thirty and eleven-thirty. Tables have also been set up on the lawn outside so we can enjoy the view of the San Jacinto Mountains that seem so close you could almost reach out and touch them. I do my best to visit as many tables as possible to say good-bye and thank everyone for their support and participation in our caring community.

The crowd cheered as each door prize was announced; they laughed mightily when the ticket for the grand prize belonged to Joan Connor, the head of Alumni Relations. It's a faded red, white and blue vest, partly made out of rabbit, which is awarded each year on the condition that the winner return it the following year. Some party pooper, in a stage whisper loud enough for everyone to hear, said this morning that it looked "ratty." This brought good-natured groans from the audience.

The winner is actually relieved to get rid of it after a year! In accepting the prize, Joan said the garment would be hanging (she probably meant hiding) behind the door in her office, available for viewing by those who dare to dream that they might be next year's winner!

There's always a wonderful spirit of camaraderie and fellowship. As I made my way among the tables greeting alumni, I noticed that Beatrice, Claire and Paula, along with her husband, Robert, were together at one table. Robert is a wonderful man and never stops referring to himself as "grateful Rob" for the gift of his wife's sobriety. Even in public he calls her his "dream girl." She refers to him as "the love of my life."

At the next table I greeted Harriet and her husband, Laurette and her partner, and Jacqueline and Michael. They were sitting with Joan, the alumni director. They were passing around the "rabbit vest" and pulling Joan's leg by expressing their disappointment at not having won the door prize.

Our six women have a combined total of seventy-five years of recovery. They carry the message to others of "what it's like now" to be sober. They could all testify to the truth of the Big Book's injunction: "No matter how far down the scale we have gone, we will see how our experience can benefit others."

♦   ♦   ♦

Claire asked Paula if she'd had any contact with her mother since her last treatment experience. All were curious to know what had happened with that extremely difficult relationship.

Paula

A year ago I received an envelope in the mail from my mother. There was no personal message inside. Instead, there was an excerpt from a church bulletin, about forgiveness. The story told of a woman who was so touched by a sermon on forgiveness that after the service she asked her husband to drive her to the home of her father with whom she had not spoken for years. She harbored a great deal of anger and resentment toward him for the way he had treated her in the past. She wanted to tell him that she forgave him for everything he had done.

When the father opened the door, he looked at his daughter. Before she could speak, he slammed the door in her face. That would have been enough for most people, but she remained resolute.

She rang the doorbell again. When he appeared a second time, instead of saying the words that she rehearsed, "Father, I forgive you for all your past injuries to me," she simply extended her arms and said, "Father, I love you."

I was touched both by the story and the fact that my mother had decided to share it with me. We had not spoken since my sister Judy's wedding, almost ten years earlier.

I took the story and the gesture to mean that perhaps, after all these years, she was hoping I could find it in my heart to forgive her.

I had a lot of feelings about the whole thing, one of which was terror at the thought of seeing my mother face-to-face. At the same time, I wanted to acknowledge her gesture, even though every olive branch I'd offered in the past had been rejected. I talked with my sponsor about it and decided to send Mom some flowers. I told the florist I didn't want to send something that would die in a few days or a week, I wanted something that would last, a real plant. I enclosed a card that read, "Dear Mom, thanks for the article. I love you so much. God bless you."

A week and a half later I received a card from my mother, thanking me for the plant, adding that she hoped she could keep it alive even though she'd never had a green thumb. She also wrote, "Judy gave me some pictures of you, which I showed to my friends, who said you were very good-looking. I pray for you each night. Lovingly, Mom."

She was eighty-three years old. This was the first time she'd ever used the word *love* in regard to me. Nothing pejorative like *ugly, troublemaker* or *fat*. She couldn't bring *herself* to say I was "good-looking," only that her friends had described me that way.

I decided to send her a Christmas card. I wrote in it that she was in my heart, thoughts and prayers every day. I asked God to bless her and signed the card, "I love you, Paula." She sent a card back, again signing it "Lovingly, Mom."

We've come a long way, and if that's as far as the healing process can go, it's more than enough for me after all these years.

• • •

Paula's story touched all of us. Nobody said anything for a few minutes.

Paula and I had talked a number of times about the role pain medications played in our previous lives. We also talked about how tough it was at the beginning to refer to ourselves as alcoholics. I told Paula how Dr. Pursch, the director of the Long Beach Center, insisted I write a press release while I was still there to the effect that I was an alcoholic. I was ashamed and tried to hide behind my husband's reputation, saying that it wouldn't look good for him. When Dr. Pursch asked the president, he said it wouldn't bother him. I don't know who I was madder at—Dr. Pursch or my husband! But I did it and now I am grateful that I did.

Paula credited the Betty Ford Center with saving her life twice and helping her to deal with the chronic pain that continues to accompany her on her healing journey. It may not seem to most people that pain and healing can walk together on the same journey, but in her case they do. When light mingles with darkness, it can create a beautiful sunrise. People with chronic pain can find strength from her story.

During her second treatment stay Paula had great hopes that Dr. Schultz, the medical director who succeeded Dr. West, would be able to provide some non-mood-altering medications to ease her pain. She was crushed, almost in tears, when he sat down with her after consulting other physicians. He said there really were no non-mood-altering meds that they could recommend to relieve the pain. But he said they'd draw up an alternative plan that would deal not only with the physical pain, but holistically with her body, mind and spirit. Both Paula and I had been looking for something magical, similar to our medication pills, but really there was no magic. The magic lay in a change of lifestyle.

Paula had to learn to take care of her physical needs on a daily basis: walking on a treadmill, exercising in her pool, stretching and attending yoga classes regularly.

There were times during the dark days when she thought she would never walk again. Now, as her team score on Friday indicated, she's rather good at playing golf, although she does have to pace herself. She has a set of relaxation tapes, which help to calm her whole body. And she is no longer embarrassed to take her little pillow everywhere so that when she sits she can relieve the pressure on her coccyx.

Just as important is the relief from her emotional pain. As her recovery continued she discovered that dealing with her trapped anger and resentments and then releasing them was a sure guarantee of reduced physical pain. Paying attention to the Twelve Steps, especially the last three—a daily inventory, prayer and meditation, and helping others—makes all of us feel alive and gives Paula a special sense of "wholeness."

◆   ◆   ◆

Jacqueline was the first to speak after hearing Paula tell the story about forgiveness and the new, tentative relationship she had with her mother. As she was listening to Paula, Jacqueline remembered a little incident that put the landscape of her recovery into sharper focus. It happened about a month before the reunion, and has the markings of a "spiritual awakening," an eye-opener that reveals details of the landscape that had previously escaped her notice.

As is the case whenever Jacqueline speaks, the sparkle in her hazel eyes captured our attention immediately.

Jacqueline

I tried to adhere faithfully to the instructions I'd been given when I left Alina Lodge. I was not to change the family's routine when I returned home. My aftercare plan said that I was to accommodate myself to *their* schedule. I pledged allegiance to that, as well as to attending my daily AA meetings. Since December 1994 I had been going to meetings seven days a week, usually twice a day. I especially loved the 6 A.M. meeting.

Then one day I had a rude—and probably spiritual—awakening.

While I was at the early morning meeting, our baby-sitter, Julia, would help get the girls up and ready for the day. When I returned I'd drive Emily to school, drive back home and then walk Anna to her school.

When Julia was days away from giving birth to her own child, she was unable to work for us any longer. I continued to rise at four-thirty to get ready for the six o'clock meeting. Michael would get the girls up; they were responsible for getting washed, dressed and fixing their own breakfast. I'd then waltz in and start barking out orders to wash the dishes, brush your teeth, get your school packs ready.

Sometimes the girls would start crying when I pushed them too hard. They complained that they had to do everything in the morning. I ignored their complaints. Then I got hit with the flu, so badly that I was unable to go to my morning meeting. When I got out of bed, I'd get them up, make their lunches, then their breakfast, clean the kitchen and help them pack. My presence allowed the girls a more leisurely pace.

They said they were so happy that I was there to help them get ready. That made me think. I sat down in the kitchen with a cup of coffee and took an inventory of what I had been doing the past five and half years since I returned from Alina Lodge. Instead of fitting into their schedule, I was manipulating them into mine. That morning AA meeting had become so important to me that I forgot that the girls were still children and needed their mother in the mornings.

The only thing sacred about that six o'clock meeting was that come hell or high water the others would be able to count on me to be in my chair when the meeting opened. Neither my husband nor the girls had complained, because they didn't want to threaten my sobriety by suggesting that a meeting at another time would do the trick.

I was using my recovery to change the family schedule, something that I had been warned against when I left the Lodge.

It was an eye-opener for me, one of those spiritual awakenings that come so unexpectedly. Had I not gotten sick, I would have continued in my self-centered way for I don't know how long. It also made me wonder whether I was being manipulative in other areas of my recovery.

Meetings are essential to the recovery process, but there is nothing sacrosanct about the time of the meeting, especially if it interferes with my duties as a mother. It was a good lesson for me.

The truth is, I had been hyperactive since leaving the Lodge. Some days I didn't have two minutes to myself. For five and a half years I'd been going to bed between eleven and twelve at night and getting up at four-thirty in the morning. I'd been functioning on about five hours sleep a night. The body and mind can do that for just so long. Lack of sleep is probably the reason I got so sick with the flu.

I remember something Mrs. Delaney, who ran Alina Lodge, used to tell us week after week in her lecture: It takes two years to get into sobriety, another two years to get our brains out of hock, and three years after that to get our brains unscrambled.

It finally dawned on me that in addition to renewing my pledge to accommodate myself to the family schedule, I should also start taking care of myself.

· · ·

Everyone at the table nodded in agreement with Jacqueline's insights. Sobriety is the most precious gift we have. It has to be a priority in our lives. An important tool in maintaining that sobriety is attendance at meetings, but the time of the meeting isn't set in stone. As I sat there listening to the comments of the others about priorities, I remembered a story about forgiveness—similar to Paula's—that Jacqueline told me one day when she was volunteering in our Alumni Office.

· · ·

In the fall of 1999 I was taking Anna to her new school. After dropping her off and walking back to my car, I recognized the police officer who'd arrested me for drunken driving five years earlier. He'd just left his child at the school and was about to open his car door. Something moved me to walk over to him in the parking lot, excuse myself and say, "I'm sure you don't remember me, but you arrested me five years ago for drunk driving."

The officer was quiet and alert, not quite knowing what to expect. I managed a smile and said, "I just want to thank you and let you know that after that I went into treatment and turned my life around."

I could see he was both relieved and moved by what I told him. He relaxed and said, "It's not often I'm complimented for arresting people. I really am very happy for you. I have personal experience with alcoholism. My brother is one of those people who just can't seem to take that first step to get help for himself."

It was tough to respond to that. There are *so many people* out there who aren't ready to take that first step, and you really can't force them to do it.

· · ·

As Jacqueline finished her story, I saw Laurette look at her with a great deal of affection. Jacqueline had been one of the few straights who could make her feel comfort-

able about being a lesbian. Jacqueline used to point out that in the Fellowship there's no distinction between straights, gays and lesbians. We all have the same Higher Power and the same standing before Her.

Laurette is usually the last to speak up—if she says anything at all! I hadn't seen much of Laurette since she stopped working for us and left our family, but through the grapevine I knew she was doing well. Listening to Paula talk about her mother, Laurette decided to share recent experiences with her family.

Laurette

"You can't stay sober today on yesterday's sobriety." An old chestnut, but a true one.

It was another gift of my sobriety that after leaving the Fords, I was able to reconnect with my family. Even though our relationships are far from perfect, I see things differently now.

I can tell my mother that I love her and respect her for doing the best she could. I met my father at my brother's wedding and I shook his hand. At the time, he made a lot of promises, but I have not heard from him since the wedding. His indifference hurts, but I now have a program that helps me deal with that pain without drugs and alcohol. My grandfather is very old, and I try to visit him as much as I can.

I was asked to be the godparent at my niece's baptism. I felt awkward because I hadn't set foot in a Catholic church in a long time. She's a beautiful child. I love her dearly and will be there for her always. I have great fear about her growing up in our family, but I know as long as I stay sober, I can be an example for her.

After the baptism was over, my aunt ran some old family movies on a VCR. One of the first scenes was my grandmother at my own baptism.

Not to be outdone, my mom shared a bunch of photographs. I watched the movies and looked at the pictures with mixed feelings—

yes, I loved my grandmother so deeply, but I also felt anger. I thought, "Why the fuck do I want to sit here and look at this stuff and be depressed about 'the good old days.'"

Because you know what? They weren't good days. They were nightmare days. I still wonder whether preserving memories of the past with home movies and photos is a good idea.

Hopefully, someday I'll be able to look at the past in a different way and be happy and smile about it.

To this very day, I feel the loss of my grandmother deeply. I still get angry that she's not here for me, to care for me, to protect me. My search is filled with anguish: "Who *is* there for me?"

I still haven't brought closure to the grief I feel about her loss. Maybe I never will.

◆ ◆ ◆

I feel special affection for Laurette. She has large almond-shaped eyes and, when she allows it, a wonderful smile that lights up the room. But she doesn't smile very often; she's afraid it will leave her vulnerable. Jacqueline asked her what she's been doing since she left as our chef.

◆ ◆ ◆

When I left the Fords, I decided to pursue my interest in holistic health. I find that people are becoming more conscious of what they put into their bodies. I'm managing a vegetarian restaurant. I'm into organic food and have a private campaign going against pesticides. I want to start a business that will allow me to use my own experience to promote my beliefs about healthy eating.

There's a certain urgency about this for me now. This past month I've been diagnosed with hepatitis C. I'm certain I got it thanks to needle use. If it's not treated immediately, it could kill me.

I've become very passionate about telling people to be careful about what they are eating and doing to themselves. My doctor has urged me to try certain drugs, but I told him no. I've chosen an alternative way—better food, drink and exercise. I've started keeping a journal of my eating habits, my daily exercise routine and other things that I am doing to improve my health and measure my progress.

I'm neither a revolutionary nor a crusader. My method comes from the AA program, which I have internalized and extended to all areas of my life. It's one step—and one day—at a time. It's progress, not perfection—a life lesson that I learned not in the streets or in church, but in the fellowship of Alcoholics Anonymous.

◆   ◆   ◆

Laurette looked at all the recovering women around the table who had helped and supported her. They loved her because she was so honest and so straightforward. She had a special bond with them because they all accepted her sexuality and made her and her partner feel welcome.

For a long time, Laurette was ashamed to discuss the fact that she's a lesbian. Her mother had told her never to talk about it and never to use the l word. At the Betty Ford Center, one of the chaplains was a lesbian, and she offered to talk to Laurette about "the issue." But Laurette wasn't ready to do so.

The breakthrough occurred in one of Ann's aftercare groups. Half the group was composed of lesbians, so Laurette felt comfortable being open and "out" in that sympathetic environment.

As her sobriety grew stronger over the years, so did her self-confidence and self-esteem. She was able to work on her issues. One of the great gifts she received as a sober person was the promise to "comprehend the word serenity and to know peace." Her sexuality is no longer a shameful thing. She often tells others that she couldn't have kept it a secret and remained sober at the same time.

Secrets are a virus that attacks our soul's respiratory system and prevents us from breathing the sober air that keeps us alive and healthy. Laurette eventually fell in love with a wonderful woman and had the courage to introduce her as her companion to her mother, brother, grandfather and friends.

Laurette and her partner had some tough times finding their way together. As

Laurette says, "We were both very stubborn and fixed in our ways. But we discovered that we had choices, and found solutions to the difficulties we encountered."

When they had their commitment ceremony, Laurette was nervous that nobody would come. Fat chance! Seventy friends came to celebrate with them and to demonstrate their love.

Laurette used to hate it when some of her friends (including me!) would tell her, "You have such a beautiful smile. Why don't you turn it on more often?" Now, she says, she has plenty to smile about every day.

◆   ◆   ◆

Claire was the next person to speak up. She remarked dryly that she thought that when people got older they were supposed to slow down a bit. But that's not the case, she said, when you're associated with the Betty Ford Center. As the years pass, she gets more and more involved in her volunteer work at the Center. Just this weekend, she'd spoken to the patients Friday afternoon and then again at the banquet Saturday night, after receiving the Volunteer of the Year Award.

Claire has the reputation at the Center of being the "go-to" person for "the tough nuts to crack." Those tough nuts are the patients who, shortly after they arrive, decide this isn't the place for them, or that they don't really have a problem. Claire's well known at the Center and throughout the Coachella Valley for her dedication to recovery and for helping those in need.

Claire

Thanks to treatment, I was reborn into another world. My senses were alert, my heart was strong and my spirit was alive. That first year I was very tight with AA. In fact I was so busy with it that I didn't allow myself to do anything else. My husband couldn't stand it, and eventually walked. The most important thing for me was the healing that continued with my daughters.

When I finished treatment I rented a condo for the month of

February so that I could be here to receive my ninety-day chip. The next year, I rented it for two months, the following year for three months, and then I sold my condo in Kansas City and moved to the desert full-time. I've been here ever since.

When I was in treatment, my counselor, Ray, and I were talking about meditation. I said I found it difficult. He told me to look at the mountains, which he described as "God's houses." I've never forgotten that, and when I look at the mountains my Heavenly Father and I carry on quite a conversation.

I'm not loyal to a particular church, really. I loved singing with my family in the Methodist church of my youth, but out here in the desert I've taken a very ecumenical approach and frequent any one of three or four churches in the area.

What has really defined the past fifteen years for me is the Twelfth Step and the many opportunities to pass on what I've received and the rewards that come from doing just that.

There wasn't time to tell the story at the banquet last night, but a year ago I received a call from the Admissions Office. Malcolm said, simply, "Claire, we've got trouble." I said, "What is it this time, Malcolm?" He said an older woman had just shown up but they wouldn't have a bed for her until the next day. She wasn't willing to stay at the perfectly decent (but bare bones) Holiday Inn Express on Highway 111 where participants in the Family Program stay.

What Malcolm really needed was someone to baby-sit her for the evening. I told him I'd be over shortly, but couldn't resist getting a dig in. "How is it that even with that expensive computer system, you still overbook?" He laughed. He knew that I knew that it's the hardest thing in the world to maintain a steady flow of admits and departures.

By the time I got over to the Center, it was late afternoon. The woman in question was not a happy camper. She said her son had made the arrangements, and now everything was mucked up.

I said, "Let's not worry about that. Tell you what, you're coming with me, and we're going to have a dinner party. You're going to be the guest of honor."

I'd already called one of my "babies," a younger woman I'd sponsored who was also a registered nurse. She said she'd join us for dinner and that if the woman wanted a drink, we should give it to her. I said darn right, I didn't want her to get the jitters or anything worse.

Sure enough, our lady had a drink, but she didn't eat too much, which I could understand. Then we came back to the Center because I thought it would be good for her to see the Friday-night chip ceremony, where alumni receive their chips to signify so many days, months, years in recovery.

After that we took her to a coffee spot where the AA regulars meet, then to the Holiday Inn Express. She was pretty shaky. I had to sign in for her. As my friend and I were preparing to leave, the woman begged us to stay. I told my friend to go home, where her husband and kids were waiting. Only my cat was waiting for me.

But God bless her, my friend stayed. Finally, about 1:30 A.M., we were able to leave the woman with the promise we'd come back at 7 A.M. to have breakfast and check her in at the Betty Ford Center.

I learned later that she called her son that morning and told him that two dames had picked her up and then abandoned her in "a dump" (the Holiday Inn Express). Anyway, we finally got her to the Center and breathed a sigh of relief that we were rid of her.

When we arrive at the Center as patients, we think we're never going to laugh again, never going to sing or dance or make love again. Getting sober is going to mean the end of all the good, fun stuff.

Just the other day an old alcoholic who's finally agreed to come into treatment asked me, "Claire, will I ever laugh again?"

I told her, "Not only will you most certainly laugh again—you'll remember the next day what the hell it was you were laughing about!"

It's so symbolic of our recovery that while in treatment we dance the hokeypokey, chant out odes to recovery as we gather in circles, talk the ears off one another and wear all our emotions on our sleeves in group and at the medallion ceremonies. Those are the real signs of the transformation we undergo as we move from the "rookie" seat in the pit to the "ejection" seat next to the granny— which is the last stop before leaving.

◆ ◆ ◆

Like Claire, Harriet also liked to laugh. Her laugh is as infectious as her warm smile, which accompanied her everywhere.

Harriet stayed at the Center as a patient for several months. She says if she hadn't had that Extended Care opportunity, she probably wouldn't have made it the first time around. She says it was a case of her Higher Power looking after her. How exciting that even though we discontinued that original Extended Care program shortly after Harriet finished treatment, now we've got it back. Since 2000, if a patient needs to stay forty-five or sixty or ninety days to really get her/his sobriety in place, we can offer her/him a program and a home. After their thirty-day primary-care treatment stay is over, they move into lovely nearby homes with sister and fellow patients where, under close supervision, they "work the program." What a blessing this is.

It was an ongoing concern for Harriet that her heavy drinking had impaired her mental capacity and her manual skills. In extended care she was allowed to do some volunteer work and was given permission to help in the Alumni Office. Joan Connor had her assemble the mailings and the little bags of toiletries that were given to the patients. As she performed those tasks over many days and weeks, Harriet's physical dexterity grew better. Joan was delighted to hear her humming and happy, doing something useful for others and working on her own physical and mental recovery.

At night she was allowed to practice typing in one of the offices. A member of the Center's management team helped her write a résumé and did a mock interview with her.

Harriet started to train for the California test for paralegals, but she couldn't get the old adrenaline back. Besides, physically she wasn't ready for it—she was still missing a beat and a step. Her road to recovery after leaving the center was difficult, but she was able to put into practice what she had been taught.

Jacqueline asked Harriet to tell the others at our Sunday-morning breakfast table how difficult it had been for her when she first left the Betty Ford Center.

Harriet

My friend Barbara and I were the last patients to leave Extended Care before the program was closed down. We had a beautiful medallion ceremony with our counselor, Patty, who took us for the customary tea at a swank restaurant. We reminisced about the good times and the trying times, how frightened we were, how manipulative we could be of the staff and of one another and how powerful the secrets could be. We talked about the love/hate relationship with the staff and finally about our fears and hopes for life after treatment.

I talked about Chris and the letter I'd received from him that almost broke my heart. Barbara talked about her husband and the anxiety she felt about returning home, like a tourist carrying a passport into a new and strange country. As the three of us looked at one another over our teacups, the memories were bittersweet. We promised to keep in touch, and Barbara and I did; she and I connect with each other once a month.

My personal care plan called for me to go to AA every day for ninety days. I fell into a home group at Fellowship Hall. I would walk there every single morning to attend the 6 A.M. and the 7 A.M. meetings. They also had a 10 A.M. meeting for women, which I would attend if it didn't interfere with the part-time job I held. Others commented on and applauded my regularity as a positive marker of my recovery.

Speaking of markers, I'd collect chips wherever and whenever I could. I got a chip for fifteen days into treatment, which I gave to someone else for her fifteen days, and which she then passed on. I wonder where it is now? Who knows, it could be in Japan or in any one of fifty other countries.

I got a chip for the Family Program, and for my thirty-, sixty- and ninety-day sober benchmarks. I loved the chip ceremonies. They were rituals celebrating the anniversaries of my recovery and the fullness of the life I discovered. They were made out of materials that were rooted in the elements of the earth upon which I was once again solidly grounded.

After treatment most people feel they've been "fixed" and the only thing left is the shouting from the rooftops. I had that feeling but, to be honest, I was really frightened. I knew I had to follow the rules.

The first time I walked into Fellowship Hall in Palm Desert, I was excited, chatting nervously, trying to act normal. To make conversation I asked an old guy who was making the coffee how long the meeting lasted. He barked at me, "Your whole fucking life."

At the time I was appalled both by what he said and how he said it. It was a sobering thought that provided comic relief, because it's true, recovery is a lifetime process, a never-ending upward spiral. I had to watch myself very carefully lest I fall back into that pattern of circular thinking that could interrupt that upward spiral.

About three months into my sobriety, the craving came back so strongly that I felt it was about to rape me. I was into that circular thinking all over again: I didn't have a job, I didn't have a car to find a job, I didn't have a job to pay for a car, etc.

In the past when I got "stuck" like this, I would turn to my dear, loyal, sympathetic friend, alcohol, who had always taken care of these problems. This time I spoke to one of the women at an AA meeting. She said that I needed to pray. She gave me a very simple prayer and told me that when I recited it, I had to stress each single word:

God is my only source—
God *is* my only source—
God is *my* only source—
God is my *only* source—
God is my only *source.*

I had to write it down to make certain I had it with me at all times. It served as a circuit breaker. It interrupted the vicious circle of my thinking. Every day upon waking, I ask God to direct all my thoughts, so that I might just follow directions, step by step and day by day.

The funny thing is, I'd never been much for prayer. I remember when I was in the fourth grade I prayed that my teacher would be sick so that we wouldn't have a test that day. It worked; my teacher didn't show that day. As a matter of fact, it worked so well that she had TB and died. I was frightened by what I had done, and I didn't dare pray after that.

The next time I prayed was when I fell on my knees in my room in the middle of all those empty bottles. Now I pray a lot, and I very much like to recite the promises in the Big Book. They mean an awful lot to me, and all of them have come true in one way or another.

When I got out of Betty Ford, I was poor. I rented a room from a woman in AA who occasionally drove the bus for us when we were in extended care. It cost $100 a week. My stepbrother, Tom, sent me a small allowance, which bought my food and my no-name, generic cigarettes.

It was a long walk to the meetings at the Fellowship Club, but I didn't mind, as long as it wasn't in the midday sun. I stayed in my $100-a-week room until my sponsor found me a place in a run-down apartment building that was being rehabilitated, although the work wasn't finished yet. It seemed the perfect metaphor for my own life— a derelict who was being transformed, with the work not finished yet.

An important part of the program is to give back something of what you've received. "No matter how far down the scale we have gone, we will see how our experience can benefit others." I always thought that particular promise applied to me. About a year into recovery I was asked to tell my story once a month at the AA meeting held in the James West building auditorium on the Betty Ford Center campus every Tuesday night. I remember before those meetings I would get on my knees in the ladies' room in the West building and ask for God's grace.

One meeting in particular stands out in my memory. A woman in the audience approached me after I'd told my story and wanted to talk. She was in treatment, and I thought my fame was beginning to spread. I felt like a guru with all the answers, and I said that I'd be happy to help her in any way; she could ask me anything.

What did she want to know? "Where did you get your blouse?" Talk about a bucket of cold water in the face! But it was an important lesson in humility.

◆ ◆ ◆

At this point Harriet said that she knew that she was talking too much, but after listening to the others speak about their mothers she wanted to add something.

◆ ◆ ◆

Shortly after I left treatment, I received a couple of boxes in the mail from my mother. One contained three of my suits and some jewelry that I'd asked her to send me. When I opened the second box, I put my hand to my mouth and uttered a little cry. There was my forty-five-year-old Raggedy Ann doll. It was kept together with Scotch tape, Band-Aids and Ace bandages. How wonderful it was that my mom had thought to send me my favorite doll despite all the conflict and pain of the past! I sat down immediately and wrote her a thank you note, still unable to sign it "with love."

Soon thereafter I was talking with my stepbrother on the phone and told him the neatest thing had happened. When he heard about the doll he started to groan and said, "Oh, my God." He said my mom and sister had patched the doll, but then, feeling it was beyond repair—"like you"—they decided to have a little funeral service and bury it by putting it in a box and sending it to me.

I wasn't all that surprised when I heard the explanation, but I chose to interpret the doll another way. I considered it a blessing to have it back. In a sense the patched-up doll symbolized me. I was still breathing, still alive, despite the wear and tear, the spiritual scratches and bruises. What had been buried was my addicted self, my dark side. My real self was recovering and getting better by the day.

My relationship with my mother has never mended, and I'm sad about that. When I was a little girl, I thought family was and would be the center of my life. As I entered adulthood my career occupied that hallowed ground. Then alcohol moved in. Now AA is the "center." I know that everything will be okay, as long as I keep AA as the focal point. I now love my life and I thank the Betty Ford Center for getting me where I am.

·   ·   ·

When Harriet finished talking, there was a long but comfortable silence, some sighs and finally some stirring around the table. People from the other tables were leaving and our six storytellers realized, sadly, that it was time for them to say good-bye. The hugs were long, the good-byes subdued and brief, as the couples were anxious not to prolong the sorrow connected with parting. Laurette and her partner walked to the parking lot with Harriet and her husband. Paula and Robert walked with Claire and Jacqueline to the Cork building to participate in the family workshop.

Beatrice lingered a bit to say good-bye to me. I thanked her for all the work she'd put into the weekend. Then she left and I walked over to the lake where I sat on a bench next to a willow tree, looking at the mountains ("God's house"), and had a quiet moment of thanksgiving.

Epilogue

L ouie, one of the McCallum Hall counselors, introduced me to an idea that I've thought about a lot. He compared the passage through treatment to the Native American "vision quest," a solemn ritual connected with dreams. It involves going to one's sacred place, in the desert or on a mountain, and fasting and praying alone for three days and four nights. The purpose was to re-vision, to re-claim and to re-member one's life dream or creative spirit. Native Americans believe that time spent with nature for purposes of reflection and guidance re-awakens us to our own life purpose. I remember the counselor saying in the lecture that a vision quest comes at a time of crisis. "Its almost like dying except that you come back from death."

He then went on to compare the vision quest to the time spent at the Betty Ford Center. "As those on a vision quest go into the desert without the sustenance of food or water, so the chemically dependent go without the nourishment of alcohol." The purpose of our journey is to re-vision, to re-claim and re-member our life's dream and spirit. We will need the support of our fellow sojourners (the Fellowship) to overcome our self-defeating behaviors, and a shaman (a sponsor) to interpret our new dreams and visions and to be able to practice the principles in all our affairs.

At some point in our journeys, those of us in recovery, having had our own spir-

itual experiences, will become healers ourselves and will tell our stories to others en-
gaged in their own personal vision quests. That is what these six women have been
doing this weekend, telling their stories, particularly the vision quest they engaged in
at the Betty Ford Center, so that they could give something back to others in gratitude
for what they have received. The "vision quest" is a wonderful metaphor and perfectly
appropriate for this place of healing and hope located in the California desert. It was
the perfect setting to confront the devils of their addictive personalities, put them to
flight and to rediscover and nurture the persons they truly are. The blessing of the vi-
sion quest is not unlike the ending to Dante's journey: "We came out of the darkness
and once again beheld the stars."

Resources

Below is a collection of organizations and websites that offer information, support and guidance to those struggling with alcoholism and other drug dependency, and to the loved ones who want to help them. If you are interested in some of the Internet resources listed here but do not have Web access, try your public library. Many libraries offer free time on computers connected to the Internet.

The organizations and websites are listed here for the readers' information and convenience. The Betty Ford Center and the publisher do not endorse them and are not not responsible for any of their programs or their website contents.

Contact Information for the Betty Ford Center

www.bettyfordcenter.org
(800) 854-9211

Treatment Referral Information

The U.S. Department of Health and Human Services (HHS) Substance Abuse and Mental Health Services Administration's (SAMHSA) National Drug and Treatment

Referral Routing Service provides a toll-free telephone number for alcohol and drug information/treatment referral assistance. The number is (800) 662-HELP (4357).

Treatment Provider Associations

Partnership for Recovery
101 Constitution Avenue NW , Suite 675 East
Washington, D.C. 20001
www.partnershipforrecovery.org

National Association of Addiction Treatment Providers (NAATP)
www.naatp.org

Suggested Websites

Al-Anon/Alateen
1600 Corporate Landing Parkway
Virginia Beach, VA 23454
(888) 4AL-ANON
www.al-anon.alateen.org

Alcoholics Anonymous
459 Grand Central Station
New York, NY 10163
(212) 870-3400
www.alcoholics-anonymous.org

Alcohol MD
www.alcoholmd.com

National Center on Addiction and Substance Abuse (CASA)
    at Columbia University
www.casacolumbia.org

Children of Alcoholics Foundation
164 W. 74th Street
New York, NY 10023
(646) 505-2065
e-mail: coaf@phoenixhouse.org
www.coaf.org

Join Together Online
www.jointogether.org

National Association for Children of Alcoholics
(888) 554-COAS
www.nacoa.org

National Clearinghouse for Alcohol and Drug Information
(800) 729-6686
www.health.org

National Council on Alcoholism and Drug
    Dependence, Inc. (NCADD)
20 Exchange Place, Suite 2902
New York, NY 10005
(212) 269-7797
www.ncadd.org

National Institute on Alcohol Abuse and Alcoholism (NIAAA)
www.niaaa.nih.gov

National Institute on Drug Abuse (NIDA)
www.nida.nih.gov

ML